Alla vita che t'arride	To the life that smiles on you,
di speranze e gaudio piena,	filled with hope and joy,
d'altre mille e mille vite	the fate of a thousand,
il destino s'incatena!	thousand other lives is linked!
Te perduto, ov'è la patria	If you are lost, where is the country
col suo splendido avvenir?	with its shining future?

"*Alla vita*" (Renato's Aria)

Un Ballo in Maschera ~ Giuseppe Verdi

THE
STONECUTTER'S
Aria

CAROL FAENZI

APERTO BOOKS

THE STONECUTTER'S ARIA
Copyright © Carol Faenzi 2005

Published by:

APERTO BOOKS
730 Fifth Avenue, Suite 900, New York, N.Y. 10019
Email: vitabella@ApertoArts.com • www.ApertoArts.com
Tel. 212 • 659-7789

The author is grateful for permission to reprint photographs from: Carrara marble quarries from *Archivi del Marmo: L'archivio fotografico Bessi,* by Daniele Canali, Aldus Casa di Edizioni in Carrara, 1997. Limestone quarries and monuments from the Indiana Limestone Company.

Design: Kedron Bryson
Illustration: Scott M. Wilson
Set in Stempel Garamond

ISBN: 0-9767949-1-8

Library of Congress Control Number 2005906590

1. Immigration stories.   2. Italian-American history.
3. Indiana history

Printed in Canada

For Joann and Goffredo,
and for my Mother

La Famiglia

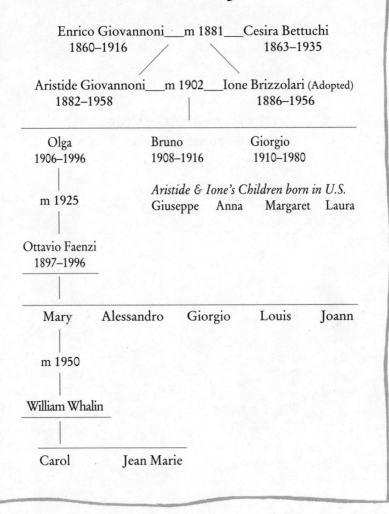

Enrico Giovannoni___m 1881___Cesira Bettuchi
1860–1916   1863–1935

Aristide Giovannoni___m 1902___Ione Brizzolari (Adopted)
1882–1958   1886–1956

Olga   Bruno   Giorgio
1906–1996   1908–1916   1910–1980

Aristide & Ione's Children born in U.S.

m 1925   Giuseppe   Anna   Margaret   Laura

Ottavio Faenzi
1897–1996

Mary   Alessandro   Giorgio   Louis   Joann

m 1950

William Whalin

Carol   Jean Marie

Toscana

Carrara

Firenze

Settignano

Genova

N

Sorano

Sant'anna
(The Farm)

Pitigliano

Roma

il Mediterraneo

italia

Toscana

THE STONECUTTER'S
Aria

OVERTURE
"On the Boat to America—Me!"

ACT ONE
1891 ~ 1929

Life in Carrara . . . Puccini and His Tosca . . .
Voyages to a New World . . . Ellis Island . . .
Labor Wars & Stonecutters

INTERMEZZO
THE 1930's

The Depression . . . Carving Stone and Singing Arias . . .
Monuments to America

ACT TWO
1940 ~ 1962

World War . . . Arrest and Internment . . .
Return to the Old Country

ACT THREE
1996 ~ 2001

A Box of Mementos . . . Quarrying Stories . . .
A Summer in Tuscany . . . Sculpting a Life

FINALE
"To the Place Where the Stars Melted"

BIBLIOGRAPHICAL SOURCES

Overture

Leaving Italy behind and going to America, but only for a little while, make some money, have a little adventure, see what all the excitement is about, come back wearing a new American suit, cash in my pockets . . . more cash than I have now anyway, only a few thousand lire and who knows how far that will take me in America?

I want to see the Statue of Liberty, those tall buildings that scrape the sky . . . I want to work with my hands on some of those buildings, leave my mark. I don't think they have much marble though, anyway that's what I hear . . . doesn't matter, has to be some kind of beautiful stone, granite maybe, yes, that would be it. And no, it's not marble, certainly won't find much white marble in America, not like Carrara . . . the kind that's pure white . . . sculptures that make people stop like they're seeing a miracle, something alive, that only God can inspire. Like when Michelangelo commanded his Moses to "Stand up!" *Dio mio, si.* I want to use my hands to make something beautiful in America that will last forever.

I wonder what I will eat there. I can still taste and smell that last meal, the one my wife made me just one week ago, seems so long ago now . . . I wonder when I will eat like that again, I don't really know what Americans eat, but I don't think it's *maccheroni,* and I don't think it's polenta, I don't think they eat garlic either. Feeling homesick already, or maybe it's the beginning of seasickness. They say you can get awful sick on these boats, but I don't think the knot I feel in my stomach is because of the sea, no, it's because I know it will be a long time before I sleep in my own bed again, with my wife again, before I will brush her hair or kiss her or tell her a joke and make her laugh, how I love to make her laugh. A long time before I see Mamma and Papa again, and I hope nothing happens to them before I can make it back. Have no idea when that will be . . . when I make enough money, is what I told them.

I will write a letter every week, maybe every day, so I know that something of me reaches them while I'm gone, I just hope they will all be all right. Sometimes now I think I must be a fool for leaving . . . just married for a few months and now alone taking this big boat away from everyone I love! What am I doing?

But America calls me, has for a long time. I have to go. I want to give my family a good life and that isn't going to happen in Italy, no, I cannot see myself trudging up to those mountains every day like my father and his before him, breaking my body and for what? *Per niente!* Not me, no. America is big enough so that even a humble stonecutter like me can find fortune! I want to send money home, lots of money so my wife doesn't have to worry and when we have children, I will know I did what I needed to do to give them a future, whether it will be in Italy or America . . . I don't know yet, many say they are going to come back to Italy, but it must be awfully good in America, because most end up staying there and bringing over the family. My wife doesn't want to come, Mamma neither, but I saw the gleam in my papa's eyes when I told him my plan, nearly jumped out of my skin . . . he's getting older and isn't so spry anymore, could I really have them come all this way, on a boat like this where they will suffer for two weeks? Cold, wind, lousy food, foul smells all around and all the time, unless you come up here on deck like I do . . . well, I'll go crazy thinking about that right now—no, I must set my sights on America, make some money, go home, start having a family of my own, do this while I'm young!

Yes, America is still young and so am I! Who would have thought that such a country would open its arms so wide to the world? Maybe America needs me as much as I need her . . . .

But it scares me to think how big it must be. I looked on a map and you could fit Italy into America dozens of times! Big— *Dio mio*! But I want to see it, see all of it with my own eyes, drink it in, ride trains and walk on its roads and see a sky that must go on forever.

The other scary thing is passing through the medical exams, so they let you stay in the first place. I have heard so many stories of people being sent back because of having this or that, or not answering questions the right way . . . what if I can't talk to someone who understands Italian? What if I answer wrong? How will I even know if I should speak or what I should say if the questions are in English? This keeps me up at night, come all this way and be sent home because nobody can understand me, what a humiliation, what a disgrace that would be, and I can't think about that anymore . . . no, it's all too much, there are too many things that can go wrong. At least I'm traveling by myself and don't have children to look after, *mamma mia*, those babies are always crying, and I haven't had one full night of sleep for a week

. . . but I feel sorry for the women who are on this boat with babies, their husbands in America . . . and I think that's how it would be for my wife and I can't stand thinking about her doing this alone . . . so many things that can go wrong.

But just look at that sea, look at that sky today, the blues blend together on the horizon and there just is no end to it. How far away is the coastline? I have stared into the sea from the port near my home so many times, dreaming about America being out there and how easy it would be to go, get on a boat, leave everything behind and just go . . . and so here I am, about halfway there now and the sky and the sea are calm and I know that this moment, right now is the most peace I will probably have for a long time . . . will I be happy in America? Will I find my fortune? Will I be one of the lucky ones?

Too late to turn back now and I wouldn't do it if I could, no, the time is now . . . I'm living at the start of a brand new century, and going to America. America! Me!

Act One

Life in Carrara . . . Puccini and His Tosca . . .
Voyages to a New World . . . Ellis Island . . .
Labor Wars and Stonecutters

*The stories need to be told, and they come
from absence and presence, from knowing
abandonment and reunion.*

Ione

I will speak first.

Everyone has a first memory, a moment remembered as the place a life begins. Mine was in my bedroom, sitting in front of a mirror.

I was about five years old when I realized I was an orphan, that my parents were lost to me . . . how they died, who they were, I never knew. Except for their last name, Brizzolari. I was Ione Brizzolari.

My dead father's brother and his wife had taken me in and during the short time I lived with them, I was unloved. I do not remember being touched or kissed by either of them, but have always believed that I must have been loved by my own mother and father. Otherwise, how would I have known it was missing?

So, this first memory: My aunt was standing behind me, pulling a hard-bristled brush through my long, thick, auburn hair, jerking the strands until I felt that my neck would snap. There was a candle in front of me and the light of the flame in the dark room reflected our faces in the mirror. She was smiling, but not at me.

There was a knot in my hair that would not budge. As she pressed her hand on my head, ready to force her way through the tangle, her hard smile caused a different kind of knot, in my stomach. Before I thought about what I was doing, I stood up straight, turned and looked up at her, right into her eyes and said, "Don't touch me."

Her mouth trembled and she seemed to be shaking. She left the room without a word.

I was shaking too and sat down, wondering what would happen to me, hoping to be left alone.

A moment later, I heard the awful door opening and in the brief glance I had of her in the mirror, a blade of metal flashed.

I thought she was going to kill me and all I could do was put my hands up to cover my face, hunching over to somehow prepare myself for the blow. Strange to think that I was calm. At least, that is what I remember.

My hair was lifted and instead of a knife plunging into my back, I heard a sickening sound of hair being torn. She was slicing off all my hair with scissors.

I never took my hands away from my face and remember hearing the blades coming closer and closer to my ears. I think I must have pleaded with her to stop.

She did stop when her fury had burned away. I heard the scissors fall to the floor and the door shut. I took my hands away and looked down. The strands of my beautiful hair looked like fallen angels all around me.

When I looked into the mirror, I did not recognize myself. Did I scream? If I did, no one came to me.

The next thing I remember is being packed up and given

into the care of a priest. He took my hand and put me next to him in his horse-drawn wagon. In silence, we left town and traveled a short distance, arriving on the same day in Carrara.

We stopped in front of a house. I glanced up at it out of curiosity, but when the door opened, I stared down, ashamed. I heard a sweet voice as the woman who answered exchanged words with the priest.

We went into the house and this woman bent down to meet my face. I could not look at her, but she lifted my chin and my gaze and hers came together. She was crying and smiling at me. When she touched my shorn head, I remember reeling back and pushing her hand away.

The priest departed and I was left in the care of Cesira and her husband, Enrico Giovannoni. They became my parents.

Their house was on the *via Carrione*, "street of the carts." It was the main road through Carrara from the marble quarries to the sea.

I remember watching the great white oxen, those gentle creatures, tireless and quiet, plodding through that street. One after the other all day, they pulled the heavy carts from the quarries like a parade that never ended. The marble was the livelihood of practically every living soul in Carrara, so the oxen were God's creatures that held our town and our lives together.

The Giovannoni house was sunny. I had been used to dark rooms, so the light coming through windows and greeting me each morning felt good in my bones.

There was a lot of laughter in that house. The Giovannonis had one child, a son, Aristide, older than I, who mostly ignored me. He dashed in and out of the house as if the music he was always whistling or singing was in his feet also. The only attention he paid me was to tease me, but Cesira would put a stop to it.

And my hair grew out again.

Cesira was a seamstress and I followed her everywhere. She taught me how to use the needle and thread, trace patterns for clothing, use chalk marks on hems and seams. I learned many things from my mother.

All kinds of people came to the house to see her for fittings. I was thrilled every time she let me answer the door. It was when the opera singers came to the house that it was the most fun.

Aristide and I would stand behind the door and listen, especially during the visits of Signora Giglia, a soprano who performed at the *Teatro degli Animosi*, Carrara's opera house.

"Signora Giovannoni," the diva said, "you know that I do not like to complain, but there is a problem with the costume you made for me and the performance is in two weeks!"

"What is the problem?" Cesira asked.

"You did not take my measurements correctly, Signora! The gown is too small!"

"Please then, put it on for me and we will see," Cesira said as she lifted armfuls of azure blue taffeta and gently guided the soprano into the bedroom. "*Prego*, Signora Giglia, slip it on and I will help you fasten up the back."

In a huff, the soprano went in.

We were giggling behind the door and our mother saw us. She put her finger up to her lips to hush us.

It took many minutes for this plump woman to come out of one set of clothes and struggle into her gown that was open in the back, for the fastenings would not come together. Cesira pulled off the measuring tape she always had around her neck and we watched as she wrapped it around the diva's strong arms, her ample bosom, waist and hips.

In between measurements, the singer pulled the fabric down and sucked in her considerable middle, trying to bend the costume to her will.

Cesira looked at her notes and said, "Well, Signora, I don't know what happened in the past month, but the measurements I took then are what I used to make the dress, so there was no mistake made."

The soprano went pink in the face as she responded, "Well! I am the same person I was one month ago, Signora, and all I know is that my gown does not fit and you must fix it!"

"As I see it, there are two possible remedies."

"But what else can be done besides your altering it? There is no other way."

"Your costume would fit perfectly, Signora, if you were the weight you were one month ago."

The pink cheeks went to crimson.

Cesira said, "I will alter the dress to your new measurements, but I would suggest you be careful with your appetite in the next two weeks. Don't come to me at the last minute to tell me it doesn't fit!"

Insulted, yet humbled in the presence of this tiny costume-maker, Signora Giglia worked her way out of the gown and, like a lamb, thanked Cesira for doing her this favor.

When the door shut and the soprano was a safe distance away, Aristide and I choked out our held back laughter until we were falling on the floor.

Cesira laughed too but said, "She knows I'm right and that I will always make her look beautiful."

And I learned from Cesira that a woman has to speak up sometimes. My mother's talents enhanced the talents of others, but she never saw hers as inferior.

Enrico and Cesira took us to the opera house many times and we would all sit together and squint when Signora Giglia hit the highest note, the seams of the dress stretched to the point of peril.

"That was close," Enrico would murmur to me as the "*bravas!*" erupted from the audience.

I adored Enrico. It seemed every time I caught him looking at me, he was smiling, as if I had done something good when all I had been doing at the moment was folding laundry or reading.

I had found my family.

When I turned thirteen, I suddenly realized someone else in the household was noticing me.

We grew up together in the same house,
Ione and I, and when she turned fifteen,
I married her.

Aristide

I was nineteen. The year was 1901.

We were never like brother and sister. I was always in love with her, and that was so for as long as I can remember.

The very first thing I noticed about Ione were her eyes— green like a cat! I have a habit of blinking hard at things I suspect aren't exactly as they first appear. I'm sure I must have blinked the first time Ione and me met eye to eye. Shortly, though, I would not be able to do that so easy because she sprouted into this tall girl and forever after, I never caught up. Never bothered me. Don't think it bothered her either.

My mother, Cesira, married my father, Enrico, when they were very young, too. That's the way it was then. I was their only child. Don't ask me why. Then Ione came along. We were enough for them probably.

Like I said, she was only fifteen when we married, but she had been sleeping inches away from me on the other side of the wall. I could hear her breathing in her sleep. I could hear her turn over in the bed. *Mamma mia*, it made me *pazzo*—crazy! My parents arranged for the nuptials before disaster occurred. I had smart parents.

Especially Mamma. You see, she was a seamstress, owned her own little shop above the house. Known as the best in town because she could sew a new suit or dress for man or woman by simply taking their measurements and understanding how they wanted to look afterwards—the *bella figura*, as we say.

I can still see her with her hand on her chin, the other hand on her narrow hip, head nodding up and down, saying, "*si, si, si*" as she looked over her customer's shape and contemplated his ego.

Later, when I began my apprenticeship as a stonecutter—*uno scalpellino*—and was crazy over Michelangelo, I chuckled thinking about how similar the approaches to their creations were, even if Mamma's was just cloth. There were no patterns, no shortcuts, no mistakes.

Ione followed Mamma around the house and shop like her shadow and learned it all. Good thing too, because years later when I left for America, Mamma's tailoring business back in Carrara kept the family alive, even during the Great War. Those were worry years, lonely years for me.

Anyway, I'm getting ahead of myself, which I have a tendency to do at times. Can't help it.

I had romantic notions when I was young and not just about marrying Ione. No, I was also going to be an opera singer. *In realtà*, I became an opera singer—a short career; but at the time, I wanted only two things: *fare l'amore* with Ione and sing to Floria Tosca.

I was learning to carve marble because that's what men did in Carrara. My father and his before that and so on. That was all there was and I did learn to love it and I still do. But I sing because God gave me a voice. It is, as they say, my get up and go.

Although I was young, I had a promising tenor's voice, and I sang around the house, on the streets, as I practiced my marble carving, worked on some little sculpture or even as I studied the books on Gothic architecture. I might have my mind on something else, but I memorized the works of Verdi, Puccini and others I loved. *La Boheme* and *Aida* were engraved upon me.

These composers were greatly admired—no, the better word is worshipped—by the *carraresi*. I would sooner go hear an opera than go to Mass, and I had a lot of company (speaking of the men anyway). I feel closer to God in an opera house than I have ever felt in a church pew.

Europe went wild for Giacomo Puccini and his Tosca during 1900 and no Italian citizen loved him more than I did. And while the Romans criticized the first performance—typical, what do they know?—the *milanese* applauded it two months later through twelve performances at La Scala.

Puccini's music spoke to our passions, our emotions about the new century—*esattamente*. He was creating something new and exciting in opera and these voices called out to us, like sirens across the sea.

It was in the same year of 1900 a wonderful thing happened. The maestro himself came to Tuscany, to Carrara, and brought Tosca to us.

You see, Puccini had a fancy summer home near Carrara called Torre del Lago and as a fellow *toscano*, having been born and raised in Lucca, I think he saw Carrara as a safe place to work out parts of the opera that hadn't quite appealed to the Romans. Safe, not because we *carraresi* don't know a good opera from a bad one, but rather because he knows we have faith in him, that we love him.

Me ne infischio! I couldn't have cared less about his reasons
. . . . I knew I would do anything to be in the audience the night
that Tosca would be performed in Carrara.

But after the excitement passed, after I had flown through
the door to share the news with my family, our squeals of disbelief
died down, our smiles turned into wistful resignation. Of course,
none of us would see it. I knew that every seat would be filled
with Puccini's entourage from Lucca and those with the prestige—
the "*prominenti*" of Carrara.

"Maybe we'll catch a glimpse of him on the street," Cesira
said kindly. "He has to eat and sleep somewhere, doesn't he, son?"

Yes, to pass him on the street, to come face to face with genius,
even for a moment—this thought gave me a little hope.

The performance was going to be on February 15, 1900. Our
opera house, *Politeama Verdi*, was new, maybe only five or six
years old then and we were so proud of it! Caselli, the city's master
engineer, made sure it had every modern improvement acoustically
possible. It was not so grand, in my opinion, as the *Teatro degli
Animosi* with its Neoclassic design, white marble Doric columns
and glittering frescoes. But our new theatre attracted many opera
companies back then, which gave me more chances to sing. This
new one was a monument to our beloved Verdi. Imagine, two
great opera houses in a dinky place like Carrara! But opera was in
our blood like the marble was.

So how does a sixteen-year-old marble apprentice get in to
see Puccini? Ha! Don't underestimate me!

It's because I spent any free time I had working in the theatre,
sweeping, taking tickets, painting scenery, odd jobs, anything, for

no money—just for the pleasure of being close to the world of my dreams.

Oh, and there was one other thing that helped: Mamma—being the excellent seamstress she was—made many of the costumes, also repaired them . . . like when the high notes caused a rip under the arm of a well-endowed soprano!

The manager of the theatre was Alfredo—good man—can't recall his last name at the moment. Doesn't matter. He liked me and I'm sure he liked that I did so much work for him for nothing besides. In fact as my adolescent voice ripened a bit, I sang in the chorus and I helped him out of some scrapes—like when a performer fell suddenly ill or there was a falling out of some kind. *Un gran casino*—a big fuss—happened all the time.

I was always prepared for any tenor role because I knew them all by heart. I was Rodolfo, Radames, Figaro, Rodrigo, Alvaro, Alfredo, Sesto, Don Ottavio, Foscari. I was hero, lover, villain. I was cruel, desperate, pure, vindictive, pious. When I stepped into a costume, when I opened my throat to sing, I let their emotions of pain or ecstasy lead me. What fun to be evil! How exhilarating to let love's passion reach such depths of despair! Opera takes the best and worst of mankind and brings it to the place that shatters you.

Anyway, that's how I managed to have a "career." I was a reliable understudy and Mamma's talents were indispensable. And don't forget, I worked for nothing! *Per niente!*

Alfredo said a few days before the performance, while I was sweeping the floor and looking dejected, "*Vieni qui*—come over here. I cannot stand to look at that droopy face. *Che cosa hai?*"

Of course, he already knew—just wanted prolonged drama before he bestowed his gift on me. Alfredo said I could listen to the rehearsal so long as I stayed invisible. And, much to my surprise, he said I could help take tickets the night of the performance!

"But wear a decent suit."

Which Mamma sewed up in no time as I danced around her singing "*Questa o quella*" from Rigoletto:

Questa o quello, per me pari sono	To me this woman or that one are the same
a quant'altre d'intorno mi vedo;	as all the others I see around me;
del mio core l'impero non cedo,	I don't surrender command of my heart
meglio ad una che ad altra beltà.	to one beauty any more than to another.

Her little shoulders hunched up when she laughed.

Then I felt bad to be going alone, but Ione and my parents knew how much it meant to me and were happy just to get the details later so they could have some *vanterie*, the bragging with the neighbors.

Mamma tugged on my sleeve as I went out the door saying, "And get a good look at how he's dressed! I want to know what his suit looks like—the buttons too, don't forget!"

Enrico laughed, "*Sì*, maybe the maestro will pull up his pant legs and show his socks too, Cesira!"

It was an unusually bitter cold but clear and beautiful night. It was not a long walk to the theatre (there are no long walks in Carrara), and I was so giddy the cobblestones under my feet seemed to propel me forward.

The light from the chandeliers overhead was as bright as the familiar faces I greeted. The *maestri* of opera carved into the four corners of the entry's ceiling all seemed to have exchanged their somber expressions for smiles. The air was thick with anticipation and wonder. The draft at the door made my fingers numb and I hardly managed to hold on to tickets, but I think it was just plain nerves really.

Puccini! And he was here.

I had not been able to go to the rehearsal because of my studies, so I was like everybody else that night in the audience, hearing only the second performance of this new opera.

Before the curtain rose, I found a place to stand, a shadowy place toward the back, happy to be alone there. And I remember the throat-catching silence that fell when Puccini entered and took his seat, not in the front row either, but on the aisle near the middle, just seconds before his opera began.

The lights went down then, but I got a good look at him. He was in the prime of his life in 1900, his thick dark hair combed back, full and glossy, his moustache bushy so that it almost completely covered his upper lip. And he was dressed elegantly as you would expect.

He wasn't as fancy as I supposed he would be for the audience at La Scala. He didn't have to be. There was no pretension here tonight. We loved opera for its great drama and sheer beauty, which let us all escape into our dreams for a few hours. We adored this man, this *toscano*, who was about to give us another *spettacolo*.

Mario Cavaradossi! Hero and artist! The arias he sang, of his love for Floria Tosca, came through me like arrows. The music had the effect of pitching me up into the air with a thrill . . . then to fall, hoping the next notes would catch me at the final moment.

E lucevan le stelle ed olezzava	And the stars shone and the earth was perfumed,
la terra, stridea l'uscio dell'orto, *e un passo sfiorava la rena.*	the gate to the garden creaked and a footstep rustled the sand to the path.
Entrava ella, fragrante, *mi cadea fra le braccia.*	Fragrant, she entered and fell into my arms.
O, dolci baci, o languide carezze, *mentr'io fremente*	Oh soft kisses, oh sweet abandon as I trembling
le belle forme disciogliea *dai veli!*	unloosed her veils and disclosed her beauty!
Svani per sempre *il sogno mio d'amore*	Oh vanished forever is that dream of love,
L'ora è fuggita *e muoio disperato!*	fled is that hour and I desperately die!
E non ho amato mai *tanto la vita!*	And never before have I loved life so much!

This was the best tenor role since Rodolfo in *La Boheme*.

But the evil Scarpia almost made me wish I were a baritone! Lusty vengeance poured out of his voice.

Già, mi dicon venal, *ma a donna bella*	Yes, they say I am venal, but it is not

io non mi vendo	for money that I will sell myself
a prezzo di moneta	to beautiful women.
Se la giurata fede debbo	I want other recompense
tradir, ne voglio altra mercede.	if I am to betray my oath of office.
Quest'ora io l'attendeva!	I have waited for this hour!
Già mi struggea	Already in the past I burned
L'amor della diva!	with passion for the Diva.
Ma poc'anzi ti mirai	But tonight I have beheld you
qual non ti vidi mai!	in a new role I had not seen before!
Quel tuo pianto era lava	Those tears of yours were lava
ai sensi miei e il tuo sguardo	to my senses and that fierce hatred
che odio in me dardeggiava,	which your eyes shot at me only
mie brame inferociva!	fanned the fire in my blood!
Agil qual leopardo	Supple as a leopard
ti avvinghiasti all'amante	you enwrapped your lover.
in quell'istante	In that instant
t'ho giurata mia!	I vowed you would be mine!
Mia! Si, t'avrò!	Mine! Yes, I will have you!

We all knew we had seen and heard something different, although at the time I would not have been able to tell you what exactly. Can't say I can now very well. Italian opera, good ones anyway, always have the same elements—love gone wrong, death of the heroine or hero, or the Church lurking in the background. Tosca, even though it was all of this, was more. The music was dark, wicked and absolutely glorious. There were moments when I felt the music alone was telling the story. When Tosca was about to leap to her death from the castle tower, all of us in the audience were willing to go with her.

I lost count of the number of ovations and encores, although I tried hard so I could give my family a faithful report. My hands lost their memory of the cold and were red with clapping, my own voice lost among the outcries of *"Bravo, bravissimo!"*

Puccini took his bows, his eyes drinking in our adoration,

boughfuls of flowers were tossed into Tosca's arms (Hariclea Darclee was not an Italian, but we overlooked it as her voice was exquisite).

But I couldn't take my eyes off of him. The great man Puccini was a hero. Our tears spoke for us.

Later as Ione let me brush her long lovely hair, her green eyes smiled at me in the mirror and I sang to her the words of Cavaradossi to Tosca:

Quale occhio al mondo può star di paro all'ardente occhio tuo verde?	What eyes in the world can compare with your green and glowing eyes?
È qui che l'esser mio s'affissa intero, occhio all'amor soave, all'ira fiero.	It is in them that my whole being fastens, eyes soft with love and rich with anger.
Qual'altro al mondo puo star di paro all'occhio tuo verde?	Where in the whole world are eyes to compare with your green eyes?

(So I substituted Tosca's black eyes with Ione's green eyes. So what? I think Puccini would just have winked at me.)

Something was keeping me in this wonderful perilous land where I had suffered so much and where I had so much more to suffer. There was a lingering suspicion that somewhere in this vast country an opening existed, that somewhere I would strike the light. I could not remain in the darkness perpetually.

~ PASCAL D' ANGELO, SON OF ITALY (1924)

 I like to think my life really began in 1921, when my family stepped off the boat to join me in America.

Aristide

Back in 1902 though—when my cousin, Andrenio "Andy" Bettuchi, convinced me I could make a lot of dough in America carving in stone, so what was I waiting for?—I had adventure. I was nineteen then, and I would have many adventures in America.

Look, on my first trip to America I was lucky because Andy was in Philadelphia to get me. But he told me stories, stories about the crook who would pretend to be your friend. "Hey, *paisano*! Need a place to sleep tonight?" And you'd say yes, you're dead tired and don't know nothing about nothing. And the next thing you know you would be relieved of your money and still have no place to sleep. If you weren't beaten up besides, consider yourself lucky.

Hey, this kind of thing even happened to people before leaving Italy! All kinds of "*amici*" are hanging around the docks promising help with luggage. "We'll carry it and check it for you, so you don't have to worry, *amico mio!*" Or a guaranteed pass on the doctor's examination that everyone feared. "This little piece of paper will get you through immediately!" And then you hand over the lire and presto! You have no lire, no luggage and that little piece of paper isn't even worth wiping your ass with. *Mamma mia*—so many people in this world out to cheat you.

Like I said, I was lucky. Nobody tried to kill me. But then I would have these nightmares thinking that if somebody did, God only knows if anyone would ever find out what had become of me. It made me break into a cold sweat thinking I could have my throat sliced and my body cut up in pieces, tossed into the Atlantic or in some garbage can in a back alley and Ione would think I took off for good!

This is what I was thinking about as Andy and I carried my trunk along the busy street where he lived. It seemed like there were thousands of Italians living there!

"*Si,*" Andy yelled over his shoulder at me as I followed him, maneuvering around the shouting Sicilian pushcart vendors. "The Irish are leaving the neighborhood now—can't stand the noise we make! Ha!"

We carried my trunk into the front door of the humble walk-up he lived in, three floors above the noisy street. As we jostled our way up the dark and narrow stairwell, he introduced me to everyone who had poked a nose out to see who was arriving.

As the doors opened and closed, I got whiffs of life there. The familiar smells of someone's cigar, or a garlic-laden casserole coming out of an oven, were heady and I felt soothed.

"Hungry, cousin?" Andy asked as he put the key into the

door. I was too famished to answer him. "Go wash up a bit and we'll have some bread and salami before we go out."

"Where are we going?"

"I'm taking you out to get some clothes. It's important you don't look like you just got off the boat, *cugino*. These ugly Irish will beat you up. And they just might anyway."

I eagerly washed off my face and as I combed back my hair, took a good look at myself in the mirror. In Carrara, I was always a well-dressed man, full of myself wherever I was. But I wasn't in Italy anymore. I admired Andy's modern American suit when I first saw him, his broad arms out to embrace me. All of a sudden, and for the first time in my life, I felt out of place.

As I followed Andy around the neighborhood to buy an "American" suit, to pick up some fresh clams for dinner, to watch him flirt with some girls we met on the street, I couldn't help feeling numb from the whole thing. I had crossed an ocean. I had arrived in America. I had been met by the dear cousin I had known my whole life, the one I played with when we were just little boys in the small streets of Carrara, splashing each other and drinking cold water from fountains that were older than anything you could find in America. The faces, the smells, the sounds were familiar to me, in that Little Italy of Philadelphia. But the city was huge! I felt insignificant for the first time.

"*Andiamo*, Andy," I said impatiently, urging my cousin to take his eyes off the pretty young women standing on the corner. I felt people staring at me, judging me, feeling sorry for me. And I was hungry! *Avevo molto fame*! I was holding the bag with the fresh bread, squeezing it through the paper. The aroma caused my fingers to pinch off a piece and stuff it into my mouth.

With a final, "*ciao bellissime*" to the girls, we made our way back to Andy's apartment and once again up the long flight of creaky stairs.

"After we eat, you can put on your new suit and we'll take *la passeggiata* around the neighborhood," my cousin said, clapping me on the back as I dropped the bag on the tiny kitchen table.

I was afraid to put on the suit. I could smell dinner cooking and I didn't want to splash anything on it. So I walked out to the kitchen in my new underwear and sat down at the small kitchen table for two.

Andy was standing at the stove in the tiny kitchen, dropping clams in a battered pot. His shirtsleeves were rolled up and I was startled to notice how muscular the scrawny kid had become. All that digging he did everyday, building the city's transportation system, put meat on his bones.

I closed my eyes and let the smell of the clams and garlic seduce my nostrils. And it suddenly hit me that, like so many of my fellow immigrants, our mammas and wives would no longer be feeding us. Being out here on the edge of the world without them— it's a good thing cooking comes as naturally to Italians as singing!

Andy turned around and laughed at the rapture on my face and my choice of dress for dinner. He leaned over and handed me a bottle of wine.

"Pour us some wine, *cugino*. Make sure you don't get stains on that holy virgin of a tee-shirt!"

"So, what do you think so far—your first day in America?" Andy asked as he gently guided the pasta into the boiling water.

I handed him a glass full of the red wine. We toasted each other, said "*cin cin*" and I took a gulp before saying anything.

Drops of the red wine fell on the tablecloth and I was thankful they missed my virgin tee-shirt.

"Andrenio, I don't know what to say. America overwhelms you. It's so big and I feel so small."

Andy grinned and said, "Everybody feels like that, *cugino*. And you! You were a prince in Carrara. But Carrara isn't big enough for you anymore. In America, you can go anywhere, across stretches of land that you cannot imagine. You will have adventure and make more money than you even know. You have a new wife, *cugino*. You cannot care for her and the *bambini*, when they come, by singing arias and keeping your nose in architecture books."

"*Si*, I would like to make money to send home. And then maybe I'll go back for good."

"So work, make money, go home, but decide later. Today is for us, to be happy to see each other again." He set the plate down in front of me—*linguine alle vongole*, the fragrant steam of the sweet clams forcing my nose down to within an inch of them.

Like a brother, he sat with me, leaned over to refill my glass and broke into a big smile. His handsome face, so full of love for me, brought tears to my eyes.

Later in the evening, as I was admiring myself in the new suit, Andy leaned against the doorway, smiling at me and said, "*Andiamo*—let's go. It's Saturday night and I have something special to show you."

We were walking and talking nonstop until Andy suddenly stopped and pulled at my arm.

"*Prego*, take a look across the street."

The first thing I saw was a long line—I didn't care what it was for, I wasn't going. I'd had enough of standing in American lines. Then I looked up and the name "Verdi Hall" reached out to me like I was home. *Un Ballo in Maschera* was the opera playing in this small building—certainly nothing like the opera houses of Italy—but it was Verdi!

"What I wouldn't give to be standing in that line," I said.

"You aren't coming with me, then?" Andy smiled at me, and started across the street.

I grabbed his sleeve, and said, "I don't have money to see an opera, Andrenio! How can you afford it?"

Andy was losing his patience with me. "*Cugino*, this is not the Metropolitan Opera House and Caruso is not making an appearance. Otherwise, you're right, I could not afford it. But a guy named Giannini—Ferruchio Giannini—opened this place, and you can hear all kinds of Italian *divertimenti*. Most of our *paesani* can afford to come, including me . . . and you."

The place was much larger than it appeared from the outside . . . I think every seat was filled and then some. The air was filled, too, with the sounds of people waiting to be filled themselves after another long week of building America. Their faces said everything, and I remember thinking "I am one of them now."

During Act One, Renato sings "*Alla vita*"—To life—and my eyes automatically closed as I transported myself back to Carrara:

Alla vita che t'arride	To the life that smiles on you,
di speranze e gaudio piena,	filled with hope and joy,
d'altre mille e mille vite	the fate of a thousand, thousand other
il destino s'incatena!	lives is linked!
Te perduto, ov'è la patria	If you are lost, where is the country
col suo splendido avvenir?	with its shining future?
E sarà dovunque, sempre	And will the passage for wounds
Chiuso il varco alle ferite,	remain always barred everywhere
perchè scudo del tuo petto	because the people's affection
è del popolo l'affetto?	is a shield to your breast?
Dell'amor più desto è l'odio	Hatred is more alert than love
le sue vittime a colpir.	to strike its victims.
Te perduto, ov'è la patria	If you are lost, where is the country
col suo splendido avvenir?	with its shining future?

I opened my eyes and glanced over at Andy. He too had his eyes closed, and right then, I didn't feel "lost" in this new country with its shining future.

And maybe life would smile on me.

For the next three years, I worked very hard. I stayed with Andy until I was able to get work in stone quarries, which took me all over the place; but I would always return to Philadelphia where there would be letters from home waiting for me at Andy's—and well, it was the closest thing I had to a home in America.

I lived, no, I worked all over the place, wherever marble or stone needed my hands, from Vermont to Colorado. I was lucky I had a skill in carving. Even so, I had no choice many times but to accept work in quarries as a laborer blasting and hauling stone. That's backbreaking work, let me tell you. But at least I didn't spend years digging for railroads or in those filthy coal mines.

In my travels I met so many immigrants from Italy, it seems I must have met them all. Everybody had a story too—told with the same feeling, yet as different as the dialects they spoke. We never thought of ourselves as Italians. You were *toscano*, as I am; or you were *calabrese, napoletano, siciliano*. Americans might have seen us all as the same lot—dagos and wops, but believe me, in those days *toscani* did not want to be known as *siciliani*. That didn't work in either direction.

In whatever city I was in, I would read whatever paper I could get my hands on that was published by and for immigrants, like *Il Progresso Italo-America* in New York (I liked this paper as it was published by a *toscano*!). Or, in Chicago, I'd pick up *La Protesta Umana*, an anarchist paper. And in Vermont, *Lo Scalpellino*, how could I not read that one? I could read about what was really behind the labor strikes, lynchings, or jailing of

Italian immigrants.

Whenever something violent happened in America, immigrants were usually blamed, many times the Italians because everybody hated us—even other immigrants. The Irish, for example. They saw the Sicilians coming in droves to take over their waterfront and fishing territories. It was bloody. So I always watched my back. I always paid attention.

I never imagined America would be like that. Nobody ever talked about how dangerous it could be. Back then, in 1902, I assumed that all of America must be like Philadelphia—crowded, dangerous and dirty. *Dio mio.* I couldn't bring my new wife, my mother and father over here and make them live in this hellhole!

In 1905, I went back home to Italy.

I thought long and hard on that boat. I watched the water. I sang to myself. I ate fruit so I wouldn't be seasick. I never was, for some reason. I let the waves carry me back to Italy in my mind. I didn't know what I wanted to do. What was the right thing?

I had been sending money home. I knew there was more to be made. But I closed my eyes on the bow of that ship and basked in my memories of Italy.

I thought of my mother, Cesira. Her body is as light as feathers but she has a will that is as deep as the marble.

My father Enrico, who will be proud—so very proud—as I tell my stories, as he admires my American suit of clothes, as I give him my experiences, those he would have liked to have himself, as we chew on our little cigars, patting our stomachs full from supper.

And of course, Ione, my wife, still new to me even though we've been married for more than three years, will make me happy that I had to endure my loneliness and will reward me with her body when we are alone once again in the dark. That reward in particular became all I could think of on that boat. You think it's an easy thing—to be a faithful husband alone in America, young, full of yourself, your desires, adventure around every corner?

I looked out over the ocean, but saw myself walking through the door of our home. I had almost forgotten smells of *la cucina*— the ripe *pomodoro*, the sweet *basilico* and of course my favorite— *l'aglio*, garlic simmering in olive oil until golden in Ione's saucepan. The mouth becomes an ocean.

I felt the hot Tuscan sun beating on my head as I walked down the small crooked streets toward the *Piazza del Duomo* to meet my friends at the café, have a little smoke, tell my tall tales (which would be very tall by the time I told them). I could already see the looks on their faces.

I saw myself going into the theatre to see Alfredo, seeing his usual frown turning into a broad smile as I came in through the door. My voice had improved and how I wanted to be on that little stage again. I wondered if Puccini had managed to bring *Madama Butterfly* to Carrara. I had memorized Pinkerton, the heartless coward . . . singing his lines over and over every day on the boat.

Yes, it would be good, this going home. America was a place to make money. It was not home.

It would never be Italy.

But I didn't stay, you know that already. Ione was soon pregnant and our little girl— *Alessandrina Olga Gina*—was born just before I left to go back to America. I couldn't leave without seeing our firstborn. Ione had been left alone too much in her life, and I couldn't leave her like that. And I wanted to have that little girl in my eyes to carry with me.

Afterward, I stayed in America for a couple of years and made a second trip back to Italy and then a third one. A result of each visit was a new addition to the family. Bruno was born in 1908 and Giorgio in 1910. I held Olga and Bruno in my arms, but not Giorgio.

So the last time I saw Italy ever again in my life was early in 1910. Of course, I never really thought, *this is the last time I'll see Italy*. I was still young. When your entire life is out there ahead of you, nothing is for the last time, is it?

But by then I saw America as the place we needed to live together as a family. Italy, as beautiful as I remembered it, was a mess. Ungovernable, it seemed to me. All you had to do was open your eyes to know how many Italians were leaving to come to the USA. Mostly it was the Sicilians and those from the regions of Italy south of Rome, the *Mezzogiorno*. It was called that because the noonday sun is so strong in the south, but also to tell them apart from those of us of the northern regions, known as the *Risorgimento*, our "rebirth." You would have to know and understand Italy's past and why we were still so divided as a people.

Until the 1860's, we Italians did not know what it meant to be a country. The Pope had the support of the French in ruling Rome and the surrounding regions. The Bourbons ruled Naples, the Austrians controlled Venice, and so on. Especially in Sicily, there had been a parade of foreign rulers for centuries and for these nobles, the common man was tied to an estate, little more than a servant. He learned to mistrust his lords and resent them, yet there was little he could do about it. The rich or even those who weren't so rich, but knew how to use fear and power, scared people into obedience and this runs in the blood even today.

But there was a man who believed in freedom for a unified, independent Italy. General Giuseppe Garibaldi was a visionary and had all the right ideas. Along with his cohorts—the Count Cavour, Giuseppe Mazzini and others of the *illuminati*—Garibaldi was inspired by the French Revolution and the ideas of independence on the rise in Europe during the 1800's. What Italian wouldn't want to kick out the foreigners? We liked the idea of throwing them out and ruling ourselves! This dream was born in the northern regions, yet the Sicilians cheered Garibaldi when his troops marched into Palermo.

Garibaldi was our hero. What a life the General led! Through the mid-1800s, he fought in mutinies, fled arrest, lived in exile in South America, married a beautiful woman there who later fought by his side in Italy until she expired in a skirmish . . . he lived in France and was a general in the Franco-Prussian war. He also lived in America. Abraham Lincoln himself asked Garibaldi to serve as a General during the Civil War. He turned down the offer, he said, only because Italy needed him first.

The Red Shirts of Garibaldi! Garibaldi and his One Thousand! With a thousand volunteers, Garibaldi defeated the Bourbons in Naples, captured Palermo in Sicily, marched on Rome to squash the Pope's worldly power, engaged the French and the Austrians in bloody battles to release their hold on Italy.

The Kingdom of Italy was born in 1861, and a King chosen, Victor Emmanuel. The seat of government was in Torino. It would still be a few more years before Venice was finally won from Austria and the Pope was removed from power. Garibaldi retired only then. America was so impressed with his valor, he was offered one of those ticker tape parades down Fifth Avenue in New York City. He refused this honor. The Jesuits had riled up the Irish Catholics . . . God forbid an Italian be honored! Garibaldi didn't want to cause a riot, so he chose the peaceful way. Says a lot about him, doesn't it?

My father told me about many of these battles to kick out the foreigners and make our own country, and there wasn't an Italian, north or south, who didn't feel romantic about the whole idea. But once the glory of winning faded, we were left with the chaos of governing ourselves.

Italy might have become one country after so many centuries of divisions, but bringing any unity to the hearts and minds of Italians will take centuries longer to accomplish in my opinion.

Just because we were called the Kingdom of Italy did not change the way life was lived. The poor Sicilian, for example, was still working on an estate, barely eking out a living. The newly formed government tried to make improvements, such as build some new schools, and roads and such. But those impoverished southerners balked: "What? You want to squeeze us for even more taxes to pay for all that?" So it pretty much stayed the way it was. They didn't like their poverty, of course, which is why so many of them left for America. The government just threw up their hands and let them.

Naturally, when the people from the *Mezzogiorno* came to America, they brought along their dislike and mistrust of authority. Some of them used it against their own people, and were called *mafiosi*. Do you know what *mafia* really means? It means having pride in the extreme, the kind of pride that a man wears like a fine suit of clothes. You know it just by looking at him, how he stands, how he struts, how he speaks, how he commands himself and others. It's not a bad word, but it's a southern word, and the secret society that does exist, the Mafia, is alive in Sicily and in America because that's the way Sicilians learned to protect themselves and their families, keeping their friends just as close, because they couldn't trust outsiders. They clung to their old ways just as those of us from the north did, but we had very different ways. Our food, our dialects, our superstitions, even our Catholic ways of worship were different. Southerners are very smart and shrewd but they're showy and believe power and fame make the man. Northerners are more practical. We wanted to make money—to hell with being feared and famous.

Can you understand now why—in those early years in America—we did not call ourselves Italians? The notion of belonging to a country was new to us. We thought of our province, village or hometown first and that was who we were, period. As time went on, it became less important to make the distinction, especially by the time I had grandchildren. Living in America was the one dream we all shared. We had to live and work in the same neighborhoods no matter what part of Italy we came from.

And it's not to say northern Italians had any reason to trust government! We *carraresi*, for example, were shaped by centuries of exploitation. We were only prized for our marble and so the endless procession of rulers used their power to control this treasure, and we rebelled when pushed too far. Anarchism runs deep in our veins. Now most folks start worrying when they hear the word, expecting the worst kind of behavior like blowing up government buildings. For me, and for most of the immigrants I knew in those days of injustice, we saw anarchy as a way to protect our freedom, which really meant protecting our families! We did it by going on strike, making speeches, marching in the streets and circulating newspapers. This did not result in killing or maiming anyone, but it was no less of a battle.

In 1908, I found myself working in Barre, Vermont. Barre was and still is known as the "granite capital of the world." The granite in those quarries—and it can go down as far as six hundred feet—is a pure, light gray stone. It's almost perfect as granite goes, strong but not too hard, smooth and reliable. Certainly not as temperamental as marble! So you can understand why sculptors liked this granite. It was used for all kinds of statuary, but for years quarrying was just a local enterprise until the railroad tracks found Barre in the late 1800s. Overnight, the whole world opened up and immigrant stoneworkers flocked there, mostly from Scotland and Italy.

There was a labor hall in Barre and when our normal ten-hour work day was over, I would quickly wash up and head over there like everyone else for something to eat and most times hear a lot of big talk and loud speeches about working conditions.

I wasn't the only *scalpellino* from Carrara who found work in Barre. Between the Italians and the Scots, there were about 4,000 of us working in some forty-five quarries, and so I found friendship with men who came from my hometown . . . . I knew some of their families, so they felt almost like brothers.

The Scots had arrived about ten years ahead of us and organized a union called the Granite Cutters International. Naturally, I was a member. Well, when I was there, the owner of the quarry operation wanted us to work with some new tools. *Molto rapido*, they said. Well, *molto rapido* or not, we knew that the dust particles that would fly out from using these things would eventually kill us. "Silicosis" is what they called it. So we rejected it when it was put to a vote. We knew the Italians were clearly the majority, the Scots the minority supporting management. After a bunch of mumbo-jumbo, we learned we were to go back to work and use the new tools! Well, we made a lot of noise, as we do so well, and another vote was to be taken.

We took to the streets to have ourselves a parade. We didn't want to fight, but we weren't going to back down either when we knew we were right. The Scots were guarding the ballot box, which we knew would be "counted" in their favor again—so we took it! The Scots tried to fend us off with their fists, even pulled off the stair rails to beat us back, but there were too many of us (we were the majority, after all, which was why we knew we had outvoted them in the first place!). Somebody got me with an elbow in the face and I came away with a bloodied nose, but as bruised and battered as we were, we all ended up singing in the streets! We sang *Addio Lugano Bella*, the most popular labor song of that time about the death of a tyrant. All anarchists, both peaceful and radical, loved this song. Part of it went like this:

> Farewell beautiful Lugano
> Farewell my sweet land,
> Driven away guiltlessly,
> the anarchists are leaving
> and they set off singing
> with hope in their hearts.
> It is for you exploited,
> for you workers
> that we are handcuffed
> just like criminals—
> yet our ideal
> is but an ideal of love.

We were also driven out of town.

I much admired in those years an immigrant by the name of Carlo Tresca. He was a feisty southerner from the *Mezzogiorno* who spent his life trying to make things better for the worker, the little guy. He had been forced to leave Italy as they were going to put him in jail for writing some unflattering article against the government about prisoners being tortured. He came to America about the same time I did, and it didn't take long for his name to be on the lips of any Italian immigrant who thought he was being treated unfairly, which was pretty much everybody.

Tresca was a Socialist and published newspapers in the early years of the century. He was one of the first editors of *Il Proletario* and later he started his own, *Il Martello* (*The Hammer*). Nobody escaped Tresca's wrath—not the police, not the politicians, not the rich owners of mines and factories—not even the Catholic Church. He sniffed out corruption where it was and got arrested many times for being so outspoken. He was always on the forefront of things, at anti-war rallies and labor strikes—right in people's faces—and I never thought he would live for very long. I would read his editorials and think it's only a matter of time before someone gets this guy in a dark place some night.

Tresca narrowly escaped death on more than one occasion, and actually lived to the ripe old age of sixty-three before he was shot in the early nineteen-forties. Either the Communists or the Fascists got him in the end, nobody really knows. Because of brave men like him, conditions for immigrant workers eventually improved. It was a war and he was one of our heroes.

But I cannot leave out the most famous case of injustice to Italians in those early days.

Since most of us arrived in America with some degree of anarchism in our blood, it didn't take long for all kinds of groups to surface. Everyone wanted social reform. That was easy to agree with. But the best way to solve it? Nobody could agree on that.

Like Tresca, many believed labor unions were the way and I agreed with that. You can get a point across without having to blow people up. And then there were the radicals. They thought the only way was to take action into their own hands. They did not want to see any organization in control. There were a lot of lunatics running around because of that belief. They thought the only way was through the individual. No organization should hold any power over the people. Otherwise, oppression and corruption would just continue. Anyway, that was their belief.

So blood was spilled when these beliefs clashed, and that was too bad because in the end, everybody wanted the same thing. And you know, it looked complicated, but it was really very simple: to earn a living fair and square and to have a voice.

I was not a radical, but I was in league with the strikers. There was just no other way to get attention. Violence was often the result, especially when Americans felt threatened. They were worried we were taking jobs away from them and diluting their culture with our strange ways. Funny, isn't it, that if most Americans would just look behind them, they would come face to face with their own struggling immigrant grandparents!

Anyway, the worst time I think was when the Russian Revolution of 1917 exploded and the Red Scare became a hunt for Communists or anyone with a foreign-sounding last name. Italians were usually at the top of this list. No matter what our politics, we were singled out as being dangerous.

If you were an anarchist, you were considered an extremist and therefore violent, which in many cases, sadly, was true. After all, Gaetano Bresci, an anarchist from Paterson, New Jersey, took a boat to France in 1900, journeyed to Monza, Italy, and shot King Umberto in the head as he was riding in his carriage, waving to crowds. Bresci was a hero to the radical anarchists in America.

And that was how a humble shoemaker and an idealistic fish peddler got into so much trouble.

During those years—and I'm talking 1917 into the early twenties—whenever robberies and murders were committed, it gave the police, prosecutors and the FBI another excuse to round up the Reds in their neighborhoods.

Carlo Tresca was active during that time, like I said, and for me he epitomized the ideal anarchist. He was the light for many of us.

A man named Luigi Galliani of Boston had a newspaper, too, an underground publication—its name said it all: *La Cronaca Sovversiva* (*The Subversive Chronicle*). He had a large following, the *Gallianisti* they were called.

Galliani was one of those extremists who were against organizing anything and would use violence to make the point that government control should be resisted at all costs. I heard him speak once in Vermont at the Labor Hall in Barre. He was a burly guy with the longest beard I ever saw. I remember it was standing room only and he was perspiring heavily as he pounded his fist on the podium. He said, "When we talk about property, state, masters, government, laws, courts and police, we say only that we don't want any of them!" So, labor unions or political parties were as detestable to him as government was. He was, I have to admit, a persuasive speaker. I picked up his paper (but then I read everything I could get my hands on). It was not a time to be wishy-washy. A man, especially an Italian, had to have an opinion. It was a confusing time and in order to fight for our rights, as we all had to, you had to believe in what you were doing.

In 1919, when Galliani was deported along with other famous anarchists like Emma Goldman and Alexander Berkman, there was a new wave of violence by some of his U.S. followers. A bomb went off on Wall Street that killed and injured many, and one blew up in the front yard of the U.S. attorney general's home. The FBI went on the hunt, and the flames of the Red Scare leaped higher.

Then in April 1920 there was a robbery near Boston. Two payroll guards were shot and killed and the take was about $15,000. Less than one month later, a shoemaker and fish peddler were arrested and charged. Their names were Nicola Sacco and Bartolomeo Vanzetti.

There did not seem to be any direct evidence, but the prosecutor, in his zeal to protect the American public, used their association with Luigi Galliani as a reason to implicate them. It's true these two were members of the *Gallianisti*. They had both gone to Mexico in 1917 to escape being drafted into World War I. They participated in lectures that promoted Galliani's ideals. But nothing I heard or read told me they were either violent or guilty of murder and robbery.

Another crime was pinned on Vanzetti while he sat in prison awaiting trial, a robbery committed on Christmas Eve the year before. Many witnesses came forward to say Vanzetti was selling eels, something any good fish peddler would be doing on that day. The judge gave him a fifty-year sentence, which was five times longer than the normal. The same judge would preside over the murder trial and so we all knew what was coming.

In 1927, Sacco and Vanzetti were found guilty and sentenced to death.

The whole world came to the defense of the two immigrants. And not just other Italians. There were petitions and letters criticizing the obvious sham of a trial. Appeals were denied; a demand for amnesty, after they had been condemned to death, was ignored. The fates of these two men were not in the hands of either the common man or the intellectual. They were in the hands of frightened people. Unfortunately, these same people had the power to turn lies into truth, hope into despair, live people into dead ones.

I have no idea if Sacco and Vanzetti were guilty of the crimes they were accused of. Fear took the place of the facts. But in my heart, I think they were framed. I read Vanzetti's final speech to the court, and I cut it out of the paper so I wouldn't forget him.

"Here is what I say: I would not wish to a dog or snake, to the most low and misfortunate creature of the earth. I would not wish to any of them what I have had to suffer for things I am not guilty of. But my conviction is that I have suffered for things that I am guilty of. I am suffering because I am a radical and indeed I am a radical; I have suffered because I was an Italian, and indeed I am an Italian; I have suffered more for my family and for my beloved ones than for myself; but I am so convinced to be right that if you could execute me two times, and if I could be reborn two other times, I would live again to do what I have done already. I have finished. Thank you."

And then they put them both to death in the electric chair on August 23, 1927. And *we* were called barbaric?

But not every story I heard was tragic.

I met a guy on a train (how many trains have I been on in America?). He was from some tiny town in Sicily, probably not even on a map. He said nobody was left there, nobody. One came, then they all came. All still lived together too. That is in "Little Italy," as Americans call it. This guy says he married a girl, a *regazza* from his hometown—didn't really know her in Italy, they met over here! Isn't that something? Come all the way to America and marry a girl who used to be your next-door neighbor in Sicily.

Mamma mia. The world was just all mixed up.

Anyway, I could never have guessed when I kissed Ione goodbye in 1910 that we wouldn't kiss again for another ten years.

There had been a plan. My father finally made up his mind he would come, so he and my mother, Ione and our three children were to make the trip in 1914 when our youngest, Giorgio, was four years old. I thought it was much too dangerous to bring over a baby, and I also wanted time to find a real home for us. I had become used to picking up and wandering whenever the work called. Life would be different with *la famiglia.*

Well, we all know what happened in 1914. The Great War threw our plans away. Visas were difficult to get. Our applications hit snags over and over.

I thought I would go out of my mind waiting. Years of waiting.

And letters came from Ione. Ione is a practical woman; she didn't write love letters. So when I got one, I was prepared for her way of telling me she loved me by describing what was going on with our children, our parents, how the money was being spent. But I wasn't prepared for the one I got in 1918.

The great influenza epidemic was killing thousands of people that year. It blew through families like the plague of old and it blew through ours hard.

My boy Bruno was dead. Nine years old. Ione didn't elaborate. Her few words told me her grief was enormous. The less she said about things, the more I could feel her pain.

The letter shook in my hands as I jumped to my very next thought: Was everybody else still all right? Ione said in her letter that only Bruno was sick. But it took more than a month for this letter to reach me. Anything could have happened in a month!

I lay in bed at night believing the entire family was on the brink of death, I one cursing me for being away, everything falling on her shoulders. For some reason, I could not imagine her being sick.

I sent a letter the very next day. I can't even tell you now what I said except I was sorry, so sorry that she had to bury our sweet little son and I was not there to comfort her. And to please write to let me know that everyone else was all right.

It wasn't long before the rest of the bad news arrived. My father, Enrico, had succumbed to the influenza. This time the letter came from my mother. Died in his sleep, she said. She had been up all night with him, and thought he was getting better. As usual, she started her work at the tailoring shop early, at sunrise, and later when she went to check on him . . . *morto*. He was becoming as cold as the marble. But she said he looked peaceful. *Grazie a Dio* for that, I thought.

"*Babbo*" I had called him when I was a child. Like when American children say, "Daddy." He had an easy laugh, a gentle way about him, handsome, a twinkle in his eye, unusually tall (something I wished I had inherited). I look like Mamma, but I have my papa's twinkle.

He didn't want me to work the quarries like he did.

Before he started having trouble breathing and took up working in wood, he would leave the house literally in the middle of the night to join his *paesani* as they climbed the mountain, to get to work on time. Home late, clothes covered in the white dust. I would swear his pores still had dust in them, no matter how hard Mamma scrubbed on him.

Removing marble in the quarries was damn hard work. Enrico handled the *lizzatura*. The *lizzatura* were pieces of wood laid down on the slope, so that with heavy ropes the blocks of marble could be eased down the mountain. Try to imagine a dozen men—men, not machines—hauling back on the ropes for resistance, while other men managed the ropes on the descent. Pull and push, letting gravity do as much work as they dared without killing anybody. *Il capolizza*, the overseer, would make sure the blocks were measured so that the load would fit properly on its sled. Each sled might weigh 40 tons. Then the *ungino*, the "man who greases," would soap the wooden slides. The rest of the crew would take their positions as soon as the *ungino's* work was done. The load then was moved down the *lizza*, until the slides had to be placed and soaped again as the marble made its way down.

But it killed many over the years. Ropes break, people hurry, things slip. The horn would go off, its sound echoing down the mountain, a terrible announcement, and we would all know the blood would follow.

My father didn't want that for me. *Dio*—he was a strong man! Fit, lean, not an ounce of fat on him. Gnarled hands, brown

from the sun, face wrinkled from the tension of ropes, weight and sheer willpower.

And to think the *lizzatura* was an improvement over previous methods. They used to just let the cut blocks go and fall all the way down! Of course, the big new beautiful pieces of "meat," as we called them, ended up broken, cracked and otherwise ruined once they stopped roaring down the mountain.

When I was a boy, Enrico (like every father in Carrara) used to tell me stories of how Michelangelo narrowly escaped death a couple of times from runaway marble in our very quarries. And to think the world would have been robbed of the Pietà, David and Moses. If God spares people, he must have been looking out for Michelangelo on those days.

Boy, did I get off track again! But it's easy to do when I'm remembering Enrico and the mountains and the marble. Nothing in America that I saw compared with the white gold of Carrara. *Niente*, nothing. Limestone? Ha! A poor imitation to use on government buildings or cathedrals. Limestone is marble in its infancy.

Picking up a piece of statuary white marble, even *i ravaneti*, which is the wasted, broken-off parts, is like holding a miracle in your hand.

I liked to look at it in the first sunshine of the early, early morning. Marble absorbs light and gives up its secrets only then. They say that's how Michelangelo used to decide which blocks of marble were fit. And he was right. Like a woman tells you indirectly how you can touch her, how close you can come, how much or how little she will reveal.

In the U.S., when I was working with limestone and carving on the façade of a building, or the rare times I had my hands on a piece of marble for a cemetery monument, I would always do the very best work I was capable of, because of Carrara. I would daydream, thinking of how new America was and how I was part of making beautiful art that would be here for years after I was long gone. Michelangelo said, "Art lives forever." His masterpieces came from mountains that held my soul and I put my soul into every carved face, hand and wing.

During those years of separation from my family, when I was on the road, I looked out and saw what a great land America was. Sometimes she opened her arms wide to me and I felt humbled. Other times they were folded and her stare was cold and hard. I saw how cruel she could be.

Where would I bring my family to live in this crazy country? During the war and the long years that kept me from my family, I had followed the work, calling no place my home. Andy was still living in Philadelphia and Ione's letters came to him. I kept in touch with him and he would send them on to me, or when I was so tired I couldn't face another train trip to an unfriendly new place, I would spend some days with him. We would go to the opera, have meals together, tell our tales, sometimes just say nothing. I wanted to breathe the same air in the same room with someone I knew who loved me, so that my loneliness would disappear for a while.

I was by then in my mid-thirties. I was lonely, very lonely. To the bone.

I kept busy. I kept moving. And at night, I would dream of them coming. I painted every detail in my mind of how it would be, that moment when distance was no longer something I had to even think about. And I knew that once they came, I would never let anything in this life rob me of my happiness. I would never be lonely again.

I was not a carouser, and while I might make eyes at a woman who was making eyes at me, I never loved anyone but Ione. I was not perfect, no. I am only a man. And I have no halo to show myself a saint even if I was born on All Saints Day. But I never lost sight of the fact that one day I would have to look into those green eyes and Ione would know everything and then where would things be? There are things you do in this life that need to be buried and forgotten. I buried those things like I buried my grief over Bruno and Enrico, and like my despair over all those nights alone in America.

And there was opera. During those grueling years when I was alone, the operas of Puccini and the old ones of Verdi kept me sane. Singing took me to a place where I forgot about my life, the work, the moment, the way my hands ached, the dust in my nostrils, the hole in the bottom of my shoe, the miserable lunch I would have that day, the flea-infested cot I would be holed up in that night, another long ride on a train to a new place.

Ever since that night in 1900 when I heard *Tosca*, I followed Puccini's career. No, I did not have the opportunity or the money to see his operas, except when I went with Andy. But I bought the librettos and later the recordings and boy did I learn them and sing them while I worked.

Manon Lescaut, La Boheme, Madama Butterfly, La Rondine, Il tabarro, Suor Angelica, Gianni Schicchi, La fanciulla del West, Turandot and of course, *Tosca*. All of them, and not enough of them.

There weren't enough of them because *il maestro* was taken before his time. I was angry when I read of his death. He was only sixty-some years old when he died of throat cancer. He left his final opera, *Turandot*, unfinished. A few years before there had been *uno scandalo* about an affair with some young servant girl his wife accused him of. Puccini's wife harangued the poor girl until she ended up committing suicide. Puccini was vindicated, for the girl was examined after her death and found to be a virgin, but all the publicity, lawsuit and so forth must have put him in a bad way.

In *Turandot*, the character Liu, a slave, kills herself and it was the last act Puccini ever wrote. So a servant girl the world would never have heard of ends up with immortality after all.

Puccini's friend Arturo Toscanini conducted the premiere of *Turandot* two years later. Someone forgettable had been hired to complete the unfinished portions. I thought that was a travesty. But then I read that at the premiere Toscanini had put down his baton at the moment of Liu's death, turned to the audience and said, "The opera ends here because at this point the maestro died. Death on this occasion was stronger than art."

I saw *Turandot* years later, and I left my seat at the death of Liu. When I play the recording at home now, I pull up the needle in the same place. The kids roll their eyes, but say nothing because they've heard the story.

I also got myself a book and sketched things—all kinds of things. People reading on trains, a child kicking a ball, a man sleeping on a bench, a beautiful woman sipping her coffee.

For my whole life, I've found it impossible to rest my hands . . . it feels funny unless I am holding something in them—my chisel or a piece of charcoal. And in those days especially, if I wasn't busy with those things, if I hadn't looked for the beauty in what I was doing, I don't know how I would have made it. There was beauty in the tenor voice of a man in love, in the polished shoulder of a marble angel looking over the dead, in the simple profile of a woman sitting alone, waiting.

I exhausted myself every moment of every single day, which turned out to be a pretty reliable way of making sure I could sleep at night no matter where I was.

I recall all the scenes of my life since leaving Italy as inseparable, so that not one could exist without the others—little lifeboats tied together preserving each memory.

Olga

It was December of 1920. I was sitting next to my grandmother, Nonna Cesira, on the train that was taking us away from Carrara. Examining her tiny hand, turning it over, I could see all the strange brown marks and large blue veins running this way and that, rising up under her skin. I was amazed at how different they were from mine and wondered if I would have those hands one day.

We had secrets, Nonna and I. One night when my mother had sent me to bed for not finishing my supper, Nonna tiptoed to my door later, carrying a warm cup of *cioccolata*. "Shh," she said, "our secret!" Her smile sealed it between us.

I wondered if chocolate would taste that delicious in America.

I looked up at Nonna's face , her silvery hair neatly wound into a knot, a wayward tendril falling down her forehead. Her eyes were closed. I turned away and gazed out the window of the train. Finger and handprints of all sizes and shapes were layered against the glass, remnants of faceless lives on their way to distant places.

I then thought to look beyond the smears, to the quickly

vanishing white marble slopes of Carrara. I turned in the seat as the train sped onward, staring back until I could no longer imagine them. I didn't know if I was sad or not. I knew I would be seeing my Papa again in a few weeks! It will be an adventure, my mother had said, a ship taking us across the ocean to America.

So why then had I heard her crying at night? I looked past Nonna, across the aisle to my mother. She was staring out the window, stroking the blond silky hair on Giorgio's sleepy head in her lap, her face a mask.

I was thirteen years old then. My father had left for America in 1910 when I was only three. I pretended to myself that I remembered him. I would look at the small photograph of him that my mother kept by her bed. I made up stories about him. I dreamt of him with one hand on a piece of marble, the other gripping a chisel, chips flying and dust floating around him, turning him into a white ghost. He would lift me onto his lap, telling me stories of how precious the marble was, how it was a miracle that the only pure marble in the world was in our mountains, and terrifying stories of how Michelangelo narrowly escaped death.

Some of these things my grandfather Enrico told me as I was growing up, but I also made believe.

There were four of us who boarded the train that chilly morning: Nonna Cesira, Mamma, Giorgio and me. The small station of Carrara was not crowded. I had imagined it would be full of people dressed in their best suits of clothes like we were, men trying to keep their families and luggage together, women holding onto squirming babies, sleepy children sitting on steamer trunks leaning against their mammas, the conductor shouting directions trying to be heard over the crowd, as people tried to find the words to say goodbye to parents, brothers, sisters, sons, daughters, cousins, to those who would then be left standing on a deathly quiet platform.

There would have been some comfort in that.

But the truth was, not many northern Italians were still leaving for America in 1920. The first surge of Italian immigrants were those from the north, like when my father made his first trip almost twenty years before.

Were we the only ones going? I looked up at my mother with these words in my eyes and my mother looked down at me, her eyes soft, liquid.

Trunks were loaded, seats were taken, tickets were stamped. The conductor punched four times and I swallowed hard, thinking there should have been one more, one more for Bruno.

Two years younger than I, Bruno was born in 1908, after my father left on the second of three trips he would make between Italy and America. Bruno had soft reddish-brown curls and the green eyes of my mother, eyes I privately desired. I thought my brown ones, the same as everyone else's, were nothing special. I felt plain.

My mother cuddled Bruno, sang to him as he slept in her arms. I watched her dab at the bubbles that formed on his mouth as he blew sounds and smiles into her face, held so close to his, her eyelashes damp on his soft cheek. His bronze curls blended perfectly with my mother's as she held her cheek to his, singing *una ninnananna,* a sweet lullaby for him:

Maria lavava,	Mary busy with the washing,
Giuseppe stendeva,	Joseph hung it out for drying,
Il figlio piangeva	All alone the baby lying
dal freddo che aveva.	From the bitter cold was crying.
Stai zitto mio figlio,	Hush my son, my little one,
che adesso ti piglio,	In a moment I'll have done,
Il latte t'ho dato,	All my milk I've given to you

il pane non c'è.	And the bread is finished too.
La neve sui monti	As snow from the heavens
cadeva dal cielo,	Fell over the mountains,
Maria col suo velo	With her mantle of blue
copriva Gesù.	Mary covered Jesus.

On my eleventh birthday, Bruno became feverish, his cheeks aflame, his body trembling. My mother and grandmother, their backs to me and Giorgio, bent over him, calmly cooling his flesh with cloths soaked in water.

"Go to the fountain, Olga, please!" my mother said without turning around.

"*Sì*, take this bucket and hurry back!" Nonna said, turning to look at me with kind encouragement.

I did not have to be told to go to the fountain of the Siren. It was said that the water was full of the Siren's healing tears, which had miraculous powers. Stung and blinded by my own tears, I stumbled through the small crooked streets and over the Bridge of Tears to find this healer, Giorgio behind me, desperately trying to keep up. He was only seven years old. I kept yelling at him to go back home, but he clung to my footsteps. I held the pail under the water spilling from the dolphin's mouth. The Siren looked down benevolently as she rode his back, as she had done for centuries.

I wiped the tears running down my chin, but they mingled in the waters and I looked up at the Siren. I was sorry, so sorry I had been jealous of Bruno's green eyes and the attention my mother lavished on him.

In 1918, many died from the influenza epidemic and Bruno, too was swept up by this plague, dead at nine years old.

In just a matter of weeks, Nonno Enrico succumbed as well.

Enrico had been *uno scultore del legno*, a woodcarver, and many homes in Carrara held his handiwork. A bureau for Signora Fregosi's dining room, a chair for a small corner in Signora Mazzuoli's bedroom, a frame for a mirror, its curved edges graceful, leaves and rosettes intertwined, gleamed as if they had always grown out of that wood.

Almost all the furniture in our home had been born of his hands. He worked in our small back yard, wood chips flying. Sometimes he would take his rest under the large fig tree. We had to give away or sell almost everything when we left for America. Mamma and Nonna must have felt like they were selling some of their children.

Nonno had worked in the marble when he was young, but after many years, his breathing became labored. One day, after he came down the mountain from the quarry, he put down his chisel and never went back.

He carved marble at home in between furniture projects. One of his friends, who still worked in the quarries, would bring him blocks of marble, pieces no bigger than what a strong man could carry with both hands. Enrico would beam and often come into the house covered in equal parts marble and wood dust.

"My father, Antonio, taught me woodcarving," he told me one day as I sat under the fig tree and watched him polish the slender leg of a small table. *Molto carino*, such a charming thing, I had thought. Later, I discovered the little table in my bedroom and knew how much my grandfather loved me.

Enrico's coffin was placed in the front parlor, as was the custom. People came and went for hours. Occasionally someone would pat my face. Giorgio stayed close to me, shy. I walked around the house, avoiding the coffin, yet I was fascinated at the idea of looking inside it. I thought, Bruno's coffin was so small.

This one took up the entire room, barely enough space for anyone to find the place to kneel and pray for his soul. I closed my eyes and thought again of Bruno, how he had looked exactly the same to me in death as he had in life. He would always be a little boy, like an angel. An angel with green eyes.

Women cried softly, but then a wail would ascend like a soprano's voice rising above a chorus.

Mamma and Nonna were very quiet, their voices hushed, defeated. I watched Nonna. She stood up straight and smiled into the faces of our grieving friends, gracious, as she always was. Once in a while, though, I would catch her staring off into space and see those little shoulders giving up. We had lost so much and in less than a month.

Enrico was only fifty-three when he died. And all he had ever talked about was when were they all going to America . . . when would the day come? He asked every day. When would he see his son again?

The smell of crushed white flowers and the heat of the room made me dizzy. I started thinking that maybe I had the plague too. I stared across the room and imagined my own body in the coffin.

The grieving finally left with their rosaries and I crept over to the coffin, Giorgio right on my heels. I took a deep breath and looked inside. My first thought was how wrong he looked. His moustache and his thick hair were combed neatly with a waxy shine that was out of place. He held a crucifix on his chest, between his hands, like a prayer. I peered closely at the crevices in his hands and fingertips that had always held the fine dust of marble. Gone. Blown away.

The journey to America that Nonno Enrico had longed for

would not come for two years.

The Great War kept us from the reunion my father had planned. Petitions for passports and visas were denied time and time again during those years.

And letters would arrive, long letters. Sometimes Mamma handed me a little sketch Papa had included in the letter. A note would be attached and he called me his *"figlia bellissima,"* his most beautiful daughter. My cheeks would burn and I let these words sink into my heart.

In the dim light, late in the evenings, I remember watching my mother, clad in a white cotton nightdress, as she bent over the kitchen table. With her long hair loosened over her shoulders, hand against her cheek, she wrote to my father so many thousands of miles away.

Finally, America relaxed and said we could come.

The day before we left our home, Mamma told me she wanted to take a walk with me down to the port. It was a long walk on a winter morning, but I was happy to be alone with her.

We held hands as we stood on the cold beach that brilliant morning, as the sounds of Carrara beginning her day surrounded us. I heard the sing-song voices of fishermen calling to each other over the water, the splish-splash of waves near our feet. I squinted at the flutter of sea gulls overhead. I closed my eyes, wishing the air were warm so I could take off my shoes and dig my toes into the sand.

Huge blocks of dazzling marble lay on the sand in the distance . . . a god's nursery, with orphans silently waiting to be delivered to the ships that would carry them to their fates. Some would become statues of saints, others would be steps in a rich man's *palazzo*, others would have humbler destinies. What will ours be, I wondered.

Mamma bent down and scooped up a handful of sand and put it in mine. As I let the cool grains sift through my fingers, she said, "Carrara is our home and I will never see it again. You must not forget where you came from."

These memories washed through my mind and in my dreams on the train.

We got off the train in Genoa. I was still sleepy until my feet hit the platform and I was slapped with all the commotion of the station. Carrara has a one-track station, a short stop on the way to somewhere else. Genoa is the major port city of Italy, after Naples, and the swarms of people, the noisy clamor of voices and train whistles dazed me.

This assault continued outside the train station and I was gripped by the wonder of where all these people were going.

Mamma explained we would be spending the night in Genoa and then we would get on the big ship the next morning. First, she said, we had to get our papers in order.

"And then what?" I asked her.

Mamma's smile turned into a frown. She did not want to be asked "then what?"

"Whatever is next," she said flatly, and I didn't ask any more questions.

We all held onto each other and squirmed our way into a small office. The sign on the door said Immigrant Aid Society. It was the first time I saw that word—immigrant—and I started to ask Mamma what it was, then remembered she didn't want to answer any questions.

As usual, we waited in a mass of people with no line and no order. I have never understood why Italians cannot form lines. But we didn't learn how to do that until we came to America.

I soon found out what was "next." And I suddenly realized why Mamma had not told us about this part.

Mamma rolled up her sleeve and I watched in horror as a doctor put a needle into her arm. She winced, but only slightly. She never took her eyes off of me and smiled when it was over, as if to say, "See? It's not so bad."

Nonna went next and looked right at the needle as it went in, as if to defy its sting.

I felt Giorgio leave my side and cling to Mamma's skirt as I rolled up my sleeve and put out my arm. The doctor nodded, saying *"Brava, signorina"* and before I knew it, it was over. It hurt, but I kept thinking that this is what we have to do so we can be with Papa again.

I couldn't watch the doctor give Giorgio the shot. Mamma held him in her lap and he whimpered, but there was no time for tears. We were scooted out of the office and told to be on our way.

Immersed in the crowds massed on the docks, I was shaken out of my belief that we would be crossing the ocean by ourselves. I held tightly onto Giorgio. Nonna never let us out of her sight as Mamma figured out how to tow us and our luggage through the maze. Mamma always figured everything out.

Strangers who pretended to be friends appeared: "Signora! Where are you taking your mother and children to sleep tonight? I know a safe place, come with me." "Signora! Give me just a little lire and I'll carry your luggage for you, Signora."

My mother gripped the handle of the bag. As a man came

forward to put his hand on it, she swung it out to hit him! The man was quick enough to back away before he got smacked.

"Go away. *Vai!*" Mamma hissed to anyone who came within a foot. Papa had written, had told her, many times in letters: Under no circumstances pay money to anyone at the docks to do any favors!

When I want to remember where I slept that night, I cannot not seem to, as hard as I try. I remember only that it seemed I slept for moments before I was shaken and told to be quick about getting washed and dressed.

Giorgio and I held hands, Mamma and Nonna right behind us, as we became engulfed among the crowds on the docks waiting to board the ship, the SS *Caserta*. The water was the same color as the steel gray sky and the wind blew my hair around, but I didn't feel its cold because of all the bodies pressed closed to us. I looked up at the ship and its size did not scare me. I had seen ships that big in the port of Carrara, but their cargo was the huge chunks of marble transported from sand to the ships' hulls, by rope, by pulley, slowly, one precious block at a time. I had never imagined that cargo could also be human. We all moved slowly up the ramps, those of us in steerage who had been called last, so that the first class passengers could be spared the unpleasantness of being so close to poverty. Having their tea already, I had supposed.

We had climbed so high to get on board, but then began the long climb down to third class sleeping quarters below. There was very little light and I felt strange when I sat on the small hard bunk next to Mamma. I saw the look on her face. She bit her lip and just sat there, but I did not see fear in her eyes.

"Mamma, it's just for two weeks," I heard myself saying. I took her hand in mine.

"We can sleep anywhere for two weeks," Nonna chimed in.

"Can I go back up on deck, Mamma?" Giorgio shouted. "I want to be up there when we pull away!"

"*Si*, let's all go," Nonna commanded.

The throngs on the deck were a mass of hands waving to those being left behind, and those left behind were waving to those who were leaving forever. We waved too, and I put my arms around Nonna's waist, feeling her small body trembling. She never stopped waving and never stopped crying, not until the port and the people disappeared from our view and all that was left was the ship, the water and the sky.

Mamma and I were sick almost the entire time it took to cross the Atlantic. The damp smells, penetrating cold, rotten food, the smell of other people's vomit, left us heaving and feverish in our beds.

Nonna and Giorgio, on the other hand, had a grand time, running around up on deck, exchanging stories with other *italiani*, enjoying the brisk sea air whenever the blustery arctic winds quieted down enough.

Years later, Giorgio confessed that Nonna had put a spoonful of brandy in his coffee each morning, this potion keeping him feeling buoyant most of the time. Nonna had obviously helped herself as well. Mamma and I looked over at the guilty one, our mouths open. Nonna shrugged her tiny shoulders and continued to attend to her embroidery and say, "There wasn't enough for everybody and besides, you two were the strongest persons."

Ha! I never knew anyone in my life who was stronger than Nonna.

Papa had also instructed us to bring fresh fruit, but it perished within days. Our own appetites perished as well. When I found maggots squirming in a bowl of food I was given, I refused to eat anything else but bread after that. I looked under and through and into everything I touched. I told my mother I felt things crawling on my skin, slimy and prickly. She searched our scalps every day looking for lice.

I never felt completely warm or dry and I sweated from sickness, a reaction to the vaccination, I suppose. My hair was saturated, as were the filthy sheets I slept in. I dreamed of snakes swimming in water. But there was no sleeping through the night. I would lie awake, as Mamma did, our stomachs lurching, listening to the sounds and smelling the misery of the dark—snoring, weeping, retching, a close smell of urine or the blood of women, babies crying, praying, soothing voices.

On that long ocean crossing, I became a woman. I saw the blood and was horrified. I tried to keep it a secret, but one day blurted out to Nonna that I was dying.

"*Cara*," she said, "you leave Italy *una bambina* and arrive in America *una donna*!"

Nonna told me that I would have this as all women do, every month, with pain for almost the rest of my life. Only when I was going to have a baby would it stop, and there is also blood at birth. A memory flashed in my head—that of seeing her carrying out bloodied sheets from my mother's bedroom. This happened on the day Giorgio was born and I had believed my mother was dead.

I felt surrounded by water, vomit, tears and blood. My new world was an immersion into life, into womanhood, a murky unknown.

There on the icy sea, Christmas Eve of 1920 arrived. Just after midnight, we ate meager portions of whatever was served, filling ourselves with dreams and memories of what we usually enjoyed at *Natale*. The fragrance of garlic-roasted meats, savory risotto and so many sweet things were recalled as we said our prayers, knowing it wouldn't be long before we would have good food again. Only one more week of this, we said!

Mamma and I said *buona notte* to the night owls and climbed down to the depths where we slept. I curled up next to my mother and we fell asleep peacefully for a change. The frigid night sea was still in the moonlight, like the most perfect white polished marble – deep, translucent and silent.

I soon fell into the same rhythm as my mother's breathing.

I was having a peaceful dream of some kind when I felt a jolt. I didn't wake, and in this sleep state, the jolt became part of the dream. It felt real, as if my head suddenly hit against something immoveable, a slam that penetrated my bones.

I heard a long and deep groan, moaning and twisted. My peaceful dream seemed to be turning into a nightmare whose phantoms won't stop chasing you. My eyes flew open. I heard rustling around me, of bodies and blankets. Loud questions filled the dark. The sounds of wonder became the sounds of panic, footsteps were scuffled, confused.

Mamma pulled me up with a hard jerk. She had hold of my hand as we scrambled and made our way through the crowded dark, pushing our way up, just up however we could go.

One clear prayer could be heard above the other cries: "*Madonna santissima, auitaci!*" Send help, save us!

Mamma lost her grip on me and we were each tossed like waves up the cold metal stairwells. I felt I was stepping on people, but I could do nothing but be carried along, clutching at whatever was in reach—hair, arms, clothing—to keep from falling under the crush of feet.

I couldn't find her. I cried out for her, but could see nothing and my voice was just one frantic cry among many others.

My nose filled with frigid open air as I reached the deck and I choked from having held my breath for too long. My heart was a drum in my chest. The only light came from the bright hard stars in the sky, but I could still see fear in all the faces around me.

The ship's crew was yelling at everyone and each other. With voices and whistles, they guided us into groups on the deck.

I stood shivering in my thin nightgown, trying to stay out of the way. I closed my eyes, listening for my family's voice. Instead, I started hearing a new word over and over . . . "*Il ghiaccio*! It was ice! We hit an iceberg!"

My tears were freezing on my cheeks. People around me began praying. I saw others wandering in circles, dazed. Others clutched at their children, one man's fist was blaming heaven. Many sank to their knees in disbelief.

I thought to myself, "I wonder if it will be a slow death, inch by inch." The water would be terrible and I shivered more at the thought of that unimaginable cold than at the December gale blowing across the ship.

I remembered it was Christmas and looked up at a beautiful sky of glittering stars. I would never see my father now. I would never know what chocolate tastes like in America. I would never be a woman in America or have my Nonna's hands.

But at that moment, I felt those hands on my face and a blanket was thrown over my trembling limbs, as my body folded into hers.

The ship's wound was not fatal obviously, as I lived to tell the story! It took on water during the rest of the trip. The pumps cried and moaned constantly. The ship limped along. Instead of trying to find sleep, we passengers in steerage fought sleep, as we imagined how close the cold waters were to our beds. Death was inches away and we were so far from Italy now.

The Captain announced it was too late to go back. Believe me, every passenger asked him. We were near the middle of our crossing, so we might as well keep going, he said. His assurance was met with very little belief. Everyone on board talked about the sinking of the Titanic, which had occurred eight years before. We felt we had just lived through a miracle.

I have always since believed that when your time is up, it's up. And I also swore to myself I would never board another boat again.

Giorgio's ninth birthday was January 10. There were no special treats to celebrate with, but Mamma promised him a party once we were together with Papa in our new home. Sunny, beautiful Giorgio. He didn't care so much. He always managed to find his own amusement on the ship. Having inherited Papa's love of opera and his voice as well, Giorgio entertained us on his birthday. He was enraptured with the opera Puccini had written about the American wild west—*La fanciulla del West*, The Girl of the Golden West—so pretending to be the cowboy Johnson, he sang:

Risparmiate lo scherno . . .	Spare your mockery . . .
Della morte;	I am not worried
Non mi metto pensiero:	about death:
E ben voi tutti lo sapete!	And all of you are well aware of it!
Pistola o laccio e uguale	Pistol or noose, it's all the same.
Se mi sciogliete un braccio . . .	If you untie one arm . . .
Mi sgozzo di mia mano!	I'll cut my own throat!

Giorgio had found a piece of cloth to wrap around his throat like a bandana, and ripped it off, pretending to cut his own throat. He fell down at our feet, twitching like a man dying with great drama. Nonna jumped up clapping. "*Bravissimo!*" she cried. Mamma and I huddled together laughing and applauding. A crowd had collected and Giorgio leapt to his feet, bowing at the numerous ovations. There were many encores. My brother made us forget ourselves.

Day after day, we looked for that lady in the harbor that meant we were in America.

In those last days at sea, I would sometimes brave the cold and go up on the deck. Always, in all directions, there was nothing but the water. I could not grasp how vast the ocean was. It seemed to me the ship wasn't moving at all.

We arrived on January 20, 1921, more than a month since the day of departure and a full two weeks longer than the voyage should have taken.

There are really no words to describe the moment when you realize your life will be changed forever.

On the ship, we had our memories of Italy still and we spoke of them all the time so we wouldn't lose them, because we believed we would never go back. America for all its riches and dreams was still the unknown, yet it was where we would live the rest of our lives. Hope, terror, gratitude, longing and regret were as real and present on the deck of that ship as the four of us standing there.

We waited on board after the ship docked at the pier on the Hudson River. We watched the first-class passengers leave the ship on their way to the immediate embraces of loved ones. A doctor had come on board to take a quick look at these well-to-do passengers and they departed for customs at the Barge office.

I looked around at those of us left behind, those of us in steerage. The people had a wild look about them and this matched the wildness of our imaginations as we were led toward the dreaded examinations at Ellis Island. Our fear was wild, for the stories that crossed the Atlantic of deportees separated from their families had embedded themselves in our minds and we believed them.

Disease, exhaustion and fear clung to us like our wrinkled and dirty clothing. Thirty days at sea, and as terrified as we had been that the ocean would claim us, Ellis Island seemed like the gates of heaven that would slam unmercifully if we were found wanting. Our want was desperate but the moment had arrived. Profound heartache or sublime joy awaited us. There would be no in between.

During those moments, when the excitement of being on deck and seeing the gigantic Statue of Liberty soar above us had passed, during the moments when I saw the first class group disembark so freely, during those moments . . . remembering the iceberg, when I thought: *are there enough lifeboats for everybody?* It was the first time in my life that I realized that in this big world, my life was not worth very much outside my family.

I squeezed Giorgio's little hand and looked down at him. His face was bright at the adventure, which felt to him as if a live opera was being performed in front of his eyes. I smiled at him through my tears. My mother and grandmother were behind us, and their strong hands on my shoulders comforted me.

We disembarked with our possessions and boarded a ferry that took us to Ellis Island. We were given large identity tags to hang around our necks. Lines began to form, our luggage was checked and we walked upstairs to the landing outside the Registry Room.

My legs felt funny and wobbly from the sudden stable surface under me. Ahead, up the line, I saw the doctors in their uniforms. "*La Batteria*" is what we called the examinations.

I was tired and I was afraid. I let my thoughts wander and I gazed at the other people pressed in around us. The line moved slowly but steadily and occasionally a voice became loud or pleading, as one of the doctors put a chalk mark on the passenger who did not pass this first round of examinations.

I shivered and wondered where they took people with chalk marks. Did they just put them back on the ship? Were they allowed to see their family?

While we waited in line Giorgio, past his amazement at hearing different languages, began to rub his sleepy eyes. I elbowed him hard, thinking that red eyes would only call attention. My thoughts leapt ahead. What if even one of us didn't pass?

I glanced behind me, at Nonna who looked tired but managed a smile and a wink.

Then I touched my own face, wondering how I must look after the seasickness and loss of appetite. "I must be green," I thought. "They don't let sick people into America" is what we were all thinking in that line—Italian, German, Russian, everyone. In the hushed whispers of each language, everyone was thinking the very same thing.

I thought of my father, who was somewhere nearby and patiently waiting for us. I would know my father immediately, I believed. I had dreamt of him so many times and I remember thinking it was possible we might never even get to see him.

I was hungry and thought about what I would eat if I could have anything from my mother's kitchen—*la cucina*. I thought about summer, when the dark green leaves of *basilico* perfumed my hands as I plucked them to adorn the blood-red *pomodori*, sun-warmed and sweet together. But no, that's not what I would have. No, it would be *zuppa di minestrone*—steaming hot and filled with savory bits of *pancetta* . . . then a thick slice of crusty bread to swipe every last drop from the bowl.

Day dreams . . . let them go on, I thought. It was the longest day of my life.

I don't remember the faces of anyone who asked me

questions, or pulled back my eyelids, or placed cold instruments to my chest. I would always remember what the hands felt like, how the voices spoke to me yet I understood nothing, only terror from not knowing if people were being kind or cruel and whether I should weep or smile in response.

When the doctor used the instrument on my eyelids to check for trachoma, I sent up a prayer that Giorgio's rubbing would not hold him back. I wanted to scream, "He's just a little boy—nothing is wrong with him!" But I made myself stand very still.

Then I saw them put the chalk mark on Nonna, and lead her away before anyone could say anything. I burst into tears.

We were told that Cesira was being held for a more thorough examination, but these words made no impact. Stunned and silent, we were guided into the Registry Room to sit and wait on long benches with hundreds of others. We would have to answer more questions and pass a literacy test.

The room was immense and not unlike the size of a ship. But on the ship hearing our native tongue and being among our own kind was one thing that comforted us as we floated out across the dark waters from Genoa. This room was filled with people who spoke different tongues and it was another jolt that reminded us we were small in the world.

Mamma took us by our hands and we waited. Her hands smoothed our hair and stroked our faces. She held herself by the elbows and rocked on the hard wooden bench. I kept hearing her say, "*Poverina, poverina . . .*" *Poor little thing.* I thought, why does my grandmother have to endure this? What will they do to her? What are we going to do if they won't let her come with us? We constantly watched doors around the vast room, hoping to see her walk through.

When our turn came to face the inspector, to our relief he

understood Italian. Mamma calmly answered his questions: "Yes, we are Italian . . . My husband and their father paid for our passage. He is meeting us here in New York, waiting for us right now. I am a housewife . . . . Yes, I can read and write . . . Yes, my children and mother can read and write . . . My mother? My mother was taken away. The doctors are examining her . . . No, I am not an anarchist. No, I have never been in a prison . . . When can I see my mother?"

"Mamma, what are we going to do if Nonna is sent back?" I was surprised to hear my own voice asking my mother this impossible question, as if I had a right. I expected a look, not a response from my mother.

"We aren't leaving here without her," she announced and her voice echoed in the lonely hallway where we waited after passing all the exams. "If she has to go back, we'll all go back, and that includes your Papa."

We were finally ushered in to see Nonna. I was relieved to see her face indignant, her chin high and arms folded. She was not in a bed and she was fully dressed, just sitting there. When Mamma opened her mouth to ask how she was doing, Nonna held up her hand and cut her off. "And so what if I have to go back to Italy? I have my business and I have my house and I will be fine! *Vai!* Go to Aristide! You are putting him out of his mind with this worry! Go on and leave me alone."

The doctor came in at that moment, examined Nonna and shrugged his shoulders as if he couldn't understand why she was held back in the first place.

Nonna was released and she took my hands. We jumped up and down and around in a circle like little girls. We had been on Ellis Island for six hours. We gathered our belongings, which for the very first time felt light in our hands, and boarded the ferry in the late afternoon, the final trip that would take us to Papa.

"Will he still be there?" I asked out loud as the ferry slowly pulled away from the dock.

Giorgio said, "Of course he'll be there. He's our Papa!"

I searched for him among the crowd on the still-distant dock, among all those waving, yelling, laughing, crying . . . heads craning up and down searching for that one face that mattered.

As the ferry approached, I heard a sound come from my mother's throat, felt her body lurch forward. She squeezed my hand hard.

"*Guarda! Mamma, guarda!*" she said to Nonna. Look, Mamma, look! Nonna clapped her hands together and cried, "*Sì, lo vedo!*" Yes, I see him. I see him! Yes!

My eyes fell on my father's face, and I knew him. In an instant, ten years fell away.

When my father held me, it felt like he was never going to let go, like I would be forever in his arms. I cried and buried my face in his chest so I could inhale him. There was a light snow falling on us and his wool coat, damp with small snowflakes, was rough against my cheek. My nose ran all over it and I was completely in love with him. Holding me with one strong arm, he lifted up my brother with the other. Pressed close in those protective arms with Giorgio, I imagined little Bruno was there, waiting for his turn, for Papa to hold him too.

Giorgio could not contain himself, looking at the spectacle of people all around him. "Look, Nonna! Those men are lucky to have so many brothers!" He had seen black men with matching red caps carrying luggage for travelers.

I remember looking at my parents and I will never forget seeing them together for the first time in my own memory . . . and feeling there was nothing any more to fear.

I'll never forget the day my family arrived and the moment my loneliness left me.

Aristide

When they didn't get off any of the ferries by noon, my heart, which was so full from waiting, sank. Sank to the depths I had imagined when I heard their ship had hit an iceberg on Christmas Eve, taking my hopes and dreams with them.

You know that I jump ahead in my thoughts, so you can imagine how relieved I was when I learned the ship was going to be all right, just delayed! Two more weeks the official told me! Yet each day of delay was an agony, a hardship to endure, a cruel one it seemed to me. Ten years was unbearable, but it was over.

I recalled my own experiences getting through customs, so when the ship came into the harbor, I expected them to be on the first ferry. Wouldn't you? A ferry arrived about every hour from Ellis Island—so yes, by noon, I was frantic. I couldn't move from my place, but my mind was imagining all sorts of disasters. As I stood there, I felt fragile, my faith felt fragile. I believed they had been saved at sea by a miracle and I wanted the rest of it now, right now.

The last ferry of the day was coming. My fingers were numb

from the cold, my heart was in my throat and I thought, "If they're not on this ferry, I am going to die."

It seemed that it took forever to come close enough for me to see any of them. But then suddenly, like a door that opens right in front of you, I saw her face. Ione's face.

So long, so long had it been since I had seen this face! But I was only allowed that glimpse before she disappeared among the crowd again. Then I noticed this small hand waving, and realized it was my own little mother!

"Ci-ci-ree!" I called out to her, which was what I have called my mother for years, from the first time I tried to say her name, Cesira, and couldn't get it right.

A young woman stood next to her, a bit taller than my mother, her serious face staring at me fiercely. How could this be Olga, I thought. But it was, she looked just like Ione. She had her arm around a young boy who had a mop of blonde hair—my son whom I had never seen!

I did everything I could to keep the tears behind my eyes. I wanted to be able to read my children's faces clearly. If I missed these first looks, I would always wonder if they had loved me in my absence.

I wanted to run to the boat, but could only inch my way through the crowd. Suddenly, they were all right there: Ione, Cesira, Giorgio and Olga. I picked Giorgio up carefully. My ten-year old son put his arms around my neck and said, "I love you Papa!" and when I looked over his shoulder at my wife, we both thought of Bruno and wept openly. I have never known another moment in my life where joy and grief were so equally measured in my heart.

As I wiped my tears away, I noticed it had started to snow. I will never forget looking into my daughter's eyes, the snowflakes gently falling on the dark hair that framed her face. She looked back unsmiling and for a moment I thought she was angry, but she fell into my arms and she shook all over in her sobs. "*Carissima, carissima!*" I patted her hair. I couldn't believe how beautiful she was.

I pulled my mother close to me and laughed out loud because she felt the same to me. I swung her gently around and off the ground. Her body was still firm and lean but when I looked into her eyes, I saw how much older she was. She nodded as she read my thoughts and whispered, "If only Enrico could have lived to see this day. He tried so hard and he loved you so much, son."

This brought me fresh tears and I have to confess, after all the years of seeing this day in my mind, I did not know how I was going to be able to turn to my wife. I waited the longest for her, I had longed for her more than anyone these past ten years. I guess I worried that if I had kissed her first, my children and mother would think I loved them less. But Ione has always understood me. She knew that I wanted her for last because I love her the most.

My mother took the children by their hands and walked away so we could be alone.

What do you say after ten years? I poured my heart out to Ione in letters, told her I loved her a million times.

The immediacy of having my family suddenly appear around me, especially my wife, completely unnerved me. I found that all I could do at first was just look into her eyes, hold her, cry with her. Words failed me, completely failed me! Touching her, caressing her, was the only thing I knew to do. The many years spent touching stone, polishing stone, in silence and in rapture, had become natural for me—so I did what came naturally. Words would have to come later.

My friend Sandro had patiently waited with me to help with the trunks and then take us to his home. The electric trolley cars were a brand new sight in New York and to us all a modern miracle. We were used to seeing horses doing the work. My mother clapped her hands in delight and was the first one to hop on board.

I saw they were all thunderstruck as they tried to take in the overwhelming chaos of the city, so I told them we were going to be living in Alabama.

"It's warm there and we'll have a garden," I said to them when I knew they were cold from the January chill. I know what it's like to remember the sun of Carrara and its brilliant flood of light, golden on the mountains. I remember it well, even if it was years ago. So I understood their fear. Their gentle world had been torn by near-death at sea, a voyage twice as long as provisions lasted, cold gales that had teeth in them and caused them to be both seasick and homesick. The long lines, the fear of the doctor's decisions—Cesira was almost sent back!—not understanding when and how they would find me—how could their hope survive all of that?

I so wanted them to have hope, to know that this dismal voyage and dirty city and cold gray skies were not what America was, at least not all the time. I told my children stories of the mountains in Colorado, the beautiful wide stretches of land, the generosity of strangers I received many times. I told them of my adventures, of labor strikes and how proud they should be that they now live in a country that has such freedoms!

I didn't hide the truth from them; not all the stories had happy endings. But I wanted them to know what life was, especially Giorgio.

*Could anything on earth compare with the
size and noise of New York City?*

Olga

We spent six days there, staying with friends of Papa, to rest,
to eat, to not have to get on a train right away to yet another
strange place. I was wide-eyed as we walked around, my head
almost always turned up toward the skies as tall buildings seemed
to reach like sopranos do for the highest note, up into clouds.

I thought the English language sounded harsh, but then the
familiar lilting Italian would surround me among the crowds of
Mulberry Street, the vendors, the fruit stands, the children running
and playing. I missed my home.

I missed the clean white look of marbled mountains against
blue sky. I missed the Monday morning market in the Piazza
Alberica, the gentle exchanges with friends as we sat on the steps
of the fountain, the smells from close kitchens calling us home to
eat. I missed the walks down narrow streets and the ancient walls
of the cathedral. I could never have imagined New York City
and how my fellow countrymen lived in a place where even
breathing was difficult. Our house in Carrara was not grand, but
I saw whole families in New York living in one room, water that
tasted bad and women and little children going to work in factories

everyday. It was true that in Carrara boys started learning how to work in the marble quarries at an early age, but everyone seemed happier and certainly they looked healthier. America, the land I thought was so big in my dreams, looked small and dreary, at least in the Italian neighborhoods.

Papa's easy laughter helped. And he told us his work was in Alabama, that we would be taking a train there, where it was warmer and that we would have a garden!

I smiled when I heard Papa say "Alabama." I pronounced it perfectly the first time, not like so many other English names that I couldn't seem to get out of my mouth. So I imagined that because the word sounded so friendly, it must be a wonderful place.

"Did you plant *basilico*, Papa? Do we have a fig tree too?" I asked him as he gave me a kiss goodnight.

The train ride was long and I slept like I had never slept before. I dreamt I was on the train from Carrara and I saw the mountaintops, crisp and white, fly by like clouds. I saw Enrico in his coffin and he was laughing. And then suddenly I was holding Bruno's hand because the ship was sinking and he was shivering. I felt the lice in my scalp and this jerked me awake and I blinked at my surroundings, not sure where I really was.

My mother and father sat in the seats in front of me, their heads leaning in toward one another, touching. They were speaking softly to each other and this made me feel safe again.

"Papa was right," I said to myself, as we got off the train and I felt the mild, humid air of Alabama on my face, so very different from New York City. The constant chatter of foreign languages was replaced by a southern drawl and the dialect of the Old South. It didn't sound harsh, this English.

There were no electric trolley cars in Montgomery. I

remember feeling the gait of the horse on yet again unfamiliar streets, looking at grand mansions and manicured lawns. Then minutes later, seeing the shabbiness and roughness of the street where we would live, the place for Negroes and immigrants.

For our first dinner Mamma wanted to make ravioli, but the market didn't have all the familiar ingredients that normally fill those tender pockets. We sat at the table that evening in silence, wondering how the ravioli would really taste with Alabama greens mixed up inside, and whatever else Mamma and Nonna were able to put their hands on.

Imagine—my father hadn't tasted Mamma's cooking for ten years! The comforting aroma of the tomato sauce swirled up to our noses; we looked anxiously at our plates. Papa tasted first and when his left eyebrow rose in a surprised arch, we all nearly cried from relief. We wanted to believe we would be able to live in Alabama after all.

Mamma and Nonna had brought what they could from Italy. The three of us couldn't wait to open up the large trunk and when we did, the fragrance of our house in Carrara spilled out with the bedding and tablecloths and clothing. There would be no way to preserve the aroma, but it was a smell we carried in our hearts. For a while, when I would sleep on those embroidered pillowcases, I was carried back to my beautiful little bedroom.

So our humble home was layered with these comforts. Hand-crocheted linens were placed on tabletops. Colanders, cheese graters and pasta cutters adorned the plain kitchen.

On the first day of school, Giorgio and I were assigned to the first grade because we couldn't speak English. This humiliation made us both work very hard.

We came home every day and shared with Mamma and Nonna what we had learned, so all of us began to speak English slowly together. Papa would correct and write things down very patiently so we would learn faster. He wanted us to speak English, so that our differences would lessen the unkind glances and remarks from those who looked down on anyone who was not white and Protestant.

By the end of our first year, Giorgio and I passed into our proper grades. We made friends with our Negro classmates. Mamma and Nonna laughed often with our neighbors . . . *queste persone simpatiche con le facce scure*—friendly people with dark faces, as we called them.

"What's wrong with being a Catholic, Papa?" I asked one evening, as we were finishing supper.

I couldn't help but notice my mother's mouth, hard and solemn. Nonna had abruptly gotten up to clear the table. Papa looked guilty.

"*Carissima*, there is nothing wrong with the way we live. There is something wrong with the way *they* live."

I didn't understand this new land. I didn't understand why we could not go to Mass. Mamma just said it was dangerous. I didn't understand why the black people were so hated by whites. I didn't know what color we were exactly, only we also were called names when we went into town.

That same evening, I started to ask "And what does *dago* mean?" but the words caught in my throat.

I paid more attention, listened to the stories as my language improved; they were terrible stories. I learned new words that were always said in hushed tones. "Lynching" and "nigger" came into my mind like blows to the head. I heard people talk about the Ku Klux Klan in such a hushed, fearful way that I felt ashamed to ask my father what these words meant.

Each and every night as the sun went down, Mamma and Nonna went to every door and window in our home, pulling down shades and locking everything up tight. I heard the despair in their voices as they spoke of crosses burned in yards and men with pointed white hoods who stole people in the night. One night, I heard them talking about the son of one of our neighbors who had disappeared and the talk was that he had been "lynched."

We had been in Montgomery for almost two years. Mamma had my brother Giuseppe the first year. The new baby brought joy to the house, but she was afraid, I think, afraid of losing what she had waited so long to bring together.

Mamma couldn't go to church the way she had in Carrara. She missed things from home that she had left behind and couldn't replace. Simple things, like a special herb for a recipe, or big things, like the friendliness of a whole town, where there was mostly kindness and sharing. We never knew we would not have those things. Mamma became friends with Mrs. Mattie Thompkins, the neighbor lady who lost her son. Before her son died, Mattie was a lively woman who helped my mother learn some English. Mattie's favorite thing to say when she got excited was, "Lordy be!" She would howl with laughter when my mother tried to say it. Mamma wasn't offended. It must have felt good to find a reason to laugh out loud. But then one day Mamma taught Mattie to say, "*Mamma Mia*" and that became Mattie's other favorite thing to say.

There were few happy times though, as I saw my mother fall into a depression, and my father tried desperately to keep us happy.

So we all felt helpless, especially Papa, and we had a bitter taste for America in those days.

When we were eating together—those were the liveliest times I remember. What is it about sitting down for a simple meal that fills our stomachs, yet also never fails to remind us of who we are to each other? For all the disappointments we had in Alabama, we never forgot that we were a family and that our being altogether again was the thing that mattered the most.

I am alone in the dark, holding my rosary.

Ione

Sitting here on the edge of our bed, I put my hand over my eyes. My head hurts. I try to concentrate on my prayers, but all I can do is ask one thing of our Blessed Mother over and over. "Please help us find a way out of this place."

I am not kneeling in the pew of a church because it's dangerous to do that here.

When I saw that Statue of Liberty, not so long ago, I got tears in my eyes. I hadn't cried since we left Carrara, not until that moment. I held my mother's hand and clasped my children to me and even though I was terrified of what was in front of us, that Lady made me feel strong, that we could make a good life here. Not that life was horrible for us in Italy, not where we came from. But Italy was changing. And my husband, he first went to America to make money, but I always thought he would come back to Italy for good. Finally he wrote to me from across an ocean and persuaded me it was for the best, to come to America.

We hadn't seen or spoken to each other in ten years. We had lost our son and our father. We had a mother who was getting older, and I didn't want to see her continue making dresses and suits every day from morning until night. I had two young children. I was tired and so lonely. I was a still a young woman when Aristide left. I feel old now.

Have the people here in Montgomery ever seen her, the Statue of Liberty? Do they know she exists? I don't think so. Not the white people anyway. We are not considered to be white and also because we are Roman Catholics, we are as low as the Negro in their eyes. And this horrible word, "nigger." It's said with such venom. *Che disgustoso* . . . how disgusting it's one of the first "English" words my daughter Olga has learned since we came here.

I don't know what this KKK means. We don't have that letter "K" in our language. But I learned how to say the word "cruel" from one of my neighbors and that sounds like a K—three times for how evil they are. I spit on them.

Aristide says they hate Catholics, Jews and immigrants in general because they think we are taking jobs away from Americans and because our religion does not seem Christian to them. He is calm as he tells me these things, as he sits on the bed next to me, speaking softly so our children don't hear us.

I ask him, "Hate and killing is Christian then in America?" He says nothing more, there's nothing to say about it that makes any sense.

But I know he sees the fright in my eyes, and I see the anger in his and his resolve to leave this place of hate before it's too late. I know he'll take us out of here, but I'm furious that we're here at all.

I didn't bring my children and our mother to America to have them all be afraid. Cesira is too old and my children are too innocent. And another baby is on the way! I did not wait ten years to be with my husband to live in a place where I can't even walk into the Church unless I go so early in the mornings no one will see me.

"We can't live in the big cities," Aristide said to me when we took the train from New York to Montgomery.

He's right. I know. I saw with my own eyes how our people live in such a place as New York City. Squeezed in dirty, filthy rooms, no air even to breathe. During the seven days we were there, we stayed with people Aristide knew and everybody looked sick to me.

Believe me, none of us looked so good after thirty long days on that ship, but Aristide said many in the cities were dying of tuberculosis. They are insects trapped in a jar. He said he saw them sometimes on boats going back to Italy, to breathe in a little fresh air again before they die.

My garden—it's the only thing that reminds me every day I haven't lost everything. I dig with my hands in the black soil and my tears for Italy sink in and disappear. I share the vegetables and herbs with the friendly people who are our neighbors, these Americans with dark faces.

My poor neighbor, Mattie. Mattie, who became my first friend in America. I'll always remember her warm smile, as broad as her shoulders, when we met for the first time. I took Olga with me to the small market for the ingredients I wanted to make our first Sunday family dinner. I was discouraged because I couldn't find them all, nervous also as I felt strange eyes staring at me. I was afraid even to speak, unable to make myself understood.

The green leafy produce looked different from the Swiss chard I was used to boiling and chopping up for my ravioli. The cheese I longed for, the sheep's milk pecorino, well, there was nothing that smelled like it, so I knew it would not have *sapore*, the taste.

Mattie was in the store and I noticed her watching me. Perhaps she overheard me mumble in Italian as I tried to decide what to buy. She walked over and stood right next to me. This simple act felt kind and calmed me. Somehow, I found things to buy. I believe there is a language of the heart that exists among women that require no words.

Since that day, we have been friends. She was in my kitchen bringing or borrowing something almost every day. We never had what you could call a lengthy conversation, but we found things to laugh and cry about just the same.

The Negroes speak so strangely, different from the English I heard in New York. But I am sure we sound very strange to them. So we all do what we can to help each other.

But that's during the day. At night, the fear walks around us, light on its feet like a fierce cat that sees in the dark and patiently waits for its prey to forget for just a moment. I go around the house when the early evening comes and push all the shutters tight, check all the doors, block out the inside light from strange eyes.

I've seen the remains of the burning crosses. I smell the smoke. Or maybe it's the fear I smell. What I see in my dreams and what I see with my eyes have become blurred in my mind. But all of it is real. I have never in my life been afraid like I have been afraid here.

Mattie's son was "lynched" about one year after we arrived. *Dio mio*, that's another beautiful word Olga—and Giorgio too—have learned.

She screamed for a whole day and night as, I simply held her in my arms.

She seldom leaves the house now, and only when I call out to her will she look up to wave back. How I miss her laugh and her big warm hugs, but I understand why she can't even manage a smile. No sound comes from her house. It's as if a big bright light was shattered.

I think about her. It makes me remember when my own son, my little Bruno, died in my arms—but the screaming came after the silence for me.

I washed his small body in silence, when the fever finally left him. I closed his precious eyelids, forever being denied looking into eyes so like my own. I held him and carried him around the house for hours. We had a Mass said, we threw the earth on his coffin, we attended his small grave, placed flowers. In all of this I spoke not a word.

It was some days after Bruno was buried that Cesira came to me, took both my hands in hers and just drew me to her. That's when my screaming began. And she didn't say anything, just held me or left me alone in my bed until it was over.

Of course, my children needed me and were a comfort to me. Mattie had only the one son and her husband is ill. She has no choice except to suffer. She will never leave this place.

I look around at what is now my home. I close my eyes and reach up to run my hand over the headboard, its hard sharp edges feel rough and a sharp pain enters my heart when I remember how beautiful my home was in Carrara. Sunshine and evening breezes that did not have to be shut out, the shine of dark wood, polished and like velvet, not even a splinter to the touch, lace at my windows, my sturdy kitchen table, the heavy marble top covering it, and so smooth. Pasta dough glided over it as I floured, rolled and cut it into shapes.

So much, so much left behind. America seduces, but her promises now seem shallow to me. Ten years of waiting and I thought it was over the day I saw that statue. How many more years now do we have to wait for the sweetness of life to find us again?

I hear Aristide coming in the door. Our children are asleep. It is quiet in the house. He will find me in the dark, he will stroke my hair, I will let him brush it as he wants, then gently he will push me back on the bed and he will say nothing to me. For so long we did not speak. Now there is again nothing that can be said until the day comes when he finds me in the dark and says, "*Cara mia, andiamo—adesso.*" We go now, my love.

The day Papa burst through the front door like a freight train caused us all to freeze in our places.

Olga

Then we saw the huge smile that made the dimple disappear in his chin, and he gathered us all around him.

As his words came out in one long excited stream, Mamma started crying, which was always the signal for me to start. Nonna reached up and took my father's face in her hands. Giorgio jumped up and down.

"Where are we moving, Papa?" he cried, and spoke for the rest of us.

"Indiana, *caro!*"

"Indiana! That's where the Indians must live, right Papa? Cowboys and Indians!"

We all laughed at Giorgio's eruption. As I looked at both my brother and my father, bursting with feeling, I realized what I loved so much about them both: they saw the world as a stage and life truly was an opera.

Worry appeared on Mamma's face as the news began to sink in. I could read her mind. I knew she was thinking, "Why should we expect Indiana to be any better than Alabama?"

Papa read her mind too. He was ready for her. Knowing Papa, he had probably rehearsed his speech on the way home from work. I remember hearing their low voices that night as he soothed her, convinced her, and assured her. Papa's optimism and enthusiasm simply left no room for anything else to exist for long.

Despite our joy over leaving, it was hard to say goodbye to the women in our small neighborhood, especially Mattie. We all knew, as we pulled away from each other and gave our last embraces, we would never in our lives see each other again. We had leaned on one another for many things those two years. We planted vegetables together, celebrated birthdays, shared our grief and times of humiliation as well. Alabama . . . that is where I first learned what friendship between women meant.

It was already 1924 when Papa moved us into our new house on Stevens Street, right in the middle of the Italian neighborhood in Indianapolis.

Our new home was small, but comfortable, with a narrow porch facing the street. I shared a bedroom with Little Nonna, which is what we had all begun to call her, as she seemed to be shrinking! Mamma delivered my little sister, Anna, shortly after we moved.

Papa's work was in the limestone quarries of Bedford, Indiana and he would travel there, coming home on the weekends. I think he just didn't have the heart to move us to some small town when he didn't know how long he would have the job.

I think this was when I began to realize how much my father sacrificed, how hard he had worked for so long to bring us here. I had only considered Mamma's, Nonna's, my own sacrifices. He was an artisan—*uno scalpellino*—and his marble-carving and work in gothic tracery mostly kept him out of coal mines and railroads while he was scraping together enough money to send for us.

Of course, sometimes he had to work in those places. He never talked much about it unless there was a fantastic story to tell. And then, well, he made it all come alive for us.

I never saw my father lose his temper. He often made jokes when things were bad. And he sang! Sang like Caruso! Mamma was so serious, but it was a good thing. Mamma was practical and Papa always saw the bright side.

When we moved to Indianapolis, I understood why immigrants stayed in clusters of their own kind, even when conditions were deplorable, as I first saw in Little Italy in New York. On Stevens Street, we felt at home instantly, surrounded by our beautiful language, our worship and our food. After the Purgatory of Alabama, living here felt almost like Paradise.

We did not want to forget our homeland, so we recreated our version of Italy as we knew it, and held on tight.

Heads nodding, hands waving wildly in mid-air to make sure the point was made . . . old women, heads down, tiny fingers working delicate pieces of lace on linen, at times smiling with a small shake of the head over grandiose statements made by the men . . . the men smoking little cigars, a smooth sip of amaretto on a late evening, a little bocce ball played in the backyard on Sunday afternoons. But everyone working hard, so hard—in kitchens, in factories, in markets—to hold on to the belief we all came to this country with.

There were changes as America absorbed our lives. My mother usually called my father "Ari" and so people thought it was Harry, and except by the older Italians, Papa was called Harry the rest of his life. My brothers Giorgio and Giuseppe, became "George and Joe." My mother's name, "ee-own-eh," had become "eye-own-ah" in Alabama, and stuck. Little Nonna said no one was going to change her name. Our family name had already lost an "n" at Ellis Island: Giovannoni became Giovanoni.

Italian neighbors and people just arriving here from the Old Country, which is what everyone calls Italy, often came to our house. They shared their stories with us, of their hometowns, their long journeys, the excitement of seeing the Statue of Liberty (and we all shook our heads at the same memory), the uncertainties felt as they were pushed and probed along through Ellis Island, the surprise—no, shock—over how difficult life in America really is. How keeping our ways and our customs were looked down upon. How bad it felt to be called a dago or a wop.

Little Nonna and I would often walk over to Rizzuto's Grocery Store. It was a short walk, but between our home and the store, which was around the corner, there were many distractions.

Especially in the nice weather, people were out on porches or busying themselves with errands, or children were playing in the streets. And in the neighborhood, everyone noticed everything and it was impolite not to speak. And really impossible besides! There was an intimacy with neighbors we had been used to having in the streets and small towns we had all left behind. For our family, it had been two long years of mostly feeling like strangers. The thirst for our passionate language was strong.

In those first weeks we lived there, the Holy Rosary parish

was close to being completed. So people were always standing around watching, anxious for it to be finished so Mass could be conducted properly—not in the basement as had been going on for years until money could be found to finish the church.

On this particular day I'm remembering, there was an unusually large crowd from the neighborhood gathered on the street and sidewalk to watch a cast iron bell being lifted up to the *campanile*, the bell tower. All eyes were riveted on the bell as it ascended with the help of pulleys from above. Men yelled at each other from above and below and all of us looking on felt the heaviness of the moment on our shoulders, holding our breath, wishing it was over.

I wandered away from Little Nonna to get a better look and noticed I was standing next to Father Priori. The bell was high in the air and about to be anchored into place. Nobody uttered a sound until we heard a cry of relief and then we all cheered.

Father Priori wiped some perspiration off his upper lip with the back of his hand, obviously relieved. He was a serious man with a round face, bright dark eyes and hair parted to one side, combed just so. But he laughed easily with the children and always had a kind word for you. He founded the church and our school. He built a playground for the children and was always finding ways to bring people together. Holy Rosary was at the heart of our lives in those days as was Father Priori.

"*Buon giorno*, Father Priori," I said to him.

"Good day to you, Signorina Giovanoni. It's a beautiful bell, isn't it? And it's just the first one!"

"How many will there be, Father?"

"Six."

"Six? Six as big as that one?"

"The last one will be the largest. I am told it weighs seven thousand pounds. It will be the largest bell in the entire city." His chest and chin jutted out in pride as he said this.

"Father, when will we hear the bells ring? I can hardly wait! I haven't heard bells ring for years."

"Next Sunday, my child. Next Sunday when we open the doors for the first time."

Little Nonna walked over to clasp my hand to remind me we still needed to go to the grocer.

When we walked into Rizzuto's Grocery, I pretended not to notice Salvatore Pezzullo, who was on a ladder arranging cans of tomatoes into pyramids.

The store was owned by Leo Rizzuto and his wife, Amalia. Salvatore was Amalia's younger brother.

We exchanged greetings with Amalia.

Salvatore climbed down from the ladder, mumbled a greeting to us and hastily retreated to the back of the store.

Within a few minutes, several more customers came into the store and Salvatore had to emerge to help Amalia take care of everyone.

I'll never forget what was said next, as Little Nonna reached into her pocketbook to pay.

She commented sweetly, "It looks like you have more business than you can handle, Signora! That's good."

Amalia, looking grim, replied, "Yes, my husband wants to hire someone to help, someone who can wait on customers, but I don't know. It's hard to find someone you can trust."

"How about my granddaughter? You can trust her and she needs work."

I nearly dropped to my knees when these words came out of her mouth. But I said nothing. I knew better than to challenge Little Nonna, especially in public.

Amalia looked me over skeptically, like I was a choice piece of veal, and too expensive.

"How old is she?"

"Sixteen and very responsible."

"I'll think about it. I'll let you know tomorrow. I want to speak with my husband and my brother."

Salvatore, who was weighing some *soppressata* for Signora Toffolo, did not appear to have heard any of this. But I noticed him glancing up at us as we left.

"Nonna!" I cried in protest the moment we were out of hearing range.

"*Cara*, you're almost *sixteen years old*," she said to me. "I was much younger than you when my mother put a needle and thread in my hands.... It's time you learned how to do something besides take care of your little brothers and sister. It will be good for you."

I was afraid I couldn't do it, but as usual, she was able to read my thoughts because she said, "Of course you can do it! Be polite, smile at people when they come through the door, put their groceries nicely in a bag and count the money."

By the time we got home, I was excited and couldn't wait to tell Papa.

He looked at me in surprise. I thought he was going to say "No."

But he only said, "*Cara*, whatever you want. Your grandmother knows best. She always does!"

I stood in the front room of our new little house watching my wife and my mother hang draperies.

Aristide

Ione was going to have our baby, any minute it looked like, and she was smiling and laughing with Cesira.

I was smiling too. I had lived for this day. Yes, I know. I have said that my life began again when they all got off the boat, but life threw me another curve.

Working for years to bring them all to America, to give them the life and future of my dreams, to see my children running carefree and happy outdoors, to see my mother relax those little shoulders, to see my wife laugh again.

Living in Montgomery had taken that dream and turned it into a nightmare. Every single day, when I left the quarry and walked through the door of our bedroom, I braced myself for Ione insisting we go back to Italy.

All I had thought about before they came was how it would be when they did. After they came, all I could think about was how miserable I had made everyone and I had no idea how I was going to fix it.

I did not want to go back to Italy. My father was in Italy and so was my son, Bruno. It was my fault they were dead. If I had had the sense to bring them sooner, things would have been so very different.

Instead of freeing my children, the harshness of people with small brains and dark hearts was thrust into their faces and they learned what hate looked like. I didn't want this for them—not yet. I wanted to see their innocence last. I had missed so much of it.

Ione never said the words I had dreaded, but they were between us, between us even when we made love, held on to each other for dear life at night, when we brought our son into the world. When she looked at me, it was like she said, "And what is his life going to be?"

I made up my mind that I would quit the quarry. I had to do something. I saw my wife slipping away, my children confused, my mother trying to hold us altogether.

The only person I could turn to was Andy. I wrote to him, my despair in my letters sounding like Act II of a tragic opera that has no chance for a happy ending.

In one of Andy's letters he told me about the quarries in Indiana and that he had heard there was work.

Andy always seemed to come through for me in my darkest moments. He was like a good librettist—change the words, change the story, change the ending!

All of these emotions were winding their way through me as I was watching the ladies adorn the windows of our house.

Ione, a pin sticking out of the side of her mouth, mumbled, "What's the matter with you, Ari?"

How could I tell her?

"Want some music?" I replied instead.

"*Si!*" my mother said. "Sing!"

I dug into my operatic memory for something happy.
"We're waiting!" said Ione.
The Count of Verdi's Il Trovatore came to my rescue.

Il balen del suo sorriso	The flash of her smile
d'una stella vince il raggio!	outdoes the beam from a star!
Il fulgor del suo bel viso	The brightness of her beautiful face
nuovo infonde a me coraggio!	inspires me with fresh daring!
Ah! L'amor, l'amore ond'ardo	Ah! Let the love, the love with
le favelli in mio favor!	which I burn speak to her on her behalf!
Sperda il sole d'un suo sguardo	Let the sunshine of one of her glances
la tempesta del mio cor!	disperse the storm in my heart!

Ione was my Tosca with Green Eyes again, looking at me like she was in love.

Olga and Giorgio burst into the house and shouted, "Papa! The neighbors are coming outside to listen! It sounds like a recording, Papa! That's what everyone is saying."

That was the moment . . . finally.

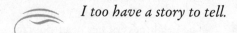 *I too have a story to tell.*

Leo Rizzuto

We have not yet been introduced, but you know who I am. I run the grocery story in the Italian neighborhood, with the help of my wife Amalia and my poor brother-in-law, Salvatore.

You will soon understand why I say "poor" when referring to Salvatore. Everyone always said "poor Salvatore." All you had to do was look at him and the word just came out. He was the kind of guy who believed he was defeated before the first punch was thrown or the first word shouted in an argument. He would wince when I came near him, expecting the worst and—poor Salvatore—the worst is what he usually got. Sometimes, I would slap him on the back just to see if he could stand up straight. Oh, he would, but because he was afraid of me, not because he had a backbone. He was sad and it cast a long shadow. You could feel it just standing next to him.

I immigrated to America and arrived in Boston in the year 1912. My hometown was Monterosso, a small, poor town in the province of Calabria. I married Amalia before I left to set up a home and business for us in Boston, before she came over.

I am a big man. I've always had big dreams and the only place big enough for me was America.

I opened a small grocery on Fulton street, one of the busiest Italian streets in Boston. When Amalia wrote to me that she could not leave her younger brother behind, I had no hesitation in agreeing he come along. Salvatore was twelve years old and I planned on making him an apprentice. I wasn't going to slave away all by myself.

Amalia and Salvatore were raised by their aunt and uncle. There was always a lot of mystery around what happened to their parents who were dead a long time ago. Nobody seemed to want to talk about it.

Stories of their deaths were shrouded and who knows what the truth is? I heard they drowned. I heard they were murdered. Poison, daggers, dark corners. Who cares?

Whenever anything happened, Amalia would say, "It's my bad luck." You know what I'm talking about—black cats, broken mirrors, the evil eye! Yes, we believe in bad luck, but with Amalia, she believed *she* was the bad luck.

Well, my plan was to take her away from all that nonsense. A new life was all she needed, hard work, helping me make my dream come true in America.

Amalia could not believe she had managed to actually get on the boat with Salvatore and arrive in Boston Harbor, themselves and their money and their possessions intact. All she could say was, "I can't believe we had such good luck."

I lost my temper after the first ten minutes of hearing this. I said, "Of course you had good luck! Nothing bad can happen so long as you're with me!"

And she looked relieved. Salvatore did not say a word.

Poor Salvatore.

So, life in America started out good. I taught them both everything about the business so they could run it while I concentrated on important things like getting to know the *prominenti*, you know, the influentials in the neighborhood who I would do favors for and who would then owe me one or two.

But over time, more grocers moved in on my territory. All of a sudden, the coffers weren't so full. I would scowl when I looked in the cash register and Salvatore would crouch like it was all his fault. Well, I didn't exactly try to convince him otherwise.

I would blast Salvatore because I didn't know what else to do with my anger and Amalia would literally stand between us. I never hit Salvatore or my wife, but she acted as though I was going to. All this carrying on all the time just because I yelled some at her brother.

One day, I stood in the doorway of my store and just took in the view.

There they both were, as usual. Amalia, eyes cast down, was dusting the long countertop. Occasionally, she would turn to a shelf behind her, running her hand over it looking for more dust, her belly big and swollen from being pregnant with our first child.

And there was my brother-in-law. Counting cans of tomatoes and checking things off a list in front of him. His eyes were cast down too.

God, the two of them never looked any different to me. They knew I was standing there too, probably praying I would not find a reason to yell. I wanted to yell. Why? Because the one thing I was looking for I did not see. A customer!

At that very moment, I felt a nudge behind me and a small voice saying, "*Permesso*—excuse me."

I turned aside and let the old lady come through the door. Saturday morning and we have only one customer, I thought to myself, seething. When she left, I could no longer maintain my silence.

"Salvatore!" I said, jerking my head. "*Vieni qui.* Outside!"

As usual, my command had the effect on Salvatore like a firecracker under his ass. He pulled off his apron and dashed out the door to join me.

It was crowded on the street and not enough room on the narrow sidewalks for everyone. The streets were smelly—full of carriages and horses, dogs, children, women toting bundles, fruit stand vendors with their bananas and even a couple priests making their way through the crowd.

I put my arm on Salvatore's shoulder and guided him into the nearest bar.

"*Due espressi per favore!*" I said to the owner.

I was looking for a quiet and cool place and sat down toward the back. Salvatore just stood there, as usual waiting for me to tell him what to do.

"Sit down, Salvatore, sit down."

I waited until the bartender placed the small cups of coffee in front of us. I looked around to make sure no one could hear me.

I leaned close and said, "Salvatore, how many years have you been here?"

"You mean in Boston?" he says.

I felt the pressure of the blood in my head that always comes in talking with him.

"Of course *Boston*! Have you ever been any place else since you got off the boat?"

Salvatore looked down and stirred his coffee.

I tossed back the mouthful.

"Drink your coffee, Salvatore. *Con calma.*"

"We've been in Boston for ten years . . . Leo."

I was surprised to hear him speak.

I continued. "That's exactly right. You're twenty-three years old now and I'm not getting any younger myself. Your sister is going to have our child soon. My responsibilities are growing. And I would think that pretty soon you will be wanting a family of your own."

Salvatore's cheeks turned red.

"What's the matter, Sal? Don't you ever think about women?" I would still be sitting there if I waited for an answer to that question. "I want you to know, Salvatore, that I know you've worked very hard to learn this business."

He sat up a little straighter.

"You're ready for more responsibility, Salvatore. And I need your help. I need your help to persuade Amalia."

He just looked at me with his pathetic "who, me?" face.

"Salvatore, the truth is . . . the truth is," and I looked around again to make sure no one was listening and leaned in across the table. "We aren't making any goddamn money! You do the books. You know what I'm talking about."

"We make a little money, Leo. Last month, for examp—"

"But it's not enough! I have a wife. I have a child coming. I'm responsible for you too, for God's sake. And what happens when *you* decide to get married, eh? In a couple of years, they're going to have to bury me with all these mouths to feed." I was trying to keep my voice down, when steam was ready to blow out my ears. "All I see around me is less money and more Italian grocery stores!"

Salvatore leaned back and blurted out, "Well, there are lots of places to make money in America. Let's open a grocery store somewhere else!"

Madonna! I swear I could not believe my ears. I laughed so loud, everyone in the bar turned around.

"You're a genius, you know that, Salvatore? Finally, I see you've learned something from me."

That night, after Amalia had cleared the supper table, I pulled out a couple of cigars and some papers.

"Look at this, Sal." I put the papers on the table and handed him a cigar.

"This is Indianapolis, Indiana. Ever hear of Indiana? Well, it's in the middle of this goddamn country and every single railroad line goes through Indianapolis. Guess what that means for grocers?"

Salvatore chewed on his cigar and said, "That would mean we could get our hands on anything coming or going."

I was stupefied at the change in him. I gave the kid a few compliments and his brain started working.

"And guess what else? There is a growing Italian community there which means—"

This time, Salvatore interrupted me: "—which *means* there's probably no competition like here."

I got up and slapped my brother-in-law on the back. I wasn't thinking "poor Salvatore" any more. I was thinking that we would soon be leaving all of Amalia's bad luck behind us in Boston.

I wish I could tell you this turned out to be true.

A month later, Amalia delivered our son. I said that we would name him Salvatore and she cried like the baby.

Color of love, expression of compassion
have never so miraculously come
to the face of any lady when she gazed
 at eyes susceptible of anguished tears,
as they came to your face whenever I
stood in your presence with my grieving face;
and something comes to mind because of you:
a thought that makes me fear my heart will split.
~ VITA NUOVA: DANTE ALIGHIERI FOR BEATRICE

 It is Thanksgiving Day, 1924.

Salvatore

Today is *il giorno delle nozze mio*, my wedding day, the day
Olga Gina and I are to stand in front of Father Marino Priori at
Holy Rosary and say our sacred vows.

Olga's grandmother, "Little Nonna," as she lets me call her
now, made the satin wedding gown, which of course I have not
been allowed to see. I wasn't sure for a long time if Little Nonna
even approved of me. She normally said very little to anyone, but
nothing to me. "*Buona sera, signor Pezzullo*", "*non, grazie, signor
Pezzullo*" or one of her little shrugs was all she ever offered me.

Then one day, after Olga accepted my proposal of marriage,
I was invited for dinner and afterwards, we were all enjoying a
glass of *vin santo* and a few *biscotti* at the table. Aristide (I can't

bring myself to call him Harry) stood and began to sing a little something for us. He sang from Rigoletto *"La donna è mobile"* which means "Woman is fickle."

La donna è mobile	Woman is fickle
qual piuma al vento,	as a feather in the breeze,
muta d'accento	she changes her words
e di pensiero.	and her thoughts.
Sempre un'amabile	Ever a loveable,
leggiadro viso,	graceful countenance,
in pianto o in riso,	weeping or smiling,
è menzognero.	it's deceitful.
È sempre misero	That man is always wretched
chi a lei s'affida,	who places faith in her,
chi le confida	who entrusts to her
mal cauto il core!	his heart misguidedly!
Pur mai non sentesi	Yet that man never feels
felice appieno,	thoroughly happy
chi su quel seno	who doesn't taste love
non liba amore!	on that bosom!

I felt the "holy wine" go to my head and I surprised everyone, most of all myself, by joining in when it was apparent Aristide wasn't ready to die out. My voice does not have half the power or beauty of his, but I can hold my own and pretty soon I was standing next to him, our hands on each other's shoulders singing Verdi's score like we had written it ourselves. Then Giorgio stood up and the competition for who could hold a note the longest caused me finally to gasp for air. (Aristide won.)

As I sat at the dinner table that evening, I felt a slow sinking of my body in the chair. Something inside me, a longing I didn't know I had, felt satisfied. I looked at each face, the faces of those who would be my family. I thought, how different this was, how much love existed in between the plates of pasta and the refills of wine.

Aristide, his long sleeves rolled up to his elbows, reached across to pat Giorgio on the arm after our performance. The little ones, Joe and Anna, were passed around the table to land on different laps. Little Nonna held court at the table, Olga's eyes shining in adoration of her.

Out of the corner of my eye, Little Nonna was half smiling at me and I knew at least I had amused her. I so wanted her respect. Later, Olga told me that Nonna said it was important for a woman to be married to a man who was sure of himself, who was serious and responsible. Not a dandy, she said.

We will have wonderful things to eat and drink on our wedding day. No, not Thanksgiving fare, although I have come to like this American holiday, but all the traditional dishes both our families love. *Antipasti* to start, then a first course of pasta or risotto—*funghi porcini* perhaps. For the main course, a veal or beef roast and various *contorni*—zucchini and other fresh vegetables. Then *una selezione di formaggio*, hopefully the *pecorino* I so love, and afterwards *una torta* baked by my sister, some *asti spumante* and wines for the wedding "*brandisi*"—toasts for our happiness.

I will look into Olga's brown eyes as we toast and she will hold my gaze, but not for as long as I will. I could look at her forever.

I remember her first day at the grocery store, as she tried to follow Amalia's every order. My sister can be strict. The look on Olga's face made me say to myself, "So serious, this *regazza*, but so pretty!"

I fell in love with her a few months later, on the day she asked me, "Salvatore, what do you do when you're not working?" No one had ever asked me such a question! Had I ever given thought to anything except making a living since I got off the boat thirteen years ago?

The grocery store has been my life for all these years, and I am so very proud of it. Leo has been out, cooking up a new business, meeting with his lawyer Girotti, and he's turned over almost everything to me. Let me tell you what the store looks like, then you can imagine how much my world has changed since Olga.

The store is wide and open with a high ceiling, an ink-black fan (which has a squeak that only I seem to be bothered by) that churns overhead in the summer to keep our customers cool, so they spend more time and money during August, when it's hot and humid, as summers in Indianapolis always are.

Tall, windowed cabinets that I make sure are cleaned with vinegar everyday line the wall. On top of these cabinets, I've stacked pyramids of the bright yellow and red cans of *pomodori*, the delicious tomatoes of Italy.

We also have a counter that holds our precious cigars—Bob Burns, Blackstone and White Owl. To add a little theatre to our business, I bought a large stuffed white owl that now is perched on top of the cigar boxes. As you can imagine, Leo loved this idea, his double chins following along with his nod when he saw what I had done. He gives more cigars away than we sell, which I point out to him all the time, but as usual, I am rebuffed.

"*Madonna!*" he will say, "The man just had a son, Salvatore . . . I am going to charge him for one lousy cigar?"

And he added, "The owl looks great there. You're learning, Salvatore, you're learning! This is your best idea yet—better than the stupid roses!"

I asked my friend Mario, who is a fellow member of the Lodge of the Order of the Sons of Italy, to decorate the store. He painted a big border of red roses along the walls up close to the ceiling, all around the store. And in the center, I had him paint an American eagle with spread wings, clutching a banner in its claws with the words in English: "If we please you, please tell us."

Mario did great work, but Leo had a fit and said, "No Salvatore! Roses? And why isn't it in Italian, eh?" The palms of his hands were together under his chin and he was waving them back and forth at me.

I said, "Leo, it has to be in English. And most of our customers are women."

He said nothing but "*Uffa!*" and turned his back on me, but he didn't make me change it because he knows I'm right.

So when beautiful little Olga was still waiting for my answer, looking at me with those eyes, I couldn't speak for I realized in that moment that at twenty-three years of age, I was lonely. Something was missing from my life that I couldn't name until then: Olga.

I was surprised at how irritated I was when moments later, Ottavio Faenzi appeared. I hadn't heard anyone come in, but suddenly there he was, passing leisurely right in front of me, walking toward the back of the store, toward Olga. He was a big man, with a round face, and women seemed to like his looks. His dark straight hair was starting to thin a bit on the sides even though we were probably the same age. I ran my hand through my hair, grateful I had more than he did. He was calm and soft spoken, one of those types where nothing ever seemed to bother him, like he had all the time in the world. "Otto," as he liked to be called, put on airs in his fancy suit, calling himself a chef . . . he was nothing more than a cook in some small restaurant in Mishawaka, who came in too often and ingratiated himself with Leo. The way he looked at Olga and the way she blushed was a jolt. I was already losing her and hadn't had the courage to claim her for my own!

Within a few weeks, I proposed to her, after of course, speaking with Aristide, for whom I have so much respect. They both said yes. For the first time in my life I knew what it was to be happy.

The things in my life that used to bother me, squeaking fans, fingerprints on my cabinet windows, everything having to be just so all the time, suddenly fell away to give me room—to feel, to laugh, to hold hands, to feel her breath as a whisper in my ear, to shiver from head to toe.

It's a beautiful love story, *vero*?

I saw my life ahead of me very clearly—my wedding day, prospering at my trade, a long life, happiness, a home of our own,

Sundays spent with family, holding my sons on my knees, seeing them grow strong and tall in America, smiling across the table at Olga, growing old with her, fifty, sixty, seventy Thanksgiving Day wedding anniversaries.

Leo congratulated me in his usual way—a hard slap on the back and a laugh—the kind of laugh that sounds like he was taking credit for the whole thing.

He said, "*Finalmente!* See? I told you it was a good idea to hire that girl!"

We were at a meeting for the King Humbert Lodge. The usual group was there—Leo and me, Dr. Lapenta, Girotti the lawyer, Father Priori, Mario, others.

While the cigars were being passed around, provided by Leo, of course, he slowly stood up with exaggerated effort and stayed quiet until everyone stopped talking.

"My brother-in-law here, Salvatore—you all know him to be industrious, hard-working, nose in the books—but I'm happy to say that he's discovered women . . . " Leo stopped to enjoy the laughter that erupted at my expense.

Father Priori did not laugh, but looked over at me, smiled and nodded.

Leo went on. "And in particular, one woman—Miss Olga Giovanoni—the daughter of the stonecutter, Aristide Giovanoni. They will be married this coming Thanksgiving Day."

Everyone stood up and came over to shake my hand and congratulate me on my choice.

Amalia said she was happy for me, but she was crying when she said it. My sister was like a mother to me, always protecting, always afraid something was going to happen to me. I was angry at her reaction. For once in my life, there was someone besides her who loved me.

When we were alone in the store, I asked her, "Can't you just once be happy about something?"

She was stacking bars of soap one on top of the other and my answer jarred her. The display tumbled across the floor and she wouldn't look at me.

"I am happy for you, Salvatore. And I like Olga." She got down on her knees to gather the soap.

"Really? Your face and words tell different stories, Amalia."

"I just don't want anything bad to happen."

"*Ma dai!* For the first time in my life, I feel I have good luck. Don't bring our parents' sad lives into mine!"

She looked at my face and asked, "Salvatore, what's wrong?"

"I just have a headache. Who wouldn't have one? Between your gloom and Leo's temper tantrums—who wouldn't have a headache?"

A few days later, when Olga and I were laughing at some silly thing I said, I suddenly felt myself going weak and feeling dizzy.

"Salvatore! Are you all right? Do you have another headache?"

The headaches would come and go. There was pain, terrible pain in my head and face, blinding pain. I thought at first that I had just been working too much. Olga would say that I think too much. The headaches would go away for a few days, then come back even more terrible than before. There were days when I couldn't get out of bed, nights when I couldn't sleep, moments when I thought I was losing my sight.

I kept this from Amalia and pretended that I was nervous about the wedding, but I wasn't nervous. The coming wedding was an oasis for my soul. The thought of being wedded to Olga was the only thing that relaxed me, that gave me peace.

I finally relented to Olga's wishes, and went to see Dr.
Lapenta.

"Signor Pezzullo! *Buon giorno*," he said as he entered the
examining room.

I am always impressed at how elegant a man he is. He isn't
tall, but his stature is that of a general. His pointed black beard is
always immaculate and dramatic on his face with its high brow,
the kind of face you see in paintings of counts or dukes. All he
needed was a cape.

I smiled through my pain.

Over the next few weeks, there were tests. Lapenta gave me
powders I took to help ease the pain.

"You have a tumor, Salvatore . . . in your head, behind your
ear," Dr. Lapenta said. His mouth was a straight line, his eyes
showed no feeling.

Something black flashed through my brain, Amalia's
prophecy, inevitable, here.

I heard myself ask what could be done, that I was getting
married soon. And the silence, which was probably not very long,
was heavy between us.

His words sounded measured, rehearsed. "The only thing
we can do is operate and try to remove it. If we don't, it will
increase in size and eventually it will be fatal . . . I'm sorry,
Salvatore."

Leo put his face in his hands and cried when I told him. I
had never seen him cry. Amalia refused to believe it, which made
me want to slap her. She was hysterical.

"What does Dr. Lapenta know? Leo! I want go back to
Boston, there are better doctors in Boston! I am not going to let
anyone cut you, Salvatore, no!"

She reached out to me to stroke my head, pressing her

fingertips on the place behind my ear. The pain throbbed in my head at her touch. Leo was pounding his fist into the wall, yelling at Amalia to shut up.

I had to get out of there. I had to see Olga.

I sat with her on her front porch and told her I was having an operation and that our wedding plans would have to wait for a few months. I swallowed my pain and said this to her in the same way I would have told her that I would be late for supper.

She said nothing for a long time. She asked me about the operation and what Lapenta said and she didn't cry. If she had, I don't know what I would have done. I did not want to humiliate myself in front of her. I wanted her to see my courage. I wanted her to believe that everything would be all right. I wanted to believe it too and if she did, I would have some hope.

To hell with Amalia's bad luck!

The front screen door squeaked open and Aristide came out of the house to have a smoke and say hello to me. In the dusk of the evening, we could not really see each other's faces clearly and I was thankful mine was in shadow.

Olga spoke calmly. "Papa, Salvatore needs to have an operation. Dr. Lapenta says he has a tumor and he's going to take it out. He will need time to recover, so we will have to wait to get married."

She said what I could not say.

Aristide, still standing, lit his cigar, blew out the match. He put his hand on my shoulder, patted me gently on the back.

"*Figlio mio*," he said—calling me his son! How I want to be his son.

"You are young, strong and you have a family, Leo, Amalia and us, who love you. Remember that. Remember that. *Non dimenticare*, Salvatore."

He handed me a cigar and we all three sat there in silence as the dusk turned to pitch, only the street light giving us the shapes of the trees. The cicadas sang their last song in those trees and there was an aria being played on the phonograph inside the house, a tenor's voice in painful ecstasy. Tears burned behind my eyes.

Aristide said his *"buona notte"* and went back into the house. Olga took my hand and understood: I had no words.

She made me look at her and she said, "We won't let anything happen to you. And we'll have a spring or a summer wedding and you will give us our beautiful life, Salvatore."

But to tell you the truth, I don't think I will ever be the same—even if I live through it.

So instead of a wedding day, and the white adornments of bride, church and marriage bed, I lay in a cold hospital, surrounded by the white vestments of doctors and nurses.

There is a crucifix hanging above me. It offers no comfort.

Olga was here in my hospital room a few minutes ago and before she came, I was determined to be strong, greet her with a big smile and reassure her, comfort her, talk about her day and our wedding plans.

When she came to me, I saw the mist of tears in her soft brown eyes, betraying the strength of her posture and smile. I was stunned and my body went limp. She was trying to be strong for me!

Her beauty made me forget the words I had rehearsed.

She sat on the edge of the bed. I reached for her small hand, and she brushed my hair back away from my face. She bent down and kissed me. It felt final to me, devastating.

I closed my eyes and tried with every power I had left to me to capture this, so I could take this, her, her scent, her lips, her eyes—the only things now that matter—with me, into life or death, *vivo o morto*, as God wills.

I turned my head away so she could not see the hot tears streaming down my face. I could not watch her leave the room. I preferred to see her walking toward me, the gleam of white satin at her throat, waist, wrist and ankle—soft petals of pink on her arm, leaning against her father . . . mine.

*I must speak because I was the boy's doctor
and surgeon.*

Dr. Vincenzo Lapenta

I must speak because I am responsible for saving lives.
Because I can do nothing else with my life other than to stop it,
stop the bleeding and the deaths.

I will tell you something of who I am so you will understand
the agony I have in my heart.

My father told me I would do great things. The first time he
said this to me, I was an infant, not even three weeks old.

I was born on the fourth of July, 1883 on the island of Ischia.
In case you don't know, Ischia is in the Bay of Naples. It is a
beautiful and terrible island, its history marked by four thousand
years of domination by Greeks, Samnites, Romans, Saracens,
Germanic tribes, the Spanish, the French and the Bourbons.
Ruthless pirates, popes and rulers matched the natural violence
of the place, beset as it was with earthquakes century after century.

My father was Captain Antonio Lapenta and he was one of
Garibaldi's generals. Giuseppe Garibaldi, the hero of the
Risorgimento that united Italy in the 1860's, had been dead only
one year when I was born.

My father was 43 years old then, and as there were no more
battles to be fought (at least the kind of battles that spilled blood)

his duties kept him in the city of Naples, just across the bay. So when I was born, he wanted to move his family there, to keep us near him.

My mother told me when I was old enough to remember that I was alive only because my father, for the one and only time during their marriage, refused her request. I was an infant, and she wanted to wait a few months before we moved the household from Ischia to the mainland, but he wouldn't let her.

On July 29, three weeks after I was born, the biggest earthquake of the century shook Ischia to its foundations and thousands perished. We had left for Naples the day before.

So it was that my father expected great things of me. And looking back, now that I am old and experienced in having to make rapid decisions, I know that it was a combination of intellect and instinct for danger that caused him to flee the island.

I grew up hearing his tales of battles, glorious battles. I saw his eyes blaze in the telling. I saw his grief when he spoke of so many of his countrymen dying in pools of their own blood in front of his own eyes, and he was helpless. I saw his disappointment because despite all this, Italy was far from being unified. The dreams of Garibaldi and his peers—Mazzini, Cavour and others—were lost in the continuing chaos.

The blood. The descriptions of the blood seeped into my dreams and thoughts and over time, gave birth to my passionate desire to become a doctor, a surgeon, a scientist!

My father encouraged my inclinations. I enjoyed a privileged and intellectual upbringing. I was sent to the University of Naples and received a medical degree when I was twenty-three years old.

I was not satisfied. My father, whom everyone called The Captain, told me that if I was going to become the caliber of surgeon he expected me to be, that the world expected me to be,

I would have to be educated in America.

I was accepted into Harvard the next year. I sailed from Naples, with a ticket for a first class cabin, plenty of money, and a mission to serve the world.

Obviously, my experience on board ship was very different from my fellow passengers, the immigrants in steerage. While on board, I had several occasions to use my medical skills. I went below to the crowded, airless steerage section to treat seasickness, dysentery and even a broken leg. I felt useful for the first time in my life!

These are my future patients, these poor Italians, I thought. I couldn't wait! I couldn't wait to get started and do things that would make the world sit up and pay attention, that would make my father proud of me.

I remember looking out over the water and recalling my father's stories and thinking that wasn't it good that my father could be an old man and feel satisfied he had tried to make a difference in the world?

I was a young man then. I didn't know what my life would be, but I knew that at the end of my life, I wanted to fulfill my duty, like my father did.

Excuse me for going on for so long about this. I know, I must tell you about Salvatore. Indulge me for just a few more moments, please.

After graduating from Harvard, I met and married my wife, Rose. It was clear that Boston did not need another doctor, so I found my calling in an Italian community that desperately needed a doctor. In 1911, we moved to Indianapolis and I began my practice. My patients were there!

It was wonderful tending to these people, but I wasn't satisfied. I constantly felt I wasn't living up to my purpose. The visions of the bloodied battlefields continued to haunt me, the memory of my father's eyes as he related how many died because they simply bled to death.

So I began to experiment, working in my laboratory until I could not keep my eyes open, after I had seen and taken care of my patients. Rose would often find me asleep, slumped over among vials, papers and instruments. She would gently wake me so I could get to bed.

When World War I began, I drove myself even harder. I would think of how many in Europe were dying each day and I knew there must be something I could do to save them!

And I did. I discovered and developed the hemostatic serum and it did only one thing: it stopped bleeding. It was near the end of the war before it was really put into use and I still get angry with myself when I think of all those who died unnecessarily—if only I could have figured it out a year or so sooner!

I was used to seeing my name in the newspapers. Over the years, my support of the Red Cross was mentioned, as was my appointment as Royal Consular Regent of Italy for Indiana. This or that event that Rose and I attended or hosted would usually be included as "news," although I thought teas and violin recitals were occasions too trivial to be brought to the city's attention.

However, I must confess I read with much pride the *Indianapolis Star* edition of February 3, 1923:

In recognition of his discovery of a hemostatic serum which proved of marked value during the last year of the war and in general surgical practice since, Dr. Vincent A. Lapenta, an Indianapolis physician, has been informed of his appointment as a Knight of the Royal Crown of Italy, an organization of men who have distinguished themselves in science, art or literature or who have performed some work of philanthropy resulting in benefit to humanity.

Dr. Lapenta's notification, which came from the King of Italy, carries with it the title of "Sir" and was given for "unfailing devotion to the advancement of science." About a dozen Americans have received the honor. Charles Schwab, steel magnate, for his work during the world war; William J. Guard, New York journalist, for his effective attacks on German propaganda; and Guglielmo Marconi for the discovery of wireless, are distinguished members of the order.

In addition to the Italian honor. Dr. Lapenta received from England two months ago, the title of "Fellow of the Royal Society of Arts and Sciences" in recognition of his scientific discoveries. He is Royal Italian Consular agent for Indiana, a member of the American Medical Association and the American Association for the Advancement of Science.

This was the only article that I ever clipped out of the paper. It was the only one I had ever thought worthy enough to have been mailed to my father, my father who had passed away a year before I married Rose.

Well, enough of living in the glories of the past.

For now, I wanted you to know something of who and what I am and how I could come to have so much feeling for this young man, Salvatore Pezzullo, when he appeared in my office, complaining of constant headaches.

I was not accustomed to seeing Salvatore in my office. I saw him socially, at King Humbert Lodge meetings, weddings and the like. Occasionally, when I would stop in to see Rizzuto and we would share a cigar, Salvatore would be diligently at work in the store, never one for idle gossip, like his brother-in-law.

You couldn't say an unkind thing about this young man, yet he always seemed so down in the mouth, so forlorn somehow. I always wanted to pat him on the back and ask him "It's not really that bad, is it?"

So when Leo announced that Salvatore was going to marry Olga Giovanoni, I think we all felt a huge relief. For the first time, I saw the man smiling, even whistling as he walked around the neighborhood.

I knew very soon, after examining Salvatore, that there was no hope.

I had never in my life had to give anyone news that bad. I couldn't bring myself to tell him there was no hope because he had hope and who was I to take that away?

We scheduled an operation for a tumor that was inoperable, but the alternative was unimaginable.

I saw Signorina Giovanoni in the hallway coming out of the hospital room, walking toward her parents and grandmother the day before the surgery. I will never forget her question.

"Doctor, will I have a wedding day?"

I said to her, "I will do my best, *cara*. I will do everything in my power." By then I knew my best would not be enough.

Before Salvatore went under the anesthetic, he looked at me and squeezed my hand tight, shaking it like he knew I wouldn't let him down. I so wanted to save him.

This wasn't like being tortured by the death of an unknown soldier on the ground taking his last breath thousands of miles away. This was one patient, in my hands, and I felt the crush of this truth in my soul.

And yet the boy lived! I was stunned and came out of the operating room, punching at the swinging doors as if they couldn't open fast enough. The ashen faces looked at me with a last glimmer of hope.

"He's in very critical condition—but by God, he's alive!" was all I would say, could say.

For the next three days, there was a constant vigil at his bedside, although Salvatore was unconscious. I hope he knew somewhere in his soul that he existed and was loved.

I dreaded the walk down the hallway to his room, but each time the thread of his life was there.

When Salvatore opened his eyes a little and Olga told me he gently squeezed her hand, hope was replaced by the expectation he would recover.

One week after the operation, Salvatore Pezzullo contracted pneumonia, and in mere days died in his sleep.

Pneumonia! To have had all the skill I possessed to repair him, wielding a scalpel that would have been useless in another doctor's hands—to have taken Salvatore to the brink of life again only to lose him to pneumonia was the cruelest irony of my existence. In the end, I had still failed him.

A cold December wind blew hard across the front steps of Holy Rosary, as all of us who came to pay our respects at his funeral treaded wearily up them.

I felt eyes upon me. I was glad I had the arm of my wife, who said to me later that the looks I received were looks of respect. Respect! Respect I didn't deserve. She was truly the only one who understood the depth of my grief.

We sat toward the back and I forced myself to remember him. As Father Priori struggled to comfort us during the Mass, I made myself recall everything that happened from the time I found the tumor until I covered Salvatore's body with a sheet. What didn't I see? What didn't I do that might have saved him?

I looked down at my hands and wanted to sever them.

Surely you knew I would have something to say about this, didn't you?

Leo Rizzuto

I wanted to kill Lapenta. It would have been better if Salvatore had died on the operating table, in my opinion.

When he came flying into the waiting room after the surgery and told us Salvatore was still breathing, I had to catch Amalia who was so weak in her knees she couldn't stand up.

The Giovanonis cried from joy. I cried from relief. I needed Salvatore. I needed him more than ever. I was two months away from opening a restaurant, the first Italian restaurant in Indianapolis and I was going to operate it and leave the running of the grocery to Salvatore.

I gave the store to him as a wedding gift . . . well, partly. I did expect him to split the profits with me, but hell, it was a generous thing for me to do. Since he was starting his own family, he needed to support himself.

Yes, it would take a few months of recovery, then he and Olga would marry and life would go on as planned. I went ahead with the restaurant, meeting my lawyer, paying visits on people who owed me a favor to help me "finance" the business.

I was busy doing what the head of this family was supposed to be doing, while Amalia sat by Salvatore's side everyday with Olga. Every night, Amalia, while not exactly optimistic, would give me an encouraging report on his progress.

Then he was dead. Just like that. The next thing I know, I'm sitting here in the front pew of Holy Rosary, at his funeral. My wife is gasping, bent over, a handkerchief covering her mouth. My two-year-old son Salvatore is huddled close to her. There is nothing I can do—absolutely nothing!

Why does this coffin have to be sitting right in front of me?

So what am I going to do now? How am I going to manage things now? If I'd known he was going to die, I'd have held off the plans for the restaurant.

And my wife will be of absolutely no use, not now. She'll never get over this. Never.

And Olga? She won't be able to work either—maybe not for months! Who knows how long that will take? She may never come back. Jesus.

I cannot look at this coffin, so I look past my wife and over to where the Giovanonis are sitting. Aristide has his head down, his two fingers are pinching his eyebrows together. Well, he doesn't have anything to worry about except consoling his daughter. He'll go back to his carving and singing arias and in general being happy-go-lucky. *Non ci capisco nulla!* Beats me!

I look up at Father Priori's face, pretending to listen to him . . . anything to keep me from looking at my wife or thinking about how simple everyone else's life is now except mine!

I just pray, pray that Amalia's bad luck has ended now with this. Why did I name my own son Salvatore?

Little Nonna had put my white satin wedding gown in a place where I couldn't find it.

Olga

I'd lost a husband and had not had the wedding. I wasn't a widow, but people treated me like one.

I was very depressed but it was not because I missed Salvatore. He'd promised that he was going to give me a beautiful life and perhaps he would have. I also know I would have had to bury a piece of myself.

I was alone in my room, not knowing what I was crying for, when I faced the truth, when I allowed myself to see it: *I was relieved I was not going to have to marry him.*

Days after the funeral, I made up my mind to make this confession to Father Priori. But I didn't do it. Salvatore did not deserve that. It was selfish to unburden myself and dishonor him.

It's not that I didn't want to be married. I had many romantic notions and I could recall fresh scenes of Salvatore looking at me. I would lean a little forward, my breath caught, waiting for him to tell me what only his eyes could express. But it was just a flicker, not the flame I wanted to consume me. Was he just too shy or was it that he was too afraid of his own passion? The light in his eyes would fade, the flicker extinguished.

I tried to make myself believe that the careful, warm feeling I had for him was love. It was pity and that was all it was, after all.

After we had become engaged and before we knew he was ill, I guess I had been moping around the house and Mamma stood over me, hands on her hips and said, "Salvatore is a smart, decent, successful serious man. Do you really think you are going to find someone better? What is it that you want, Olga? To marry a Sicilian? Maybe you would prefer to be an old maid?"

I didn't want to be a spinster, but truth be told, I had no qualms about marrying a Sicilian. I didn't dare say that to her. It was still a time when Italian regional differences were deep, but times were changing. I couldn't say that either.

I felt ashamed as I thought of how much Mamma had been through, all those years of waiting.

The shame was added to the pity that I believed was love.

Well, it's over, I thought. But then came the next thought . . . I might never have the romance I craved! What if people never stopped treating me like a widow?

Two weeks after the funeral, Leo Rizzuto paid a visit to our home.

There was a wet snow accumulating at that early evening hour and I remember hearing his booming voice and the stomping of his feet as he shook the snow from his boots on the porch.

I listened from behind the crack in my door, as Papa invited Rizzuto to sit.

"Ari, I know it's only been two weeks. How is she doing?" I heard him say.

"Keeps to herself . . . very quiet, but I think she's better . . . these things take time . . . How's the Signora?"

I heard Rizzuto push his breath out into a loud sigh, but he did not reply.

"Ari, I came here because I need to know if Olga still wants to work in the store . . . for me . . . in a few weeks maybe . . . when she's better . . . with the restaurant opening in a month or so, and with Amalia the way she is . . . and Salvatore gone . . . I need the help."

"I'll ask her, Leo. I don't know what she wants, but I'll ask her."

I knew what I wanted. I couldn't bear to stay in my room alone any longer with these tortured thoughts.

I went back to the store a few days later, ready to face the ghost of Salvatore, but there was a new face there.

"Olga, this is Filomena. She'll work with you until Amalia comes back," Rizzuto announced and then promptly departed.

When Leo was away from the store and there was a lull in the afternoons, Filomena would flip through pages of the latest *Photoplay*. Sighing over Valentino as a Sheik or a French nobleman, she would turn the magazine around on the counter so I could see the pictures too. Most times, I went about my work.

"Isn't Valentino dreamy, Olga? Wouldn't you just die if he walked in here right now?" and she would pretend to swoon, which made me laugh even when I didn't really want to. Sometimes I wished I could be as carefree as Filomena, but I wouldn't allow myself this frippery. Salvatore's death was still a recent occurrence and I couldn't go anywhere without people offering their sympathy. Customers who came in would be surprised to see me there and couldn't keep themselves from consoling me. What would people think of me if they saw me sighing over Rudolph Valentino?

"Speaking of dreamy, look who's here," Filomena said as she scooped up her magazines and shoved them under the counter.

Ottavio Faenzi had not been in the store for weeks, not since the funeral. He removed his hat respectfully as he walked in and stood quietly.

He lived in Mishawaka, Indiana, near Bedford, and was a

cook in a restaurant there. He came to Indianapolis to buy produce at the City Market, but would almost always stop at the store to purchase vinegars or other special things from us.

He was friendly with Leo and Leo had in mind to hire him as a cook in the new restaurant when it opened. But Ottavio always talked about the day he would have his own restaurant in Indianapolis.

Salvatore had always tried to avoid Ottavio when he came in. I think he was a little jealous. Ottavio was always turned out handsomely in a nice suit. He seemed to know how to handle Leo, unlike poor Salvatore.

"*Buon giorno*, Signor Faenzi," I finally said, breaking the silence. He was probably shocked to see me, like everyone else was.

Filomena propelled herself in his direction to pull items off shelves for him, place them in bags and write up his order, constantly chattering away. Ottavio bowed slightly as he left, putting his hat back on as he walked out.

"He's so handsome, *vero*?" Filomena said.

"Is he?" I replied.

"You don't think so? I think he has eyes for me," and she pulled Valentino back out from under the counter.

Otto, as he insisted we call him, appeared nearly every week, usually on Monday. Filomena would arrive on those mornings dressed up, and her voice and eyelashes fluttered, as she knocked things over and dropped other things, waiting for him to come in.

"What the hell is wrong with her?" Rizzuto would complain to me. I just shrugged my shoulders and laughed.

I was polite to Otto but always let Filomena wait on him. I knew he was looking at me but it still felt like the whole world was too. I may not have loved Salvatore, but I would never let anyone know that.

When I smiled at Otto for the first time, because I finally could not ignore him any longer, it felt like the sun was pouring through me after having been in clouds for so long. I fell in love with Ottavio Faenzi and I kept my secret from everyone except, finally, from him.

He began writing me letters. I'd go to the mailbox before anyone else in my family, but Papa managed a few times to get there ahead of me. He would simply pull out the letter and say, "*Cara*, there's something here for you."

I couldn't imagine that my father would approve of a new suitor, but he never asked me what it was or who it was or what I thought I was doing.

Of course everybody, especially Mamma and Little Nonna, knew something was going on. I think they were all afraid to know and I wasn't giving them an inch.

Letters arrived every week from him and filled more of my lifeboats.

I would not open the letter immediately. I wanted to be alone when I opened it, to have the luxury of his words, words of love spilled onto a page that was meant only for me.

I would run my fingertips over the sealed places and think that his lips had pressed those places. I shivered thinking about nights that would come, when we would be married and he would touch my sealed places.

My dearest lover,

We are far away from each other, but my heart is with you. I would like to have wings to reach the holy land where you are. I think only of you, Olga and I

have a burning desire to have you with me. My
intentions are sincere and honest. I will always be
faithful to you and I will not regain my lost peace until
I am with you. You well know that my heart feels rest
only when I am near you and hope that will be
forever! Many greetings to your family. I kiss you with
all my soul.

Otto

I was delirious with the delight I felt. But the ridges of my
guilt remained hard. I stopped eating. I had difficulty sleeping.

I did everything I could to keep my wits about me. But I had
a guilty secret and I could tell no one, not even Little Nonna. For
the first time in my life, there was a secret I couldn't tell even her.

She would beg me to talk to her and all I could do was cry in
her lap.

"*Signorina*, may I have a word with you?" Father Priori asked
me as I stood on the steps outside Holy Rosary to receive his
personal goodbye after Mass.

"*Signorina* Giovanoni, would you be so kind as to come to
my office tomorrow—at around three? I have a matter to discuss
with you."

I tossed in my sleep that night, feeling sick that my secret
was known and to the priest! I hated myself for being so weak.

When I arrived, I was a bit taken aback at how humble the
priest's office was. I sat in a chair across from his worn, wooden
desk—sturdy and filled with uneven stacks of paper. Shelves held
many leatherbound books, heavy as sad saints. I was surprised to
see a wedding photograph.

"My parents," Father Priori said. He pulled his chair out
from behind his desk and pulled it around to sit next to me, which

made me feel even worse. I didn't want to be this close and so vulnerable. Suddenly, I wished I had the comfort of a confession booth, a curtain that would fall between us.

He sat for a moment without saying a word, and put his hand on my shoulder. His tenderness made me cry. It became a torrent.

"My dear girl!" the priest said as he handed me his clean white handkerchief.

I took it and said, "I'm sorry, Father, sorry."

"Sorry for what, child? That you cry? That you are in pain? Cry, cry all you wish."

He sat patiently as my crying continued, until I had nothing left.

He then said to me, "I am here to listen and help. You can tell me anything, as God already knows what is in your heart."

I wanted to confess, to remove the stone. I loved Otto with an ache that gave me pain and joy and yet Salvatore would have been my husband! My husband if he had lived! And we would have had children together. But he died and wasn't I still supposed to love him?

I took a deep breath and raised my eyes to the priest's, which were kind like Papa's were. I told him everything and did not look away.

Father Priori did not once interrupt me. Finally, there was nothing else to say.

"Child, you must know and hear me—that you have done nothing wrong, absolutely nothing. Where there is love, there is God. You love Ottavio and he loves you and has asked you to marry him. How wonderful! Do you not see that this is the healing?" he asked.

I didn't.

"Olga, dear, when you came into Salvatore's life, do you know how much light you brought to him? Salvatore was a sad man. He kept his sadness inside himself and he never understood what happiness was until he met you . . . . I know that because when he came to me to speak about making arrangements for your wedding, I simply said to him how pleased I was that he finally knew what is was to be happy and he, I think probably for the first time in his life, broke down and let someone see the pain he held—the pain that was on its way out the door—because of you—only because of you."

My tears poured out again and over my cheeks and hands as I thought of Salvatore, and the last time I touched his hair.

Father Priori said one more thing. He said, "You were his gift, Olga. It was his last gift, yes, but the most beautiful one. Think, how sad would it be if he had left this life without having known what love is? And having known what love is, don't you believe that he would want you to have it too?"

Ottavio and I were married on Christmas Eve, 1925.

While all this was going on, I stayed where it was safe.

Giorgio

In the background. Where I could watch and not be asked too many questions.

On most Saturday afternoons, if you were looking for me, I would be at the Apollo Theatre, sitting in the dark.

I have to slouch down in my seat, because I seem to have grown to being six feet tall since my fifteenth birthday. I can't stretch out all the way in my bed now, my shoes don't fit and everybody is always looking up at me and shaking their heads.

Everyone in my family is short. So is everyone on my street.

Little Nonna says, "It's Enrico. He wants someone else in the family to be tall." Lucky me.

On top of that, I have blonde hair and blue eyes. Why do I look so different from my sisters and brother? Little Nonna has a theory about that too. She told me that my mother's parents, her natural parents that is, were Austrian or French or German—something like that.

So, I am always getting these strange looks. Sometimes I wonder where I belong.

I don't think about anything when I'm at the movies. My

favorite American cowboy is Tom Mix and I am so happy when the double feature is a Western. I love to watch the wild horses galloping across land that goes on forever, huge mountains and dark skies that have storms and lightning and fierce things.

Did you ever see the way Mix lassos the villain after he first makes fancy loops and jumps with the rope? Or he could leap from a speeding locomotive, and land on his horse! And at the end of the movie, his horse, Tony, would rise up on his two legs and carry him away.

I remember going to the opera on Saturday afternoons when I was younger, before we left for America. I thought that what happened on stage to make me scared or make me laugh could never be outdone. The voices themselves could chill my blood better than any shadow or dagger or ghost could.

In America, the movies are like that. Even though there are no voices, the action, the booming of a pipe organ, the way a scene can change from one thing to another so fast—well, it always takes me away from who I am and where I am.

And all of this is mine for fifteen cents. For me, it's just one more miracle that can be found *sola in America*—only in America!

My biggest worry is how to ask my parents for the money I need to buy a cornet. The best price I can find is $99.95! I feel guilty wanting it but I can't stay in the school band if I don't have my own instrument.

Maybe I can work more hours at the grocery store. Standard Grocery is the newest and biggest store to open in Indianapolis and it's close to where I go to school, Cathedral High. I go to work right after school and I've saved some money, but not enough to buy a cornet. Not even half.

But right now, that's not even my biggest worry. I have to

tell you what Father Priori asked me this morning, as I was finishing up serving daily Mass with him at Holy Rosary.

We were standing outside on the steps of the church and the last of the women bid Father Priori good day. As I also turned to leave, the priest gently placed his hand on my shoulder to stop me. I turned back. The bright morning sun made the silver threads of his hair sparkle and his dark eyes squint at me.

He said to me, "Giorgio, I hope you know how pleased I am with the way you've taken your religious duties to heart here at Holy Rosary."

I of course said, "Thank you, Father."

"Would you be willing to perform another service for your Church?"

I could not imagine what it could be. I was excited and a little scared. I wasn't used to anyone asking me if I was willing to do something, as if I had a choice about it.

"Giorgio, Bishop Chatard is going to Rome this summer. The Bishop not only received me warmly when I first came to America, his support both financially and spiritually was the reason we were able to build our church. We would still be serving Mass in the crypt if it were not for him . . . . The reason I tell you this is that I would like to do him a service and I need your help, if you are willing."

"Of course, Father," I heard myself say. I think my voice squeaked. I was getting embarrassed.

"Teach him to speak Italian, Giorgio. He has acquired some knowledge, but he wishes to be able to converse with and understand better our brothers and sisters in Rome. Are you willing?"

"Willing? I'm very happy to do it!"

"He may pay you something, Giorgio, but I don't want to

ask him. He's done so much for us already."

"I expect no money, Father."

"If he offers, take it, Giorgio and simply thank him. Let it be his choice and graciously accept it. He's a confident man and you'll find him to be exacting, yet generous."

I walked away in a daze. I was going to teach the Bishop Italian? *Dio mio.* It was quite an honor to be asked, but there are so many others like me who could do this. Why had Father Priori asked me? Why me? What if the Bishop doesn't like me, or isn't pleased with what I do? The honor began to feel like a curse. "I wish I was back at the movie house!" I think I said it even out loud.

It was almost dark when I walked into the house. I smelled supper and it felt warm inside. I went into the kitchen, kissed Mamma on the cheek and patted Joe on the head. He was clinging to the hem of her dress and his thumb was in his mouth.

"What's for supper, Mamma? Boy it smells good!"

"Gnocchi . . . and you're almost late for supper, Giorgio! Go wash up and call your father. He's in the back yard."

I kept my coat on and went back outside to find Pop. He was finishing up the annual chopping down of the fig tree. He had already cut it and was covering it with leaves and manure and whatever else to keep it safe until the seasons passed and it could be resurrected.

"Hey Pop, I didn't know you were going to do that today! Why didn't you tell me? I'd have helped you."

Papa wiped his hands off and smiled as he looked up at me.

"It's all right, son. Besides, I wanted to hear all about the movie you saw today. Was it a good one? Did you enjoy yourself?"

I shrugged. Papa frowned. He always wanted me to have a good time.

"Anything the matter?"

"I just have a lot on my mind, Pop."

"Like what?" He got up and sat on the stone bench next to the fig tree's "grave." In the dim light, I could see the small fig leaves he had carved in the stone legs of the bench. "Sit down, son."

"Seems strange to have the tree gone, Pop. I like that tree."

"Yes, it's a good tree, the fig. I have to confess I'm not pleased the fruits are so small. In Italy, they're almost as big as a fist! Do you remember them, son?"

"I do. The tree we had —it shaded the whole back yard."

"There's only one good thing about covering the fig tree, in my opinion."

"What's that, Pop?"

"It means it's time to make the wine!" and Papa's dimple disappeared with his smile like it always did when he got a kick out of something.

"Now why don't you tell me what are all these things on your mind."

So I told him . . . first about Priori asking me to teach to the Bishop Italian. I thought this good deed might impress him. I should have known better. Pop wasn't the kind of man who went to Mass with us every week; when he did it was to make Mamma happy.

He asked, "Is this something you would like to do, Giorgio? Or do you feel you must because you were asked?"

"Oh no, Papa! I should like to do it. I enjoy my duties at Mass. I want to be of help if I can."

"Then you should not worry, Giorgio. As you do with everything else, son, do your best. After all, it's *you* who understand and speak Italian. What mistake could you make?

Seems to me he's the one who should be worried!"

He was right! Well, this all suddenly looked different to me.

"*Che più*, Giorgio? What else?"

"Papa, I need to buy a cornet if I'm going to stay in the band at school."

"*Va bene*, Giorgio. How much?"

I about choked when I said, "Ninety-nine dollars and ninety-five cents."

I know Papa didn't mean it, but his eyebrows have a mind of their own and they arched way up high on his forehead.

"I have twenty-five dollars saved, Papa."

Mamma's command came from inside the house, "Aristide! Giorgio! What are you doing out there in the dark? *Per favore*, come in and wash up! The gnocchi are getting hard and cold."

"Don't worry, Giorgio. We'll figure it out . . ." He stood and looked down at me. In the twilight I could see the kindness in his face." . . . after all, we've figured out much bigger problems than that, haven't we? All we have to do right now though, is eat. *Andiamo.*" He patted my shoulder as we walked in, and I realized I was taller than my father.

What a relief. *Si, mangiamo.*

I was spending every Saturday morning with Bishop Chatard, after Mass and before the Movies.

The first time I was admitted into the Bishop's study, I was surprised at how small it was, made really for only for two or three people. There was a desk, with a nice brown leather top. There were two high back chairs, also in leather. The larger one, the color of garnet, with wide arms was where the Bishop sat. The second one, for me, faced the desk.

The Bishop was a large man and he filled the room when he

entered. I was always startled at the whiteness of his skin and hair, so used I was to greeting dark faces with dark eyes. His voice did not match his size. We called this *sottovoce*, and yet, when he spoke, you felt the power of his words.

The light was not bright in the study, but it was enough, especially when the drapery was open and it was a sunny morning. There were many shelves with hundreds of books and a simple wooden crucifix hanging on the wall. The room smelled of leather, tobacco and musty old paper. I liked it.

In fact, I looked forward to my Saturday hours of devotion, devotion to God as I attended to my altar duties and as I taught the Bishop my first language.

The Latin and the incense and the bells, the chanting and repetitions made me feel I belonged. I admired the robes that Father Priori wore, and I could see myself with the same vestments, offering Christ's body to those taking holy communion.

I wondered if my passion for serving God was true because a few hours later, I knew I'd be coming out of the Apollo, dreaming of adventure and holding a beautiful woman in my arms.

This worried me.

At the end of our last lesson, Bishop Chatard said to me, "George, I leave for Rome next week and I want to thank you for all your help. I will never speak Italian as well as you, but at least I have been armed with enough to not become completely lost in conversations!"

"I'm pleased if you're pleased, Father."

He asked, "Were you ever in Rome, George? Before you came to America?"

"No, only Carrara, where I was born. Of course, we were in Genoa to get on the boat."

"May I bring something for you from Rome? I should like to."

I remembered Father Priori's words of advice.

"Yes, Your Excellency. Thank you."

He continued.

"I should be pleased to . . . . George, you seem so content in your duties. Father Priori speaks so highly of you, tells me that you have such sincere devotion . . . . Have you thought about what you will do when you finish high school?"

"I think about it all the time, Father. I can't say that I know what I want." This was as honest as I could be.

"Well, we all must follow our calling. Is it possible, George, that God has called you to the priesthood? Have you ever felt that?"

The heaviness of this question fell on me. I wanted to answer properly.

"Your Excellency, there are times when I pray . . . that I feel this, yes. There are other times when I'm not sure."

"It's normal to have doubts. It's a big decision. But God does not call everyone for this life and I would admonish you to pay close attention and listen. You will come to know what God's will is. You can be sure of that."

I was relieved. The Bishop at least didn't think I was foolish.

"If that day comes, George . . . I want you to know that I would be pleased to sponsor you at St. Meinrad's Seminary. I think you have the makings of a fine priest. And I think I am a pretty good judge of that."

I thanked him and told him I would pray about it.

He said he had something else for me, opened one of the small drawers of his desk and removed an envelope. He stood up and came around the desk.

As I stood up to take my leave, he smiled and handed me the envelope, instructing me to open it when I got home.

So guess what was in the envelope? There was $25, which, after what I had saved and what Pop gave me, was just enough to buy that cornet!

For now, all I have to do is learn how to play it.

I knew I was going to like Otto the day I asked him to let me drive his car and he agreed.

Aristide

He said okay even after I mentioned to him I had never driven a car in my life. He shrugged and said, "Why not? Try it."

It was a beautiful Sunday afternoon. Otto and Olga were visiting us from Mishawaka. We said goodbye to the women who were busy making dinner and we took off in the shiny Ford, Otto at the wheel. When we were out of sight, we stopped the car and traded seats. Otto didn't seem worried, so why should I worry?

I immediately knew what I was doing.

I said, "What's the big deal about driving? An imbecile could handle this, *vero?*" Otto shrugged in agreement.

I kept one hand on the wheel, but as I was talking, I needed my other hand to make my points. I was having a great time. Otto didn't say much, his hand resting on the door, smoke from his cigar trailing out the window.

We drove out of the Italian neighborhood and headed to the center of town. As I guided the car around Monument Circle, Otto pointed out the Columbia Club to me, but I was mesmerized by the Soldiers and Sailors monument spiraling up to the sky.

The carvings of eagles and engravings of brave deeds made me wish I had had a hand in it. And to see it from a car at a speed that let me take in all the angles almost at once, gave me a thrill. I drove around it at least three or four times until I was a little dizzy.

As usual, I lost track of the time and we realized we were late getting back home. So we headed back and on Merrill Street, I accelerated, a little too hard and it spooked me. Instead of engaging the brake, I engaged the wrong gear, lost control of the wheel and smacked right into a bunch of trash cans!

Mamma mia, what an imbecile I was! I jumped out of the car and ran around to the other side to see if there was any damage before Otto even opened his door. I thought, how is it the man can be so calm? And naturally, every Italian on Merrill had to come out onto their porches to see what all the noise was about. *Madonna*!

There was only a small dent and minor scratches, and after apologizing and telling him I would pay for everything, I started worrying about what we were going to tell the women.

We decided to say nothing.

We sat down at the table with the family. I started feeling nervous, so I poured myself another glass of my red wine, poured one for Otto too. Why wasn't he nervous? Otto leaned toward Olga, smiling as he slowly twirled long red strands of spaghetti onto his fork.

Ione kept looking at me. What is it about guilt that makes a person lose control of his faculties? I can't keep secrets from Ione. We were children together. She knows me through and through.

I noticed that I kept rubbing my forearm. It hurt and when I finally just looked down at it, there was a bruise the size of a bocce ball there.

Ione put down her fork and said, "What's wrong with your arm, Ari?"

"Oh, just a little bruise. It's nothing," I said breezily.

"You didn't have a bruise when you left the house, before you went riding with Otto."

"No, I guess I didn't." So far, I was agreeing with everything she said, a safe position.

Otto spoke up, "We had a little accident. I wasn't looking where I was going for a minute and we hit some trash cans."

Did I see Ione roll her eyes? I know I saw my mother roll hers.

Otto Faenzi was calm, cool. Thank goodness one of us was.

As stricken as I was over Salvatore's death, I knew in my heart Otto was the right man for Olga. He made her happy. What more could a father want?

Other than I wished they were living in Indianapolis. Otto was still a cook at Clark's Restaurant in Mishawaka and I knew that Olga was homesick. We saw them on most weekends in Indianapolis, as I was still working for the Indiana Limestone Company in Bedford during the week.

The three years before the Depression hit were filled with so many good things. Ione and Olga were both pregnant for much of that time! I loved being a grandfather! And even though I was still away during the week, when I walked into our house, it finally felt as if we had built a home for ourselves. I hadn't felt that way since I lived in Carrara, not really. The smells of something garlicky and wonderful simmering on the stove, a faint odor of last night's cigar, the fragrance of clean laundry just folded from hanging in the sun outside—smells that are like layers of life that welcome you the moment you put your foot through the door.

We got three more girls in the family and one boy. Mary Helen was Otto and Olga's firstborn, followed by a son, Alessandro. Margaret Ann was born to me and Ione, and we took to calling her Maggie. Her sister Laura followed in 1928.

We had a full house and when we were all together, I never saw so much squirming, crawling and rocking going on in my life. But *mamma mia*, I was happy!

I was, however, a little worried about Giorgio. My son was on his way to becoming a priest. Or perhaps on his way to making the decision. I wasn't against the idea, no. Every man has to make his way in life according to what gifts God has given him. But I had a sense that Giorgio had one foot in church and the other foot in the world. That's a tough spot to be in. I would never have interfered if he decided to go to the seminary, but as it turned out, destiny made the decision for him.

When he graduated, he enrolled in Central Business College, which surprised me because I thought with the Bishop's offer to sponsor him, he would have gone to St. Meinrad's right away. That's when I suspected he wasn't sure. I loved that boy, and I let him go his way.

In 1929, when the Crash came and millionaires started jumping out of windows, we Italians, like other immigrants and everyday Americans, had no such thoughts about dying, only a simple wish to keep working and keep food on our tables.

This was also a time when government and university buildings were being erected and gothic architecture was having a renaissance in America. Despite the horrible economic conditions, the government made sure new federal buildings were amply decorated. The Treasury Department funded these projects—and *grazie a Dio*, because otherwise, I don't quite know how we would have eaten.

The Indiana Limestone Company in Bedford gave me an ultimatum. If you want to work for us, they said, you have to be available all the time, to go on the road, to work on weekends. They were letting workers go and wanted to keep the ones who could be sent on projects requiring artisans, but who'd also be doing double duty as common laborers.

Ione and I talked all night about it. We decided to move the family to Bedford.

There is irony in life that cannot be explained.

As usual, Olga and Otto came to Indianapolis for the weekend, now toting my beautiful grandchildren with them.

Olga wore a secretive smile on her face. I was expecting to hear she was going to have another baby. I would have bet money on it.

This is what I heard instead: "Otto got a new job! He's going to be a chef! Tell them, Otto, tell them!"

Otto said, "I'm surprised I got it, but yes, I am going to start working for the Columbia Club next month as one of their new chefs. We're moving to Indianapolis."

And Olga beamed around the table, expecting to see our smiles.

Our faces were frozen. I looked at Ione and she looked at me. Giorgio just kept staring down at his plate of pasta. Only my mother was laughing, nearly doubled over.

Olga exploded. "*Diamine*! What on earth is the matter with everybody? You shouldn't be that surprised!"

Ione said, "You tell her, Ari."

I said, "*Cara*, we're moving. We're ... moving to Bedford."

I don't even know how to describe the look on her face, but

it made me start talking faster. I couldn't sit in my seat. I leapt up and started pacing to and fro in the dining room, explaining.

"We have to! The company told me if I want to keep my job, I have to live there, be there all the time because they'll be sending me out on jobs—on jobs all over the place! If I'm not there and ready to go, they'll give the work to someone else!"

I stopped to look at her and said, "I had no idea! But—*Dio mio*! Otto—the Columbia Club—that's great news! Congratulations! *È fantastico*!" I held my arms out as Otto stood up to embrace me. My daughter sat like a stone there in her chair.

Giorgio stood up, asked to be excused and walked right out the front door.

"*Cara*," I implored Olga, "I'm sorry it happened like this. I wish I could change it."

She said, "And what's the matter with Giorgio?"

Ione answered because I couldn't. "He has to leave college to help your father in the limestone quarry."

What a day.

I was devastated over the news.

Olga

My family moving to *Bedford*. After the tense and crazy supper, we cleared the table, had coffee, played with the children—and avoided the subject. It was just too fresh and I was too angry.

That night in bed, my eyes wouldn't close. I turned away from Otto so he would think I was sleeping. He moved over and wrapped his arm around me to pull me close.

He whispered in my ear, "Olga, I want you to listen to me. Your father is a good man. All his life he has worked in stone. He is as happy doing that as I am in the kitchen . . . think about how you would be feeling right now if your father had said he lost his job . . . think about that."

His words, so few really, landed on the selfish spot in my heart and melted it.

"It's Giorgio we should be feeling sorry for," he said.

Does my sister ever think of anyone else except herself?

Giorgio

Ever since Salvatore died, everyone treats her like she's going to break if she gets even a little bad news. I could understand that going on for awhile, but she married Otto, who I think is a prince, and well—she has to grow up. She has two kids already but she still acts like one herself.

What about what I'm having to give up? No one seems to think my having to quit school is a sacrifice. And what if they knew what I was really thinking about doing?

I haven't told anyone that I've seriously been reconsidering the Bishop's offer to sponsor me at the seminary. I'm still not completely sure about it. But I thought there was time to decide! I could keep going to school until I decided. Now there is no time, no time at all.

What happened to this country? Banks closing, food lines, no jobs because the stock market crashed. How does that happen? Greed is at the root of it, Pop says. But I don't understand how a man can have millions one day and nothing overnight. Where did it all go? Will it ever come back?

I saw Father Priori this morning. When I made the

appointment with him, I'm sure he thought it was because I was ready.

I decided to just be direct.

I said, "Father, I can't accept the Bishop's offer. I can't be a priest. Not now."

He said, "When did you come to this decision?"

I said, "Last week when I found out my father would lose his job unless we moved."

"To Bedford? Where he's working now?" he asked.

"Yes, and I must go too. I can't let him go and do this by himself. Cannot."

His shoulders slumped, but he continued.

"Giorgio, times are very hard. It seems every day I hear about one of our neighbors who's out of work. We have those who are sick, infirm, jobless, alone. Yet the Church is the one place all can go for solace, for God's peace. And I know you have felt that peace here."

I'd promised myself that I wouldn't cry in front of him. But his words were so true for me. Every time I put on my robes, lit the candles, listened to his benediction . . . peace filled me. My eyes were getting tears in them.

He went on with some quiet force in his voice.

"I understand your father needs your help. You honor your father and God by not neglecting your duty. You know, I was already a priest when my father became an invalid. That's one reason I came to America. I knew I'd be able to do things in this great country that I would never be able to do in Rome. I supported my family the best I could for as long as my parents were alive. I could not serve God to the detriment and neglect of my family. And neither can you."

This stunned me. I hadn't seen my duty to my family as being the same as serving God.

He smiled gravely and continued.

"Giorgio, I have a question. Would we be having a different conversation if you were not going to Bedford?"

How to answer this?

I said, "Father, my intention was to accept Bishop Chatard's offer. I won't lie and say that I haven't had many doubts, but if I'd had more time to consider it, I believe I would have overcome them."

Father Priori leaned back with a sigh as if I'd said something final. "My son, our time and God's time are not the same. As humans, we think we always know best, that we are ready or in many cases, not ready for the things life presents to us. I have another story to share with you."

He moved his chair around to sit next to me. Just like Pop would do.

"My first assignment in America was in Bedford, did you know that?"

Surprised, I shook my head.

"To make a long story short," he said, "I had such a miserable experience there that I decided to go back to Italy, feeling like a complete failure. It was 1907 and it was a bad economic time, like what we're going through right now. Everybody was scared. I was trying to hold together the Italian immigrants and form some kind of a rag-tag parish, but they were being run off with threats and fighting and shooting. It was a bit like the wild west, I'm afraid." He chuckled.

"I kept thinking," he said, "that I was too unsure of myself, too inexperienced, too late to help them! But I learned that how I saw myself was not how God saw me. I did not fail in Bedford, Indiana. It was not the right time. God didn't let me go back to

Italy either. Bishop Chatard instructed me to come to Indianapolis, so confident was he in me. This experience humbled me, Giorgio and taught me that sometimes we need to accept things, and have faith that it's God's way and God will have things happen for us when *He's* ready."

I've been thinking about what he said over and over. Some of it makes sense to me, especially the part about serving God by helping my family.

No, I couldn't live with myself if I let my father try to support all of us alone.

But there are moments when I feel pure devotion to what is higher and greater than I. Moments when I feel a deep sense of belonging that is communion with God . . . and nothing else matters.

So maybe I'm not ready. Maybe I just make the best of it.

How can I be as old as I am and yet feel so young?

Aristide

I'll tell you.

My son, who has had his lower lip dragging on the floor ever since I told him we were moving to Bedford, walked into the house this evening with his head held high.

"Papa, there is something I need to tell you," he said.

I said to myself, Uh-oh—maybe the Bishop got to him today. I braced myself for the news.

"I want to learn how to carve stone, Papa—to be a *scalpellino*, like you."

When Giorgio smiles, the whole room lights up, like the sun just came out. And the sun had just come out.

I closed my eyes and shook my head. Never in all the time since I reunited my family did I ever once let myself believe or hope that any of my sons would follow me into the mountains. America opens up all kinds of doors for people and I saw my children having so many choices it would make heads spin. In Carrara, there was one choice.

Enrico followed his father Antonio into the mountains, and I had followed mine. True, I wasn't a quarryman, but working the marble can take many forms when it's in your blood.

I have spent many a night lately, thinking about what it was going to be like being on the road again. I shuddered thinking of the lonely nights far away from my family and it scared me.

I couldn't find the words to tell my son how happy I was. Humbled, I put my arms around him and held him tight to me.

"I love you, Papa," Giorgio said.

What was I really happy about? Was it that he wanted to be like me, or was I relieved that this time I would not have to work alone? It was both.

Intermezzo

The Depression . . . Carving Stone and
Singing Arias . . . Monuments to America

They were Otto's only relatives in America.

Aristide

The Baldonis lived in Bedford, and we found some comfort with our "in-laws" after we moved there.

Otto had an older sister, Zelinda, the first one of his family to leave Pitigliano, their hometown in Tuscany. Zelinda dutifully followed her husband, Giuseppe Baldoni, to America, together with their firstborn son, Alessandro. Like so many of us, families were split between those who came to America and those who stayed behind. Otto and Zelinda had nine brothers and sisters who were on the farm back in the old country. What makes some go and some stay? For me, even though I had a burning desire to go to America, I had a small family and always knew we would be together again, somehow, somewhere. But to leave, knowing you would never again lay your eyes on your own mother or brother, tells me you saw no other way for yourself. When I look at Otto, I see a man who has made peace with that. I like to think that in finding us, in Indiana of all places . . . well, Otto found again what he lost.

Maybe that's why he doesn't talk about where he comes from . . . why he prefers to listen and keep most of his thoughts to himself. *He doesn't want to remember it.* Come to think of it,

Zelinda isn't one to reminisce either. Maybe they are just plain happy to have made lives for themselves over here. Maybe what they found in America was more than they had ever dreamed was possible. I know that is true for me.

So one night, we were having a smoke on his front porch, the women and children inside making their happy noises. I looked over at my young son-in-law, his round face expressionless in the shadows of the twilight.

"Ever think about going back?" I asked, breaking the silence between us.

He looked at me surprised, but took a moment before he said, "Never."

This was the way it was with Otto. Even when you asked a question, he only gave you a word. So I just kept on asking.

"So, Otto, tell me what was your hometown like— Pitigliano."

"Small. Poor."

I wasn't going to give up so easily.

"And your family? You have a bunch of brothers, don't you?"

Olga had told me that Otto was the eighth child. His younger brother, Settimo, was number seven. I about fell down laughing when she told me this. I imagined his mother running out of ideas for names and deciding to start numbering her children! When you're on your way to having eleven children, it makes some sense.

"*Si.* I have six brothers and four sisters."

"Have you ever been sorry you came? Ever wondered what your life would have been if you stayed in Italy?" I asked him.

"No. I just knew I didn't want to be poor the rest of my life."

I nodded and understood. He was barely sixteen years old

when he knew what he wanted, or perhaps when he knew what he did not want. Good thing we all didn't know what we were in for though. It's easier to be brave when you don't know what's ahead.

I think about the ten years of separation and ask myself—if I could do it all over again, would I have stayed in Italy, to have had that time with them, time that will never be recovered? The children's laughter coming through the seams of the house, the clatter of dishes and female voices, the aroma of coffee and cigars, a soft summer night, all of us together. Maybe that is where the lost time goes, into what you have now. It felt like a reward.

These were tough years though, the thirties. And it meant another ten years of working away from my family, but better this time around because I had a home to come home to and I had my son with me.

Giorgio had taken to the stone like a natural. I looked at his hands and recognized them as my own when I was young. He liked to sing as he worked, just like me, and he would begin something, or I would, then most times other stonecutters joined in. Those who didn't encouraged us with shouts of "*Bravi! Bravi!*"

In the mornings, just like we warmed up our hands and our chisels, we warmed up our voices. This called for something cheery—not too fast or demanding, but what we call *allegro non troppo*. By the middle of the afternoon, when we didn't think we had anything left in us, we would sing something that was *scherzo*, sprightly and lively and humorous. There are no happier arias to be found in Italian opera than those of Gioachino Rossini. The music is merry and ecstatic, even when a knife is being thrust against someone's throat!

A favorite was a Rossini aria from *L'Italiana in Algeri*, the Italian Girl in Algiers. It's the story of two separated lovers,

Lindoro and Isabella, who find themselves in a foreign land under the domination of a buffoon of a sultan. The sultan tries to force Lindoro to marry his wife so he can have Isabella for himself. Lindoro panics and stalls for time. You can hear the *staccato* in his voice, his nerves all jangled as he tries to find excuses.

(O povero amor mio!	(Oh my poor love!
Che imbroglio è questo!)	What a mess!)
Se inclinassi a prender moglie	If I felt like taking a wife
ci vorrebber tante cose.	I would want so many things.
un'appena in cento spose	Hardly one bride in a hundred
si potrebbe combinar.	could be found with all of them.
Se dovessi prender moglie	If I should take a wife
ci vorrebber tante cose.	I would want so many things.

And of course, *Il Barbiere di Siviglia*'s Figaro!

Ah, che bel vivere,	Ah, what a lovely life, what
che bel piacere,	great good times
per un barbiere di qualità!	for a first rate barber!
Ah bravo Figaro! Bravo,	Ah gallant Figaro! Bravo,
bravissimo!	bravissimo!
Fortunatissimo, per verità!	A most fortunate man, indeed!
Pronto a far tutto la notte e	Ready to do anything by night
il giorno,sempre d'intorno,	and by day, always present, he
in giro sta.	makes the rounds.
Miglior cuccagna per un barbiere,	Greater good fortune for a
vita più nobile, no, non si dà.	barber, a more illustrious life
	doesn't exist, no.
Rasori e pettini, lancette e forbici,	Razors and combs, lancets and
al mio comando tutto qui sta . . .	scissors, all await my orders
	here . . .
Tutti mi chiedono, tutti mi vogliono:	Everyone asks for me, everyone
donne, ragazzi, vecchi, fanciulle.	wants me: ladies, boys,
	old men, girls.

Qua la parrucca...
Presto, la barba!
Qua la sanguigna...
Presto, il biglietto!
Figaro! Figaro!
Ahimè, che furia! Ahimè,
che follia!
Uno alla volta, per carità!
Figaro... son qua! Ehi, Figaro!
Son qua!
Figaro qua... Figaro là
Figaro su... Figaro giù
Pronto, prontissimo!

Son come il fulmine!

The wig over here...
Quick, a shave!
A bloodletting over here...
Quick, a message!
Figaro! Figaro!
Alas, what frenzy! Alas,
what madness!
One at a time, for pity's sake!
Figaro... I'm here! Hey
Figaro! I'm here!
Figaro here... Figaro there
Figaro up... Figaro down
I'm coming, I'm coming right
away!
I'll be there in a flash!

When we conjured up Figaro, no one could keep from joining in. With every stanza, one or two more voices would go up into the air like bright flares until it was a full chorus.

We worked very hard over long hours and in all kinds of weather, and there are times when you can do nothing but concentrate on the fine point of your chisel as it hits the stone just so and you are completely alone in that moment... but singing gave the mind a chance to breathe . . . so you could go on.

It's hard to describe the sensation of feeling chisel against stone. Stone is ancient and contains echoes of things that have been dormant all that time. Carving stone, finding patterns and figures within it, is like waking something up that has been beautifully sleeping its whole life. It feels alive under my chisel.

Giorgio understood this, felt this and it surprised him, I think. Stonecutters have a language that is all our own. We were always trading tools around, too because we wanted to make exactly the right stroke, just like wanting to hit the perfect note.

A piece of stone, especially marble, is like a blank canvas or a blank piece of paper. The artist sees his creation there, with eyes no one else has. Even if I was carving a simple flower around an archway, it was how I saw the flower and it was mine.

And there is nothing in the world like marble, pure and white and clean. I grew up with marble and its eternal nature is part of its allure for me. With one misguided stroke, a block of marble is ruined. It can be very unforgiving. For that reason, I have known stonecutters who won't touch it, preferring granite or limestone. But I never met a stonecutter from Carrara who didn't love it as I do.

Giorgio has the same passion in his blood, like the veins of marble running through the Alps in Carrara. We might never go back there again, but it is where we came from and it is who we are.

Our employer, the Indiana Limestone Company, sent us on many projects, mostly in the East. We spent a lot of time in Pittsburgh, carving on the University's Cathedral of Learning, a forty-two story Gothic structure that is the tallest college skyscraper in the free world. It was thrilling for all of us Italians, whose dream was to be able to recreate the Gothic architecture that we think is the most beautiful of all. I suppose it appeals to me because its form inspires, like the marble it is made of. The arches, for example, curve gracefully and then point straight to heaven. In one way it's simple, yet the repetition can make your head spin. Have you ever visited the Cathedral in Milano? It's impossible to completely take in the number of spires on that church. It's as if all of humanity is clustered around the pearly gates.

Many of us came to America and did a lot of the dirty work with our hands, but our souls knew what beauty was. This was not dirty work. This was art.

Mr. Andrew Mellon was a rich man, a banker who became secretary of the United States Treasury under three presidents: Harding, Coolidge and Hoover. In the early thirties, just before he became ambassador to Great Britain, he wanted some fireplaces carved in his mansion, which also happened to be in Pittsburgh, so Giorgio and I were given that project to work on. There were a total of seven red sandstone fireplaces in that mansion of his!

It seems he was quite a philanthropist, supporting groups like the Red Cross and YMCA. And he gave so much money away—millions in fact—to build an art gallery in Washington, D.C. I liked knowing that I was at least working for a man who, like the patrons of old, had a love of art . . . a modern day Lorenzo di Medici!

We also were privileged to work on the Chapel that was part of Duke University in Durham, North Carolina. It was a Methodist church, but we didn't care, it was Gothic! To be able to use my hands on something that spoke so strongly to my Italian soul . . . I found a part of myself that had gotten lost somewhere.

The sculptures in the Chapel were quite a group—Thomas Jefferson, Girolamo Savonarola and Martin Luther, plus a bunch of important Methodists! I chuckled as I thought about how they would have gotten along if they were alive. How Savonarola got in there, I will never know. He was a fanatical priest who harassed the Florentines, most notably Lorenzo di Medici, and condemned the city for its excesses. He built a big bonfire in the Piazza della Signoria and those citizens who believed his doomsday speeches tossed in everything that was beautiful and profane. We have fewer Botticelli paintings today because the panicked artist was caught up in the fray and his works went up in flames in the so-called Bonfire of the Vanities. Old Savonarola ended up being burned himself on the very spot a few years later.

I cannot tell you how overjoyed I was that my son was able to see this kind of work with his own eyes and help make it with his own hands. I had feared that we faced years of backbreaking labor in quarries, with only rare moments of actually being able to carve. I would sometimes watch him and feel a lump in my throat that I missed his first steps, his first words in life.

It was 1934 and we were in Washington, D.C., working on the National Archives Buildings, a monster of a thing. Andrew Mellon hired the architects and since it was being built during the darkest days of the Depression, the granite suppliers were pitted against the limestone suppliers, each fighting for the job. As it happened, the base of the building is granite, but the neoclassic structure is all limestone.

Giorgio and I, along with scores of other carvers, worked on the column detail—Corinthian, my personal favorite because it has ornate scrolls and leaves and flowers at the top, my specialty.

One night, I took my son to see the Lincoln Memorial. I wanted him to see what I believe to be the most important monument in the United States. Just like the Statue of Liberty, it's difficult to put into words what it means to me . . . . I feel humbled and grateful. Humbled, because despite all the prejudice that continues, despite all the injustice that continues, we have these majestic symbols that remind us how much further we need to go. Grateful, because I have found such a good life in this country. There is room for me in America.

As we walked slowly up the stairs, only the two of us at that late hour, I looked above me at a black and moonless sky. Lincoln was lit up like a bright star and he was looking right at us. His stare looks into your heart, as if to search for what's there. My throat went a bit dry and I began telling Giorgio about how the sculptor Daniel Chester French hired the Piccirilli brothers, fellow sculptors from Carrara, to carve the statue. And when I said I was proud to have been able to work on the monument, too, he stopped abruptly on the step, turned to me and said very softly, "Pop, you never told me that. Why not?"

So why didn't I?

It was during those years when I was working alone, before my family all came over. I was in so many places and along the way, I made the acquaintance of Attilio and Furio Piccirilli. They had four other brothers and the family had immigrated from Carrara twenty years before I did, so they were well on their way to establishing a reputation in America. They had a studio in New York City, which is where they made the statue of Lincoln by carving it in 28 pieces of Georgia marble.

I didn't lay a hand on the statue—the Piccirilli brothers held on pretty tight to that job—but I was able to get some work on the limestone columns. Pretty ordinary work for my skills, but an extraordinary opportunity for a poor immigrant. I would have dug the foundation just to say I had a hand in it.

When my family arrived, as my children were growing up, I never looked back. Never thought to recount to them any of what I had been through. I seldom talked about the work, or the strikes or the hard days that beat me down, or the astounding moments when I was lifted and humbled at the same time. No . . . when I walked through the door of my home, and beheld my family there, I got caught up in what they were doing. What had happened before was behind me.

I tried to explain this to Giorgio and when we reached the top and were standing in front of the enormous statue, he put his hand on the back of my neck and squeezed it and we didn't say anymore. Our eyes moved to the words carved above Lincoln that say that in this temple, just as in the hearts of the people, his memory is enshrined forever.

What is it about that long-dead President that moves me so? I think it must be how simply he said things and how true his words were. He was a humble man, but a great man. He freed oppressed people. For myself, being an immigrant, someone who slaved away, sweated alongside black, Italian, Irish and others, I felt the unity in our oppression, but also the knowledge that this country was giving us the opportunity for better lives, for ourselves, yes, but especially for our children. I want my children to have that chance. It's why I brought them here and why I teach them, those born here as well, to understand what a great country this is—despite the oppression, despite the hard times. It is all worth it.

Tell me, please, is there any beautiful structure of stone in the United States that doesn't have the stamp of Italians on it?

I would have to say those were the best years, even if there was a depression going on. America was building testaments to its beauty and power and the special talents of stone carvers were in demand. Michelangelo had his popes. We had the United States government and rich bankers. And I felt like I recovered my years of separation.

The years passed and the work changed. I carved a large sculpture of the Blessed Mother for Mount Carmel, the Italian cemetery in Hillside, just outside Chicago, of which I am quite proud. This guy, a friend of mine, Sam Rosselli, did most of the monument work at Mount Carmel with his brother Alfredo. They were carvers like me, and had hired me before. This time, I was to carve the statue out of granite. She was to be fifteen feet high and stand near the entrance.

I wanted to carve her in marble. Granite doesn't yield—details like an eyelash, a fingernail can be shaped in the marble, but granite fights you. Who wants to fight with the Blessed Mother?

"Rosselli, let's do this in marble!"

"*Impossibile, amico mio.* The owner wants granite and the block has already been purchased. What do you want to do, go to Carrara and follow Michelangelo's ghost?"

"In my dreams I will go there. *Va bene*, but I am going to pretend it's marble anyway."

I made my hands believe they were chiseling marble. I fooled my eyes into seeing the luster of white in front of them. I understood what Michelangelo meant when he said he felt hungry for marble after having to endure work on projects he did not love, like painting the Capella Sistina. Can you imagine, having his kind of talent for painting such a masterpiece, yet wanting nothing else but to have his hands in the marble? My talent is a pale comparison, but I understand the hunger.

Toenails and fingernails appeared and surprised even me.

Rosselli whistled, "How did you do that?"

"I told you: I am carving marble."

The Chicago Daily News covered our story when the sculpture was finished and there was a photo of Rosselli and me standing next to the Blessed Mother, who towered over us. A big deal was made over her fingernails.

And it was a big deal! If you don't believe me, take a good look the next time you see something made out of granite. Notice what's missing.

Marble is what humans are made of when they live forever.

When I think of the ten years I worked
with Pop, I always have to say, "Was it
really ten years? That much time already?"

Giorgio

I look at these years and I never worked so hard in my life, certainly not before, and not after either, not even close. I was pushed to limits I didn't think I possessed. First of all, when I told him I wanted to be *uno scalpellino*, I never dreamed I would ever be able to carve like him.

I had expected quarry work, carrying stone, handing him his tools, fetching this or that for him, under a hot sun or cold rain, all pretty much miserable. Sure, I knew he would teach me a few things, but I never imagined that my hands would ever pick up a chisel. That when I stood back, there would be something beautiful looking back at me.

I was amazed. He was not. And when that happened, I realized what a gift I had given him and also myself.

Life on the road with Pop gave me an appreciation for what he did for us, all those years before we were able to come over. I would sometimes lie in my bunk, in whatever poor place we had found for ourselves, listening to his soft snoring or sometimes his talking in his sleep. I could not imagine doing what we did and being alone.

Of course, you are always working with others, but at the end of the day, there would be no one to say good night to. Every night, no matter how tired we were, we would kiss each other good night . . . *buona notte, Papa . . . sogni d'oro, figlio mio . . .* sweet, golden dreams, my son.

Every morning, we would quickly wash, get our tools together, have some coffee and bread or, if we were lucky, some sausage or cheese. He would pat me on the back or I would pat him and we were off with our crew. Most times we worked side by side and almost every day, Pop would come up with one of the old arias and in a second I was singing with him.

I learned so much from him. He could measure something once with his eyes or his thumbnail, and I swear, never miss the mark. He had so many chisels, each one it seemed made for only one kind of cut. He knew before he used one if it would work or not. We carved our initials or names on the chisels so we could always claim them back from those we traded with. Pop was the "old man" among other old men and he was respected, for many reasons . . . . He was from Carrara and had studied architecture. He was not famous, but he had been in this country a long time and could talk about the early struggles, he'd been in so many of them . . . the strikes, the speeches, the marches, the battles! By the time we started working together, he'd had thirty years worth of such stories! We would sit at dinner with a bunch of men, weary from the day, and Pop would regale them with his stories. I watched their intent faces, spoons held in mid-air as they listened to him, hands waving in the air about a bomb blowing up somewhere or fistfights with the Scots or police roundups of Italians after a robbery.

Pop would sometimes wink at me as he was waiting for their reaction, and while I'm sure he was telling the truth, the stories

were not without embroidery . . . . and you know something? That's how Italians like their stories, just as they like their opera— full of drama, distress, passion and spectacle!

I was so proud of him. I had never imagined what his life was like for all those years before we were reunited . . . . and being able to work with him when he was in the prime of his power with stone, was something I knew I would carry with me for the rest of my life.

For the most part, I put away what I had dreamed of back in Indianapolis—music, business, and yes, the priesthood. To be honest, I never had much time to think about them. I was worked so hard during the day and was so exhausted each night, that there was no room or energy for anything else.

My confusion over my passions, and which ones were going to win out, stopped when I found a passion for stone and when I had my father to myself. Sometimes I wondered what it would have been like if my older brother Bruno had lived. Would he have been the one traveling all over the country with Pop instead of me? Which road that was left would I have taken then?

During the times when we got to come home, I tried to pick up the pieces of myself that were there. I sang sometimes on the radio, opera of course. I sang the Ave Maria at weddings. I picked up my cornet to see if I could remember how to play anything. On the rare occasions I went to Indianapolis, I made time to see Father Priori who was getting up in years and retiring.

I started playing tennis. My arms and hands were strong from working stone and I had a very powerful backhand. My dreams couldn't surface so long as I was concentrating on hitting that ball. Or maybe it's more honest to say any regrets I had about my dreams were pushed away.

But I don't think that works for very long. Passion changes form and time allows passion to become what it was meant to be.

I met Mary Elizabeth. Mary Elizabeth Dussard. I was playing tennis at the Southridge Tennis Court and we noticed each other, smiled and started playing doubles. She had style, strength and a subtle smile. I didn't know I was falling in love. It was 1936 and I was still working in the thick of things and couldn't see beyond that. But something awoke in me, something that I used to feel when I went to the movies every Saturday.

But in these years I grappled with my guilt, guilt that came from the path I had turned away from, and which still called me when I had time on my hands. I felt like God was on one side of me and the world was on the other, each pulling hard on different sides of my soul. This storm kicked up something fierce whenever I was close to Mary. I could feel my heart beating and what I thought was panic was love, now that I can look back on it. The storm blew over when I was away working.

I sometimes remember what Father Priori said to me about God deciding when and if we are ready for things to happen.

Pop was getting tired. I could see it in his eyes even though he still laughed and joked often, even though he still could sing an aria like nobody I've ever heard. The work was petering out and so was he and so was I.

And Mamma, who had spent the same ten years raising the kids, taking care of the house, taking care of us in between our trips, saw the same fatigue in him. It became time to make some decisions.

I think Pop never saw himself doing anything else in his life except carve stone and I'm sure he believed that in his last moment on earth, he would be in the middle of an aria, his chisel still in hand.

When Little Nonna died, it set everybody back. Despite our noisy family, there was a dark, silent space where she used to be and you could feel it. She was like the main wall of the house that held the whole thing up. We all used to look her way when things happened, all our heads turning at the same time to see what Cesira thought. She might not say anything, but the way she put her mouth or set her shoulders told you exactly.

We were all three sitting at the kitchen table soon after Little Nonna had passed from us, when Mamma told Papa that she wanted to move back to Indianapolis. Olga had five children and my mother wanted to be closer to them.

"*Cara*, of course we can move back to Indianapolis," Papa smiled to reassure her. "I'll just go back and forth like I used to, so long as there is work to do."

"No more back and forth, Ari! Please, not any more. How much longer do you think you can go gallivanting around the country?"

"As long as Giorgio can do it, I can do it!"

And he looked over at me for my vote of confidence.

I looked down, then right at him and said, "Pop, Mamma is right."

"Right about what? That I can't do my work anymore? That I can't support my family?"

"Pop, there's no work anyway! If I don't quit, they'll fire me. You too, you just don't want to see it."

He knew I was right about this. There was no more work for stone carvers and I was almost grateful there wasn't because I didn't have the heart to tell him he wasn't up to it any more. If I had, there would have been a torrent of argument about how Michelangelo worked into his nineties and died in the middle of chiseling the last Pietà.

So we were to move back to Indianapolis. But before I left, I asked Mary Elizabeth to marry me, promising her that we would make our home in Bedford.

Those few months back in Indianapolis were wonderful, like a homecoming. Otto was prospering as a chef at the Columbia Club, had managed to keep that job all during the Depression. Olga's five children—Mary, Alessandro (who we called Alex), George, named after me, Louis and Joann—were growing up, but were so close in age to my own brother and sisters—Joe, Anna, Maggie and Laura—I most times let three wrong names spill out of my mouth when calling out after one of them, before I got the right name!

Pop was down in the dumps for a while. He was without his work and needed something to do. The kids kept him busy, so instead of holding a chisel, he would hold them on his lap or take them by the hand, tell them stories, tickle them, sing to them, or rock them to sleep.

I would have given anything if he could have retired and just enjoyed his life, but money was short and he had to find work.

When he came home to tell us he would be working for the Stokely Van Camp factory, I felt something inside me sink.

Mary Elizabeth and I were married at St. Francis de Sales Catholic Church on August 19, 1940 and moved to Bedford.

The day before I got married, I watched my father get ready for work. It was quiet that morning in the house. He put on his hat, opened the front door, unlatched the gate on the fence and walked up the street to the factory alone. He wasn't whistling or humming, there was no bounce in his step. I wondered what he was thinking about.

I remember the many mornings we woke up together, had our coffee and went to work, tired but happy to be in each other's company, our chisels swinging at our sides, knowing that at the end of the day, we would have made something beautiful together.

Well, I'm not feeling so young now.

Aristide

It's not the amount of time that's gone by, but what has happened in the past couple years that has worked on me.

I hardly know where to begin. Which part of the news is worse? That my mother passed away, or that I have had to give up the work I love? Or that there is little money and I've had to take a job filling tin cans with peas and carrots?

Cesira's death came like a thief. She was never sick a day in her life, never complained that she had a headache or was tired or anything. So when she said one day that she wasn't feeling well, we all thought well she's certainly entitled to taking to her bed to lie down if she wishes. Why shouldn't she be tired?

She stayed in bed for two days and died in her sleep. The doctor said she had a heart attack. Olga —it broke her heart. I couldn't console my daughter. Ione and I sat and looked at each other, not able to really believe that she went so fast . . . the person who seemed the most likely to survive anything.

I am glad my mother didn't suffer in her dying. I just expected to have her longer. Those little shrugs that closed mouths. Those hands of hers.

For a long time, I would swear I could still hear her sewing machine humming away in her little room upstairs where she spent most of her time.

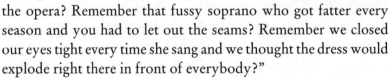

Not too long before her death, I went in to see what she was working on. She was making the uniforms for Joe's high school basketball team and there was bright blue shiny material scattered on chairs and in baskets.

"Mamma," I said, "remember when you used to make costumes for the opera? Remember that fussy soprano who got fatter every season and you had to let out the seams? Remember we closed our eyes tight every time she sang and we thought the dress would explode right there in front of everybody?"

Her little shoulders would start shaking as we laughed out loud and for those few moments, we remembered how different our lives had been in Italy.

Ci-ci-ree, Ci-ci-ree.

Then when everyone was looking at me and telling me I was getting too old to keep doing my work, I just couldn't believe it was over for me. When I first came to America, I did whatever kind of work came along to put a little food in my mouth, and enable me to send most of my money home. I dug some ditches, paved some roads, labored in some quarries—humble work, but I was young then and I knew it would not last forever.

It's sure different when you're old and know that the work is now never going to be better, that all you have to look forward to is retirement!

A factory! *Dio mio*! Enrico surely must be turning over. What monotonous work, inside a windowless place working alongside nice, but mostly sad people who don't want to be there either. How I miss the outdoors. Colorado! Vermont!

I feel like a caged bird who has lost his song.

I don't let any of my family in on this. I have never forgotten the promise I made to myself many years ago: that once I had my family back, I would not allow anything to rob me of happiness.

And you know, I have six children and five grandchildren and I get to see them all the time. This is my reward. I can come home and have supper with them every night at six o'clock sharp, which is Ione's rule. I ask them about school, their friends. Sometimes I just sit back in my chair and try to take it all in. Everybody's talking at the same time. Everybody passes plates of pasta or cheese or bread back and forth while they're eating and talking. Annie laughs. Laura cries. Maggie pouts. Joe slouches and Ione tells him to sit up straight. I reach over and run my hand over his head and get a smile out of him. I wink at Laura and get a smile out of her. I cup my hand around Maggie's beautiful face and lift her chin and she can't avoid me, so she smiles too.

"Oh, Papa!" she says.

They're growing up. This time, I am not missing anything.

Act Two

World War . . . Arrest and Internment . . .
Return to the Old Country

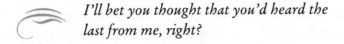

I'll bet you thought that you'd heard the last from me, right?

Leo Rizzuto

That after poor Salvatore's funeral, my life and business prospered. That Amalia's bad luck had ended, buried in the ground with her brother.

And I did—prosper, that is, even during the Depression. I'd been running a bootleg business through my "restaurant" during the Prohibition, and well, when the law was repealed in 1933, I had myself a nice bundle of cash.

Movies and bars are the best businesses to have during a Depression. Escape can come on a screen or in a bottle. Anyway, I did all right for myself. All those favors and knowing the right people. That's how you get along in this world. You didn't find me standing in any food or unemployment lines, hat in hand.

I closed the grocery store because it was smarter to put all the work and money into the tavern, which it became safe to call it when Prohibition ended. My son and daughter were growing up and of course, they both helped with the business. They worked away and I made myself indispensable in the neighborhood. I got myself tied into everything—politics, the Church and local causes—that would make my reputation. I was feared. I was respected. So I was able, with my friends, to make things happen so that the Italians could get some respect too. We'd put up with insults for too long in this country. It was time people understood what made us the proud people we have always been.

Would there be an America in the first place without Christopher Columbus? On Discovery Day, I saw to it that we were given some attention. Mayor Sullivan gave me an award ... and not just me. Medals of merit were handed out to a group of us—the tailors DaGrazia and Manzoni, my lawyer Girotti and also Piero Mazzalo who owned a produce business. We all stood with the Mayor when he shook our hands and gave us our medals. There were photographers, a crowd, everyone smiling and applauding us.

In the Indiana State House, there is a bust of Columbus and don't you know that it was me who twisted the right arms to finance the work?

Twisting arms sometimes is how things get done—although my size usually made that unnecessary. Hey, I'm not going to live forever. I want my boy Sal to be known and respected. I want my daughter to marry well and I would be the one to find her the right husband.

My daughter's name is Simonetta and her smile breaks my heart. She seems to be the only person in the world who can turn back my rage when I get upset. She doesn't cower in front of me like everyone else does (even my wife). My daughter just looks at me and smiles like *un angelo*. Sometimes she puts her hand on mine and says, *"Papa, Papa, non preoccupati, per favore."* So I stop worrying and squeeze her hand back and I feel better.

Most Italians in America—we stayed with our own kind, still married only Italians. For so long, even marrying outside of your Italian province was unheard of. A Sicilian marrying someone from Genoa? Wouldn't happen, just wouldn't happen. Then it seemed that so long as southerners married other southerners and northerners stayed with northerners, no eyebrows got raised. But as the kids who were born in America started growing up, hell, they didn't care if an *Irish* came along, God forbid. No one saw anything wrong with this—at least the younger ones didn't.

I will be damned if my daughter marries anyone except of my choosing. He will be Italian, of course. He'll be smart enough to do what I advise and make my daughter very happy, give me lots of grandchildren. They'll all live here with Amalia and me, just like it's supposed to be.

When I see what's happening out there in the world, it makes me sick. Pretty soon, all tradition will be lost, blood lines will be watered down, consumed in the big black cauldron that is America. They can call it melting pot, but not in my family. And they all know it.

So, you can understand that I blew up completely when I started noticing that my daughter's head was turned by a common Irishman who would stop in the tavern for a beer with his friends. I didn't like him the first time he came in. To be honest, I don't like having anybody but other Italians in my joint; or, if they're not Italian, then someone in politics who can do something for me and then I don't care what country they came from.

But this guy was a punk. He had a slouch and a mean smile that mocked me, like he was going to laugh in my face any minute. I waited on him, took his money and did what I could to encourage him to get the hell out, especially if I knew there was a chance my daughter might be around.

She was in high school in 1942 and I wanted her to worry about her studies and helping her mother and me. I didn't want her socializing with silly young women who might give her strange ideas and certainly didn't want her out on the street being ogled by every young creep in the neighborhood. None of them were what I had in mind for my Simonetta. She was developing into a beautiful woman and I knew what they were thinking when they looked at her. It made my blood boil. But I couldn't keep her locked in her room, even though I wanted to.

This guy was like an insect that just keeps buzzing and you keep swatting and he always gets away. It got to the point that I outright scowled at him whenever he would come in, but that seemed just to make him want more. When I saw that arrogant Irish mug, my fists clenched and I wanted to reach across the bar, drag him over and bloody his face.

My daughter was embarrassed by his attention and she should have been! The way he looked at her, his eyes roaming up and down, leaning back on his stool so he could enjoy every last movement of her ass as she came through the tavern to go upstairs to our home—it made me yell at her to hurry up! Of course, she was not used to being yelled at by me and she flinched and looked at me scared and . . . well, I knew something bad was going to come of it all.

The comment that put me over was when he had the stupidity to say to me when he was leaving, as he threw his coins on the bar: "How'd a fat dago like you ever wind up with such a beautiful daughter?" He laughed and bolted out the door. "Scrawny son of a bitch!" I yelled out after him. I swore to myself he would never enter my place again and if he did, he'd be sorry.

I didn't see a trace of him after that, not for many weeks. Maybe he'd fallen into a dark hole some place, like a cockroach crawling into a crevice.

It was too quiet. And it started making me nervous. I have

antennae. I know when something is up. I can feel it crawling around under my skin. My daughter started avoiding looking at me, gave me hurried answers.

I found myself asking Amalia, "Where's Simonetta? Why is she always late for supper?"

My wife, who never gives me a straight answer about anything, said, "She has extra work at school. Sometimes she has to stay after."

"What extra work?" I would ask, but there was no answer—because it was *bullshit*!

I decided to find out for myself. I took a ride over to her school and parked across the street as the kids were coming out. It didn't take long. I spotted her and she was laughing with a bunch of her silly girlfriends and I found myself all choked up looking at her and that beautiful smile that always melted me. I would give my life to protect her. I wanted her to have everything.

It didn't take long for me to spot what I had hoped to God I wouldn't see. The cockroach. He was with his stupid friends waiting across the street. They hadn't come out of the school. They all looked like dropouts. His face I didn't need to see. The slouch told me it was him. Smart ass. I felt my hands clenching the steering wheel.

He just waited, smiling and joking, but looking right at her. She looked at him from across the street, bowing her head in her shy way, but then she broke away from her friends and started walking toward him! It was everything I could do to stay in the car and watch this. Since when does a woman go after a man? And he's not even a man, he's a no good son of a bitch and I was humiliated, *humiliated* watching my daughter, my princess, sashay over to him like a common whore.

I started up the engine and pulled my car into the street. I swung over, reached to open the passenger door and yelled at her to get in the car.

She was completely surprised to see me, of course. She looked at me, she looked at him. He didn't move a muscle. Just smirked at me, and shrugged his shoulders at her. I raised my voice and she got in.

She clutched her books to her chest and looked out the window, tears, her sweet tears, running down her face and I wanted to take her into my arms, like I did when she was a little thing, when she would fall down or her brother would tease her too much. But I was so angry— no—I was really just plain afraid, afraid I was going to lose her.

"Simonetta, *tesoro*," I began, forcing my voice to be as soft as I could, "what are you doing going after scum like that?"

She sniffled and said, "Papa, he isn't scum. He thinks I'm beautiful."

"Of course you're beautiful!" Well, so much for trying to keep my voice down. "Don't I tell you you're beautiful ten times every day? So now you have to cross the street so that someone will tell you you're beautiful? Someone who's a drop out, who drinks beer and makes jokes with his stupid friends? This is the kind of man you think has even the right to look at you, much less tell you you're beautiful? *Dio mio*, I didn't raise you to do that. He's not even an Italian! No, no and *no*! I am not going to allow it, Simonetta."

She kept up the crying and I couldn't get another word out of her. What's wrong with women? Why can't they just do what we tell them, then everything would be fine. It worked for centuries. I know best. I will not let anyone touch a hair on her head until she's dressed in white and the priest gives his blessing.

I have her life and happiness all planned out. Can't she see that?

Before we got out of the car, we sat there for a moment. I knew that I had to say something, something to make her think, for christ's sake.

"*Cara*, haven't I always taken care of you?"

"Yes, Papa."

"Don't you know that I only want you to be happy and have a life and future that gives you that happiness?"

"Yes, Papa."

"Please promise me you will not speak to that boy again. I don't know what I will do if I see you with him."

"I won't, Papa, I promise."

Jesus, how I wish this was the end of the story.

You'd think that living long enough
to suffer through one World War
would be enough.

Aristiðe

When World War II exploded, I would never have dreamed that Italians would be branded enemies of America. I thought we were long past that.

Of course, it looked bad. During the years leading up to the War, Italians on both sides of the ocean were proud that Mussolini was not only straightening Italy out, but making her into a world power again, worthy of respect! We all yearned for that, deep down, even those of us who considered ourselves American. The days of the Medici, the Serenissima, the Roman Empire! The origins of a Republic, which the American constitution itself expresses so beautifully, the way our legal system works, the scientific discoveries of Galileo and DaVinci—so many gifts has Italy bestowed on the world. And this doesn't include the masterpieces of Michelangelo, Raphael . . . too many others even to name! Of course, we wanted to see Italy have another renaissance!

But the centuries of powerful families controlling regions of Italy isolated us, divided us and the result was—despite the unification of the country in the 1860's—a sorry state of affairs. Italy needed a strong hand. Mussolini seemed to be that man and had been for almost twenty years. Mussolini making peace with the Church gave millions of Roman Catholics around the world even more reason to admire him.

So we cheered when we read of his accomplishments, which were much more than the well-known one of getting the trains to run on time. He built railways, improved roads, education and hospitals. He finished the job Julius Caesar began—that is draining the marshes outside Rome. Of course, we only heard about the good things he did. Later, the world would come to know all about his vicious and violent regime.

The Americans liked him and supported him financially in the beginning. This helped Italian-Americans get some recognition and acceptance in those days. We were praised for Christopher Columbus as well as more modern contributions such as introducing the banana, spaghetti and olive oil to America.

It was a heady time. There were special days set aside such as Discovery Day, to honor us. After so many years of being referred to only as *wop* or *dago*, after being the lowest paid on the payroll or singled out for crimes when there was no evidence, we were given some status. Mussolini made sure that Italian-Americans felt his presence in very direct ways. He provided textbooks to our children so they would continue to speak Italian. In the Holy Rosary parish, Il Duce's photograph was prominently displayed when the American flag was saluted! What a showman he was!

But as with most despots who got a taste of power, Il Duce joined forces with the one who was fast becoming the conqueror of Europe—Adolph Hitler. Well, this turn of events knocked us off the pedestal we had started enjoying being on. Knocked us on to the floor. If you did not have United States citizenship, then you were considered an enemy. There was no place in between.

Just a few days after the Japanese attacked Pearl Harbor, *Italy* declared war on the United States! Those of us who had made America our country, who had raised families here and earned a living, had no reservations about our loyalties. I was sick when this happened, but disgusted that Italy had chosen the wrong side to be on—but then, if you look at history, Italy's usually had lousy timing when it came to war.

Our little neighborhood got a lot of attention from federal agents. They arrested several people, but when Dr. Lapenta was taken away, it sent shockwaves through all of us. How anyone could suspect Dr. Lapenta of being an enemy alien was beyond me. All those important titles he had did him no good at all. But what could be done? Who did you complain to? The police? The mayor? Many of us in the neighborhood who loved the Doctor wrote letters of protest to our congressmen. One went to President Roosevelt. I am ashamed to say we wrote them anonymously. And even though I had my own children enlisted and serving in the war effort, I was afraid. The Japanese were being herded into camps in California. The world wasn't making sense anymore.

I was proud to be an American and ashamed at the same time.

Looking back on this, I am embarrassed to admit I didn't have the courage to put my name on those letters. There were earlier days in my life when I didn't think twice about jumping into the middle of injustice. But it was only myself back then I had to worry about. I had more to risk when this happened.

Two of my children enlisted—Joe and my little Annie! All three of Olga's sons too—Alex, George and Louis. There were at least one hundred young men and women in our Holy Rosary parish who served during the war, including our neighbors' son, Mauro Agnelneri, who had become like part of our family.

I made sure I got pictures of myself standing next to each of them in their uniforms. I may look like a shrimp compared to them, but I felt tall.

I worried about them all the time. My factory work was not work that used up much of my brain, so my mind wandered and jumped to conclusions. This time, I was the one left behind while they were making a way in the world.

By 1943, all the kids were overseas in Europe . . . the house was quiet with the kids away, and so far away! Many times I found myself looking at the front door, expecting one of them to burst through it like they used to. You never knew if they'd be coming in with a scraped knee, a hurt feeling, or a grin that told you that love just hit them over the head. When they came in from the cold, I would put my hands on those fresh faces, kissing them on both cheeks and loving the smell and softness of their youth. Their voices filled my heart and I missed them so much, and was scared to death thinking of how innocent they were amidst so much evil in the world.

We kept ourselves occupied. Otto and Olga came over often and we would eat and play cards, trying to keep ourselves going while we listened to the news on the radio of bombings, battles and deaths.

Otto said one night, as he shuffled the cards for the next hand, "I got a letter from Mussolini."

As you know, Otto shows little emotion with his few spoken

words and he might as well have said he got the newspaper as usual on his doorstep.

I raised up my eyebrows, and said, "What did Il Duce want . . . your firstborn?"

"No," he laughed, "he wants me. Said I should return to Italy to serve my country."

"*Si*? And he was able to find you in Indiana?"

"My brothers sent me the letter. It came to our farm in Sant'anna."

"*Mamma mia*, I guess he's taking all ages now. I'll be expecting to find mine in the mailbox. So what did you do with the letter, *Ottavio mio*?"

"I wanted to use it for cleaning my pipe, but Olga wouldn't let me."

I looked over at Olga and she said, "It's important to keep things. I want my children to know what happened, to understand things."

She was so serious and her look took me back to when I saw her on the ferry, when she was only thirteen years old and she had that fierce look on her face, just like that. That's how I know when she's afraid.

I turned to Ione, who had been quiet all evening. She had the same look. I guess we all did.

Italian partisans took their revenge on Mussolini, along with his mistress on April 25, 1945, as they were trying to escape into Switzerland, the both of them shot against a wall and their bodies hung out for public view in Milano. It was the twentieth century, but his end came the same as for so many other despots in Italian history. The same crowds who cheered them, executed them when the show was over.

I had not intended to speak again, but it is lonely here and I cannot suffer my thoughts.

Dr. Vincenzo Lapenta

You already know what happened to me. It was all over the papers, the papers where many times my name has appeared because I sponsored a violin recital, or my wife and I gave a splendid party, or I was named Royal Consular of Italy or was given the title of "Sir."

The headline now was "Prominent Surgeon Interned at Fort Benjamin Harrison, Suspected of Being Enemy Alien." After the Japanese attacked Pearl Harbor in December of 1941, and the United States declared war, the roundups began in the beginning of 1942.

It was bitterly cold that night, the 6th of February. Rose and I were preparing for bed; our daughter Catherine was sleeping peacefully in her room. There was a very loud knock on our front door and by the time I put on my robe and got downstairs, it sounded as though whoever was knocking was going to come right through it.

I opened the door and I don't know what seemed fiercer to me—the sharp wind that blew against my face or the looks on the faces of the two men.

One of them opened his palm to show a shiny badge, the letters "FBI" flashing with unmistakable clarity. They asked if I was Dr. Vincent Lapenta and I had barely acknowledged this when they forced their way into my home.

Rose was standing behind me, shivering and silent. I was told to put on a coat and shoes, that I was under arrest for being suspected as an enemy of the United States.

My wife clung to me as I loudly protested, my hands in the pockets of my robe, my teeth clenched.

"Do you not know who I am? How dare you disturb the peace of my home!"

"Dr. Lapenta," one of them said, the wrinkled warrant in his hand, "we have our orders. You can come peaceably or you can leave your home in handcuffs."

I would not leave "peaceably."

I was turned around by force, my arms pinned together. I felt the heavy metal of the ice-cold cuffs clamp onto my wrists and all I could do was look at my poor wife to tell her I loved her—and to call our lawyer immediately. I wasn't allowed to give my daughter any comfort as she shivered on the steps of the staircase, watching this scene in absolute horror.

I was taken to Fort Benjamin Harrison, still in my sleeping gown, robe and slippers. I wasn't the only one. Twenty-seven other Italian-Americans were arrested in the neighborhood. It could have been a thousand and twenty-seven. I have never felt so alone in my life, or so humiliated. That look on my daughter's face haunted me.

The call my wife made to our lawyer was futile. Thousands of people across the country had experiences similar to mine . . . Mr. Hoover's agents, surprising people in the middle of the night, taking them from their families for no other reason than they had not obtained American citizenship.

Why had I not taken that step? I've asked myself that question a million times. My wife, who is far more intelligent and prudent than I, had implored me to do this. She was born in this country and somehow knew I was vulnerable. But that was a word that had never entered my mind. I? Vulnerable? I, who knew the laws of science and medicine and who could perform miracles in the operating room?

I was one of the heroes of the last World War on behalf of the Allies, which included Italy then. I had been given awards and titles and status. I thought I had plenty of time to become naturalized. I certainly never believed that not having it would land me in prison and branded an enemy!

Where are all my friends in high places now? The Mayor, the prominent businessmen who know me? They can no longer afford to know me.

I have been brought very low.

I am in a cell and because of who I am, have not had to share it with anyone. "Because of who I am." Who am I? I've had a lot of time to consider this also. Yes, I have all those titles. I am a scientist, surgeon, doctor, writer, speaker, inventor. I am also husband, father and son. This last one confers the most heartache upon me.

I can see my father still, standing there in front of me, proud and smiling, his arms crossed over his powerful chest, looking like the general he was. He always told me I would do "great things." He believed this since the day the earthquake shook Ischia and we were spared. In these dark days, I think about how one day would have made the difference. I might have perished then, as an infant, never having then been expected to do great things.

I don't know how long I'll be here. Who knows how long wars last?

I can make no sense out of this world, its politics, its panic. My world, the only world I have ever understood is science and medicine. Those laws don't change. And I will not change either. I still want to bring relief to people in pain, despite my own.

I am not accustomed to being idle. I asked Rose to bring my books, papers and laboratory equipment so that I can at least continue my work, which they are allowing me to do. It is all I have . . . it has to be enough.

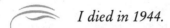 *I died in 1944.*

Leo Rizzuto

I was fifty-six years old, not exactly young, but I thought I would live to be a hundred.

The world was at war, but I didn't really care much, to be honest with you. Now that I'm dead, I can say what I want and it doesn't matter who knows the truth, one of the few good things about croaking.

Salvatore! Named after my wife's poor dead brother ... my son, my only son, Salvatore. I did everything I could to keep the bad luck from stalking him, too. Every time I called after him, every time I wrote down his name, the damned image of my brother-in-law's wooden coffin flashed in front of me. I would watch my son long after he had safely crossed a street. I worried every time he got sick. Amalia didn't dare say a word to me about her rotten bad luck, no, not after that funeral. We thought the worst had happened. But it could be worse. It can always be worse. She kept her nightmares to herself, but in the middle of some dark nights as I lay next to her, I would wake up suddenly in a cold sweat of dread.

And so when evil fate arrived again, I used all my powers to thwart its will, to protect my family . . .

It was late and it was dark in the tavern. The only light was from the streetlamps outside and I could hear my daughter's heavy breathing nearby and my wife moaning.

I took the gun from my son's shaking hands. I looked up into his face, his eyes big, and I could see the sweat on his brow and the blood coming from his lip. The gun felt hot in my hands as I looked down at the mess at my feet.

The cockroach was lying there, face up with a hole blown through his eye, half his head gone. He still seemed to be twitching a little and I heard him gasp and then he went still.

"What happened?" I asked the only question that could be asked.

Sal dropped himself into a chair and put his head in his hands.

My eyes adjusted to the dark and I went over to my daughter. She was leaning against the wall, shaking, her face in the crook of her arm. Her dress was torn at the shoulder. Her hair was wild and I gently turned her toward me.

"Are you all right, *cara mia*? Are you bleeding, are you hurt?" I almost didn't recognize my own voice, I was so scared.

"I'm not hurt, Papa. I'm not hurt," she murmured and I felt the blood drain away from my heart. I turned to my wife, sitting and rocking back and forth, still moaning *"Che sfortuna! Che sfortuna!"*

"Amalia, for crying out loud, stop it. Take her upstairs and put her to bed. I will be there in a few minutes."

I watched my wife and daughter go up the stairs and Simonetta turned around once to look at what was left of this jerk.

"Go on. Get into your bed," I told her. Sal and I needed to be alone.

I sat with my son and listened as he told me what happened.

I can't stand to picture the scene anymore, so I'll tell you that Sal came in late and as he walked through the door of the tavern, he heard scuffling in the dark. He heard his sister screaming for help and he saw the silhouette of a man pushing against her. My son knows that I keep a gun under the bar and he got hold of it and told the man to back off.

The fool didn't know what was good for him, and not knowing Sal had a gun, lunged at him. The gun went off and well, the result was oozing all over the floor.

I knew that I had minutes to think of what I must do. The police would have to be called. Jesus, it was a miracle they hadn't shown up yet after all the screaming Amalia had done, not to mention the fucking gunshot in the dead quiet middle of the night! Of course, I had heard it as I was getting out of my car. If I had only gotten home a few minutes sooner!

I told Sal to go clean up and get into bed. I called my lawyer and told him there'd been an attempted robbery, that the kid had pulled a gun on me, that I had wrestled with him and the thing went off, killing him. After all, nobody knew who the gun belonged to, no way to trace it to me.

I went upstairs and told my wife and daughter the story I was going to tell the police. They were to keep their mouths shut and if asked any questions, they had been asleep and had come downstairs when they heard a shot. I would be damned if my daughter was going to be linked in any way to this character—the cockroach—he'd gotten what was coming to him.

I told Sal that I'd be calling the police and that he needed to tell them he cut his lip falling down the stairs when he came down after hearing the shot.

"But Papa!" he said, "how can I let you do this? I killed him!"

I said, "Sal, there is not much time. The police will be here any second." I grabbed his shoulders. "I'm so proud of you, *figlio mio*, for protecting your sister's honor! You did exactly what I'd have done if I'd gotten home before you did. Thank God you came when you did! He deserved to die, Sal—you hear me? *He deserved to die.* Now I want you to do what I tell you."

It was a very long night. I was arrested and charged with manslaughter. There had been no witnesses, the kid was a minor, there was no evidence of forced entry and I guess the cops didn't buy that a guy my size would have no other choice except to shoot the bastard.

My lawyer told me not to worry, but he looked very worried when he said it.

As you know, it wasn't a popular time to be an Italian. If the likes of a Dr. Lapenta can be hauled away as an enemy . . . well, anything could happen.

When the eyes of the lily-white jury fell on me, I could read their faces. They saw Benito Mussolini and Al Capone wrapped into one.

His bawling mother, on the stand, said I had taken away her son's future. The kid had no criminal record except petty larceny and if you didn't know better, which I did, you would have thought this kid walked around with a halo, escorting little old ladies across streets. I was coming out of my skin. She said I deserved to be locked up, that I was probably mafia!

My lawyer leapt to his feet to object, but the jury had made its decision with that single accusation. I could see it. I could feel it.

When the verdict "guilty as charged" was read out loud, the words hit me like a hundred bullets in the chest. I didn't look at my wife, my son or my daughter when they led me handcuffed out of the courtroom.

My sentence? Ten years for manslaughter. I was up for parole after one year of my rotting in that place and knew it would be a fucking miracle if they let me out. It was 1943, and we were still at war, Italians getting their asses kicked all over the world.

Sal enlisted and there wasn't an hour that went by that I wasn't grateful that he was not touched by any of this. And I was also tortured that something might happen to him. Amalia's bad luck, sprung from the grave like Lazarus again.

When I wasn't thinking about that, I thought about my daughter. I never asked how it came about that the rat was in the tavern in the first place. I didn't ask because I didn't want to know. I made myself believe she was followed home and then assaulted by him. If it happened any other way, I couldn't bear it.

The memory of her smile was the only thing that kept me going in that cell. My heart hurt all the time.

After a year, the parole board denied my plea.

I wouldn't allow anyone to visit except Amalia, whose raven hair turned completely white since the trial. She brought me news of our children. They were all trying to keep the business going until I could get the hell out of that place.

When I was not thinking of Sal or Simonetta, I would think about my life, the years I spent in America, the hopes and dreams I had which came true for me, despite Amalia's bad luck.

Hell, I didn't want to be remembered for killing a teenager! I want people to remember me for the wonderful Italian foods they bought in my grocery store that reminded them of their home towns, for the good times they had with friends and family in my tavern, drinking a beer, a glass of chianti, for the cigars I passed out to celebrate weddings and new babies. I want to be remembered for the Christopher Columbus sculpture, for the opportunities I gave other immigrants who came to me because they heard I was a good man.

I *was* a good man!

In 1944, after two years of war and prison, they let me out finally, but my old life was gone. Only a few people came around, always looking at me like I was some kind of ghost. There'd been all kinds of stories about what really happened that night. But I knew. I went to my grave with it, as will Amalia and Sal and Simonetta.

My beautiful daughter—she doesn't smile anymore.

In Italy, I would have been honored for what I did, including plugging someone who was trying to rape my daughter! America made my dreams come true, but we never really understood each other. And this broke my heart when I finally realized it, that I was an Italian in a country that could not embrace who I was.

I see it all so clearly now. Too bad this happens only after you're dead.

One day—not so long ago—I was looking out over the water to where my father was standing on the dock, seeing his face, knowing that at last I had found him.

Olga

Then there is today, as I sit next to his bed in a hospital room, as he takes his last breaths.

In between these two days, thirty-eight years have passed.

I lost my first love, married my true love, had five children, gained a second brother and three sisters, lost my Nonna, and lost my mother.

Mamma died two years ago, in 1956. I think I have cried every day since then. She went like Little Nonna did, like a sudden wind that blows around you, then is gone.

I look at my father's face. He needs me so. He's been like a lost child since Mamma died. He looks peaceful in unconsciousness. I hope he is. I hope he's dreaming of us sitting around the table, laughing, or maybe he's on that little stage again in Carrara singing his heart out or—most likely—he is carving.

After Mamma's funeral, we all spent a lot of time with him, his house was so empty, his life with such a hole in it. Otto and I would have him over for supper, Annie and her husband Don would too and they would play cards and try to get him to smile. He went to visit Andy and it would cheer him up until he had to come back to that house. He didn't smile any more. He didn't sing any more. Nonna gone, Mamma gone, children gone. He was seventy years old.

I gave him something to do. I told him I wanted a birdbath for the back yard and so he could come over everyday and work on it, carving it, sweet little stone birds perched on the side. He wasn't working at the factory anymore and there was just simply too much time on his hands, his beautiful hands.

He announced he was going to Florida. He said his bones were cold and he wanted to visit friends there he hadn't seen for years. We were all so relieved to hear it.

He stayed about a month.

I still cry to remember the cross words I used with him, just a few weeks ago, when he returned. How I wish I could take them back because I haven't been able to tell him I'm sorry.

He had come by my house early in the morning to have some coffee with me. He burst through the front door like he used to and I was so happy to see his old self. He gave me a kiss and sat down at the small kitchen table while I was washing up some dishes in the sink, my back to him as we talked.

I asked him about the trip, told him this and that about the kids. There was a silence, and then I heard him sigh and say, "Olga, guess what? I'm getting married!"

I felt my hands go numb in the soapy water and when I turned around, I guess I still had hold of a dish because it slipped and crashed on the floor. I couldn't say anything. I just looked at him.

He looked down, his strong hands clasped in front of him on the table. "Olga, *cara*, . . . I'm lonely."

I am ashamed to say I completely lost my temper. I started picking up the broken pieces of china and said whatever came into my head, "You can't do that to Mamma. What's wrong with you?"

He put some photographs out on the table and said, "Just look at this nice lady."

I said, "How can you talk like this? I don't care who she is or if she's nice!"

He begged me to look at the pictures, but I refused. I said, "I don't want to look at them, Papa! You can't do this. Your family is here, not in Florida. Why do you want to go to strangers?"

He just said, "*Cara*, I'm lonely . . . anyway, I gave her a ring already."

I wanted to kill him. I didn't say another word. He kept trying so hard to convince me, patient as he always was. But I was having none of it. He left. I fumed for days and then just a few weeks later, he was admitted to St. Vincent's Hospital. The doctors said he had advanced prostate cancer.

He doesn't have much longer. He has been unconscious for days. I watch his face and see traces of his dreams float by. I think about how I spoke to him, and know it was because I wanted to keep my mother's memory alive. I was not ready to see Papa with anyone else. I would never be ready, but how I wish I'd have just kept my mouth shut. He, more than anyone else, deserved to live his last days as he wished. He gave us so much, gave up so much,

gave himself less all his life so that we could have everything. He was happy and proud to do it!

And I took his last hope away from him. This makes me remember Salvatore. I remember sitting next to his bed too as he lay dying. How cruel it would have been then to take away his hope, to have dashed his dreams before he left this world. No, it was better that he had them to hold onto, to have a reason to go on living. When he died, he at least knew that I had loved him and isn't that how we all wish to die? To know that we are loved?

Papa knows he is loved, but he wanted a second chance, a last chance to have someone in his life to talk to, to sing to, to sleep with. And I made him feel so bad.

So, I sit here and ask my father to forgive me. I hold his hand. I wipe his brow. I make sure he is covered. I sing to him. I don't know what else to do. I wish Nonna were here. She would know what to say.

What is he doing with his hands? I wonder if I should call the doctor in. But he's smiling. He has lifted his hands and he's doing something with them. He's mumbling, but I can't understand him. Is he carving in his sleep? No, it doesn't look like that. It's like he is holding something in his fingers and the other hand is guiding something between them. Is he conducting an orchestra? No, it's more like he's threading a needle, but it looks so, I don't know, so musical, like an invisible ribbon between his hands.

I lean down close to him because I want to hear what he's

saying. The noise from the hallway is loud, so I take a deep breath, close my eyes and put my ear as close to him as I can without getting in the way of whatever it is he's doing in his sleep.

Ah, yes. He's threading a needle.

"*Ci-ci-ree, Ci-ci-ree*," he's saying. Nonna. He is thinking of her right now. She taught us all how to thread needles, just about the same time she taught us how to tie our shoes. And she would have taught him too, when he was little.

Oh Papa, be a boy again in your dreams! Go back to Carrara, be in that sunny house, chase Mamma around the room, play . . . and sing.

I have dreams about my mother and I talk to her.

Olga

For some reason, Nonna doesn't come to me in my dreams, and neither does Papa.

Most of the time Mamma and I are taking a walk. The night I dreamed we were on the beach again in Carrara, I decided I was ready to go back to Italy.

I said, "Otto, I want to go to Italy."

He was reading his newspaper; a puff of smoke from his pipe curling around the edge, but he didn't reply.

"Ottavio. Don't you want to go to Italy? See your brothers?"

"No," was all I could get out of him.

"You haven't seen your brothers or sisters for fifty years. I want to go to Carrara and I want to go to Pitigliano, to meet your family."

He knows when I'm serious and have my mind made up. But he wasn't backing down.

He said, "*Perchè?* Why?" He lowered the newspaper and stared at me. "So I can remember how poor I was?"

"We're not poor now. We can go back. It's time."

He raised the paper back up, the smoke rose again. "If you want."

"I want," I said—and right then started making plans.

How do I describe what it was like to go back after all those years? Why did I long to go in the first place? I was keeping a promise I had made to my mother, yes. But I was also going for Otto, even though he wasn't exactly willing. Something was telling me that it was important we go and that was reason enough for me.

Otto and I had never been on an airplane and as we looked outside the window, as we flew through clouds, I was happy I had lived long enough that I could fly across that ocean.

I watched Otto's profile as he tried to shoot with his movie camera through the small window, at the traces of earth and water below us. It was the summer of 1962. He was sixty-five years old and had just retired from the Columbia Club . . . thirty-five years there! We had taken the kids on short vacations over the years, but we had never taken a big trip like this one together. The next six weeks stretched out in front of us, an extravagance to me. But he deserved it.

We were met at the Rome airport by Otto's brother Francesco and his son-in-law, Goffredo. The brothers both broke into big smiles as they each added fifty years to the faces they remembered. I stood a little behind Otto and did not try to hold back the tears as they hugged and kissed each other. Francesco was small and wiry, easily disappearing into Otto's larger embrace. Francesco kissed me on both cheeks warmly, and then Goffredo stepped forward, a robust young man with deep dark eyes and a brilliant smile that made me like him in an instant.

Goffredo was married to Otto's niece, Alma and they had two girls, Rossella and baby Monica, just born. In the days we spent with them, they became my family.

So many things were returned to me that I either had forgotten about or long ago gave up hope ever having them again . . . simple things like large ripe figs, aged *parmigiano* cheese that crumbled and melted in my mouth. Rich gelato made of fresh cream and filled with pistachio or chocolate . . . small cups of steaming espresso, bitter and delicious. It wasn't that these were new tastes and smells . . . it was just that in Italy, the tastes, smells and textures were so pure and so rich . . . over time I had gotten used to American ways. Italy woke up my senses.

These things from my childhood, the first twelve years of my life . . . to have it all right there with me once more helped me to feel young again, yet to experience some things for the very first time.

I had never in my life been to Rome, although it is now a day's driving distance from Carrara. In those days, Rome meant St. Peter's to me, a world away, and I saw it only in my dreams. Of course, years later when television came into our living rooms, I watched the Pope stand over the huge crowds to give the blessing at Easter or at Christmas, always wondering what it might be like to be there.

On Corpus Christi, the feast that celebrates the Holy Eucharist, Goffredo, Otto and I found ourselves in St. Peter's square among thousands who were waiting for Pope John to pass. It was hot that July day, hot like a steam bath, and there were a couple of times I felt faint from standing so long under the sun. Pope John made a procession through the crowd and he brushed by us, his purple robes and golden mitre magnificent and radiant in the light. Everyone stood back to make way for him and the crowd grew silent.

I never walked so much in my life as I did in Rome, but always around the next corner would appear something that made my eyes open wider. From one typical busy street, full of people darting in and out of shops or cafes, we suddenly stepped into the huge Piazza Navona, where marble gods emerged from fountains that were their playgrounds. The sound of the gushing water soared above all the voices as we walked to one of the fountains to sit and rest on its edge for a while. The mist from the blowing water felt so good in the summer heat, I could have stayed there for hours just watching the parade of people.

We walked past the expensive shops on *via Condotti*, my head spinning from the seductive displays of beautiful fabrics, jewelry and fashion in the windows. Everything glittered and I had to stop in front of each one.

"*Zia*," Goffredo called to me affectionately, "*Zio* and I will go wait for you on the Spanish steps. Take your time. We're going to have a smoke."

I was happy to have some time alone to wander. I knew Otto wanted to sit and enjoy one of those small Tuscan cigars Goffredo bought for him.

I watched Goffredo tenderly take Otto's arm as they turned to go to the end of the street, where the magnificent steps rose above the expansive scene and where hundreds of people gathered. I was grateful for Goffredo's attention to us. I liked that he called us aunt and uncle, *zia and zio*.

Goffredo had taken time off of work so he could drive us out to the countryside, to Pitigliano and to the farm called Sant'anna, where Otto was born. Otto's older brother, Adelmo, nicknamed Memmo, still lived on the farm with his family. Otto's sister Gesuina had written us before we left the United States, to let us know that Memmo had suffered a stroke and was hardly able to speak or walk.

I felt anxious about this reunion as we all drove out of Rome stuffed in Goffredo's small car. It wasn't very comfortable, but Goffredo kept us laughing most of the time, with a few stops to stretch our legs and drink something. And he drove so fast that I felt carsick at times, so I was happy to get out of that car and be still for a few minutes. It gave me the chance to look, really look at the beauty around us, of the hills that were lush and green, the neat rows of grapevines and olive trees, silvery and peaceful. There were a few billowing clouds, white and clean above the tall cypress trees . . . so quiet, so restful.

"*Andiamo!*" would soon be the command from Goffredo and we'd roar off in the little car.

When the farm, Sant'anna, came into view, I saw the same rolling hills, cypress trees, olive trees and vineyards enveloping us. Why did I think it would look poor? Why was I surprised it was so beautiful?

We emerged from the car, hot and sticky. Memmo's son Gino and his wife, Luigina, were the first to come running out of their house to greet us. They were so happy to see us, everybody kissing and hugging, grabbing our bags, herding us into the house—and then all of a sudden, there were so many more relatives! Memmo had eight children and most of them were married and starting to have children too, so you can imagine the crowd that surrounded us!

We came in through the door to see Memmo sitting in a wheelchair. The moment he and Otto saw each other, Memmo broke down into sobs that made us all stop talking. And I thought, how sad that he couldn't really say to his brother what he had waited fifty years to say. Otto pulled up a chair to sit next to him as the family gathered around. Otto just kept holding onto Memmo's hand and asking him things he could nod his head to. Memmo broke into a big smile and it was all right after that.

We took a walk around the farm. I was able to go into the very house Otto was born in. From the outside, it looked like a hovel and then I realized why I had expected the farm to look impoverished. That was all Otto had ever said about leaving Italy . . . *that he did not want to be poor.* I always wondered how he could have left his poor widowed mother behind. It seemed a selfish thing to do, yet Otto didn't have a selfish bone in his body.

Standing there with him, at the door of his boyhood home, I suddenly understood. His widowed mother simply could not make ends meet for the eleven children she was left with. Otto wasn't being selfish. He didn't want to be a burden to his mother. He left, knowing he had several strong brothers to work the farm and protect her. And that's exactly what happened.

All these years I had known and lived with Otto, and yet it was on that day I understood better what made him the loving man that he is.

I took a deep breath as we walked into the small home—but I was amazed at how modern and clean and pretty it was on the inside. I was glad for Otto that he could see it like this. It was good they had not just torn it down, that they kept it. Italians do that. We keep the old things that hold a memory, tinker around with them until they shine again.

It made me happy to see Otto walking around, pushing Memmo's wheelchair and pointing out to him and Francesco all the things he remembered from his childhood. Maybe in coming back here, in seeing it again like this, reuniting with his brothers who had beautiful families like we'd had, maybe now he could return home and not think of how poor he had been in Italy.

Luigina, Memmo's daughter-in-law, stuck by me all day. By the time we had to leave, she asked me if I would write to her. I liked her directness. She had been very kind to make a list of all of

Otto's family for me—I couldn't possibly have remembered all the names. I looked at her round, ruddy face framed with dark curls, piercing brown eyes and sweet smile. I reached out and patted those curls and promised I would write as often as I could. She was young, just starting her family, and I think she was very excited at the idea of receiving a letter from America.

The family loaded down the car with a basket of cherries, bottles of wine and olive oil until the four of us could barely squeeze in.

Saying goodbye felt like an impossible thing to do. It was painful, especially for Memmo. When he said goodbye to his brother the first time, they were young and just beginning their lives. There was hope that they would see each other again, one day.

But this time, there was no such hope. Yet these words could not be said out loud as they parted. I have thanked God every day that we took this trip when we did. Six months after we got home, Memmo died in his sleep.

Goffredo put us all up in an *albergo*, the Guastini in nearby Pitigliano, to spend the night before heading back to Rome the next afternoon. I couldn't believe my eyes when I saw Pitigliano the first time. The whole town is built on and out of the same volcanic rock and sits on a cliff overlooking a river far below it. Goffredo said it's at least 4,000 years old, built by the Etruscans. How on earth did Otto ever make it from a place like that to Genoa to get on a boat? I hadn't thought about it before, so I asked him.

"Natale Baldoni and I made it to Florence in a horse-driven cart. Then we took a train to Genoa . . . and I got on the boat."

As usual, my husband didn't say more than he needed to.

I tried to imagine how a sixteen-year-old boy who had never

been off the farm would feel when he saw a glorious city like Florence. The excitement of traveling on a fast-moving train, the hustle and bustle of the Genoa train station . . . going through all the lines, looking up at a ship—something he would never have seen before—and then two weeks later coming into New York harbor, the Statue of Liberty looking down on him.

We hadn't ever talked about it! So I asked him what it was like.

"Yes, it was exciting, but everybody had the same story, more or less, nothing special. I never thought much about it."

He was right, in a way. All immigrants have the same story, more or less. But he's wrong that they aren't all special.

After a sleepless night of listening to a donkey cry its heart out, we got up early and Otto, Goffredo, Francesco and I made our way through all the old winding streets to see what Otto could remember. He walked right to the church where he was baptized. He even remembered the house where his father had been born. Goffredo was amazed at his power of recollection. I didn't want to take my eyes off Otto as the familiarity of a place he had forgotten suddenly lit up his face.

I wondered—how much would I remember when we got to Carrara?

Goffredo took us to the airport for a flight to Milano. We would see him again in Rome at the end of our trip. He had become like a son to us. He and Alma had asked us to be godparents for their newborn, Monica. In just a few short weeks, I had gained an extended family, a family I would come to love as much as my own blood.

On the train from Milano to Carrara my heart was beating fast. As we pulled into the train station, Otto held onto my hand

and I was already getting out my handkerchief.

We were being met by one of my father's cousins, also named Aristide, and by Marisa, her husband Giuseppino, and their two children. Marisa was my second cousin, related to my father's side of the family. It all gets to be very confusing, but nobody worries about it. We're all cousins!

As I came down the steps from the train to the landing, I held my hand to my eyes against the blaze of sunlight, looking ahead, hoping I would recognize faces I had seen only in photographs.

Suddenly, this small man who looked very much like my father was running toward me, his arms open. He nearly swept me off my feet, laughing and talking enthusiastically. I saw Papa for a moment in this Aristide's beaming face.

Marisa and her family were right behind him. She gently put her arms around my neck and we both started crying. I had never met her, had only seen her wedding picture when it was sent to my mother a few years before. She was beautiful. Her husband, a big strong fellow with a serious face, first clasped Otto's hand, then kissed him on both cheeks, and kissed me too.

Their children were toddlers and looking a bit frightened at all this excitement. Giuseppino scooped them both up in his big arms, handed one to Marisa and picked up one of the pieces of luggage. Aristide put his arm around my shoulder, pulling me in close. When he started talking, it was all I could do to keep from laughing out loud, the resemblance to Papa's way of saying things, all excited and bursting with energy, the same, the very same.

Old Carrara looked unchanged to me, as if it had been four years instead of forty that had passed. This shouldn't have surprised me. Cities made of marble endure through time and outlast generations of people.

I longed to go to the opera houses, both of them. The one I remembered the most, the opera house of my early childhood, was the *Teatro degli Animosi*. While Otto took his *pisolino*, afternoon nap, I wandered around alone. The town was deathly quiet. I walked up the steps of the *Teatro*, expecting to find it locked, but the massive door swung open when I pushed it. A custodian was washing the marble floor of the entrance.

I nodded to her and asked if I could go into the theatre for a few minutes. She shrugged in a way that said go ahead.

The theatre was dark. It took a few moments for my eyes to adjust, but then the rich redness of the seats covered in velvet, the golden fringe of the heavy red curtain became brighter. I sat in one of the seats and looked up at the stage. It seemed smaller now, I suppose because when I was a child the stage was the biggest thing that existed for me.

My mother had told me stories of how Aristide would perform on that stage, how much he loved to do it. I closed my eyes and tried to imagine . . . the flurry of excitement behind the curtain as props were set up, the performers stepping into their heavy costumes, the musicians preparing themselves, rustling the sheets of music in front of them . . . the crowd starting to gather outside, streaming into the theatre to take their seats . . . ladies and gentlemen of the small town greeting one another . . . drama in the air, the anticipation of a beautiful evening. And my father, a young man, waiting for his turn to sing.

I remembered going to the opera with my mother, brother, and grandparents. For us, opera was a necessary part of our lives, not something we did to be fancy or put on airs. The beauty of the music was like beauty of the marble. It sustained us.

I found an old friend in Carrara, a lady I had indeed forgotten about . . . the Siren and her dolphin. She was still sitting where I had left her, by the River of Tears, her waters were still flowing from the dolphin's mouth. I remembered the day my brother Bruno died. I put my hands into the water and let it run through my fingers. I remembered so clearly how I had stood there with a bucket and a prayer that God would spare him.

The next day Giuseppino took us all up into the quarries. Now that is what had changed. Heavy trucks barreled noisily on the main street, the *via Carrione*, coming down from the quarries, filled to the brim with great blocks of marble. Empty trucks, gears groaning, made the steep way back up. The streets constantly had to be repaired, Giuseppino told us.

"I remember the days when oxen did that work," I said.

"*Si*," Aristide chimed in. "Me too! Carrara was a quiet town then. I moved away when all that noise started."

Aristide lived in Arenzano, a lovely coastal town north of Genoa. He hadn't been back to Carrara for years, he said. But he wasn't going to miss the chance to see his American cousins.

Giuseppino was a civil servant, which enabled him to take us into the working quarries that were off limits to tourists. I was grateful to be able to get as close as I could.

I had never been up there. Seems strange that I hadn't been, but I wasn't allowed to go with Enrico when I was a little girl. It wasn't a place for women. All I could do back then was look up at the white mountains and imagine the best I was able, what could happen to cause a man's sudden death up there?

"Aristide," I tapped him on the shoulder, as we were looking at the machinery that sliced the marble with diamond saws. "Do you remember when a man would blow a horn from the mountains and everyone in town could hear it?"

"*Si*, Olga, those were always terrible days. Your father used to tell me that it would send a shiver through the whole town. All the women screamed, wondering which one of them was a widow."

Giuseppino had overheard. "That doesn't happen anymore, not since we got rid of the *lizzatura*."

"That's a word I haven't heard for years!" I told him. I instantly recalled a day when I had asked Enrico how the marble got from being in the mountain, to being loaded onto an oxcart. I remembered he had laughed at my question.

"Beautiful little girls shouldn't worry about things like that, *cara*." But I was determined to know, so he pulled me onto his lap and explained it.

By this time, Otto's curiosity had got the better of him. Giuseppino put an arm around Otto's shoulder, and began telling him the history of marble quarrying.

I stooped down to pick up a small piece of the sparkling stone and thought about how old it was. I thought about how long men had been cutting marble out of these mountains . . . *centuries*. I thought about how far back my own ancestors had lived here and spent their lives quarrying marble . . . could have been many generations of Giovannonis born here. I didn't know, would never know, but it didn't seem as important as knowing that my father and my grandfather had left their mark on these mountains, were two of the thousands of men who had left their footprints, and even their very blood, in these vales of white gold.

I looked down at the footprints I was making and would be leaving behind too.

Act Three

A Box of Mementos . . . Quarrying Stories . . .
A Summer in Tuscany . . . Sculpting a Life

"Carol, your grandmother is in very critical condition."

Carol

I was attending a business retreat in June of 1996 when I received the phone call.

Stunned, I told the women I worked with about my grandmother, and they wept. Anyone who knew me well also knew what Olga, my *nonna*, meant to me.

She had fallen on the back steps a week before. It was a neighbor who finally heard her calls for help, with my grandfather hard of hearing and still asleep. Nonna had been warned not to go down steps by herself, but she'd wanted to water her roses.

Nonna had seemed to be all right when I spoke to her on the phone just days before, only somewhat disoriented. She would mumble inaudible things. She told me she had talked to her mother—who had been gone for forty years. I'd told her as soon as my meeting was over, I would be with her again.

I broke speed limits to reach the St. Louis airport and get the next flight home to Indianapolis. I prayed I would reach her in time. From the sound of my Aunt Joann's voice on the phone, there was not much hope.

Joann's son Scott picked me up at the airport. His red eyes avoided mine as I searched his face for a hopeful sign.

"Is she still alive?"

He shook his head. I had run out of time.

Aunt Joann and my mother Mary were waiting for me at the hospital. I asked them if I could see her. Yes, they said. We waited for you.

I went into a room where my grandmother's body lay on a table covered by a sheet. She looked so tiny. Her eyes were closed but her mouth was open a little, as if she were going to speak.

I looked at her hands. Remnants of the light pink polish I had put on her nails a few weeks before were still there. Her hands had crocheted a thousand miles of lace. The last time I'd been at her house, she'd given me a stack of little white washcloths, each trimmed in different colors of crochet, along with a plastic bag of frozen gnocchi. Before I got into my car, I looked again at her and waved. She stood on the front porch, with empty clay pots on the steps below, waiting to be filled with red geraniums when summer came. Familiar tears stung my eyes as I left, as always wondering if it would be the last time. And so it was.

I put my hand on her forehead. Smooth, cold. I stroked her hair and kissed her. *Nonna.*

The viewing and visiting lasted two afternoons and evenings. The salon always seemed full, as I saw familiar Italian faces, many who had peered out of the photographs my grandmother kept over the years . . . second cousins . . . those who in some way knew my grandmother and wanted to come.

I sat with my grandfather, who never left his seat, friendly with all those who passed by, shook his hand or kissed his cheek and said they were sorry. He was very quiet.

I asked him what he was thinking. He said simply that she was very special and there wasn't another woman like her in the world. I never saw him cry.

My grandmother had a beautiful summer day for her Mass and funeral. I wanted to say a few words at the service, and made notes in a business-like fashion. But as I stood by her draped coffin and looked into the eyes of my aunts and uncles, I just spoke from my heart.

I said she had given me many gifts . . . a love of Italy, of opera, a talent for cooking without a recipe. She told me to have the courage to travel and seek my dreams. *Do it while you're young*, she said. *Don't be afraid!* I had the certain knowledge that she would love me no matter what. I could not believe she was gone. I knew that if we looked in her freezer, there would be enough ravioli in there to feed everybody in her whole family. She always had plenty of everything for those she loved. Nonna saw me through many trials. She was fierce in her protection of me, yet never held back in telling me if I was wrong. And I always came out on the other side intact and wiser because she was there.

Few of the people at that funeral Mass really knew what I meant by "trials," knew what I meant when I said my grandmother had given me strength.

I had been raised as one of Jehovah's Witnesses. My mother had left the Catholic Church when she met my father, whose curiosity about this particular religion meshed with my mother's disillusionment with her own. The Catholic Church provided no answers to the mysteries. The Witnesses had an answer for every question.

The promise of a new world order, an earthly paradise, imminent, exclusive—only for those who worshipped Jehovah—

meant surviving Armageddon, never growing old, living forever. My parents, during the early 1950's, embraced this promise.

In order to be found worthy, the Witnesses denied themselves worldly pleasures and pursuits. There were no birthday parties, Christmas presents, Easter egg hunts, Halloween mischief or Thanksgiving dinners . . . there was no display of patriotism permitted, no friendships formed outside the Kingdom Hall, no encouragement for a good student to go on to college, or permission to engage or indulge in anything that would distract from studying the Bible or preaching the Good News. And yet there was love within the confines of those insulated walls. For a child like me, who was full of wonder and curiosity about everything that went on around me, this created turmoil. Rather than be humiliated, I would hide in the bathroom to avoid the playing of the national anthem in the school gymnasium, for which I was forbidden to stand. I was excused from activities at school that would compromise my faith, yet my heart longed to be a part of them. I sat in study hall alone, humming to myself, as the chorus of "Silent Night" from music class echoed down the empty corridors.

I was a goldfish in a bowl, swimming around busily, well cared for in my sheltered world, living in a typical middle class suburban neighborhood in Indianapolis, but with my nose always pressed against the small window on the big world, wanting to belong there, yet not believing it possible . . . without literally losing my life in the process.

At barely eighteen years of age, I married, which is what every exemplary young female Jehovah's Witness was expected to do . . . devoting ourselves to the ministry and our husbands. Jeffrey, my husband, though he held the position of congregation elder, claimed to hear the voices of demons, driving him to shove me against walls and try to throw me out of a moving car.

I wanted out of the marriage, but not out of the "Truth" (as the Witnesses called their religion). I staged my own adultery, because it was the only grounds for divorce in my religion. My plan was to admit the wrongdoing, repent and thus be allowed to remain. I knew I would have to endure an inquiry about my sin, conducted by a panel of elders, but I saw no other way out.

We were in the basement of the Kingdom Hall. I sat upright in a hard chair, trying to keep my composure, in front of three men with grim faces, holding Bibles and notepads on their laps.

"And how many times did you have intercourse with this man?" one of them asked me in a flat, quiet voice. The skin of my scalp prickled and the air was impenetrable as cement.

The coarseness of the question made me wish I could simply vanish.

"Only once," I replied. I could not meet their gaze. *And yet, I thought, this single, sinful and selfish act was tender and giving, unlike the brutal treatment I was accustomed to receiving from my husband.* I hadn't imagined that my innocent accomplice would have known to be patient with me, and that he would sense the terror beneath my disguise of confidence. I had been awake that entire night, thinking *so that is what making love feels like.*

All did not go according to plan. Jeffrey forgave me, something I had not thought possible. When I reported his violence, and suggested he get psychological help, I was told, "The Bible is there to counsel and solve our problems." The elders pronounced that a bad marriage was not grounds for divorce. I was forgiven my trespass. The final disgrace was having to sit through the public announcement before the entire congregation that I had engaged in immorality, conduct "unbecoming a Christian."

I was angry and found the courage to proceed with a legal divorce. I couldn't live with a man whose forgiveness would be short-lived, whose abuse would return with a vengeance. The Witnesses refused to recognize the civil divorce, but neither could they do anything about it. The price to be paid for divorce was that I would not be eligible for remarriage. I was twenty-three years old, facing a life of celibacy. I seethed under the surface of my obedience, and yet I could not leave them. Where would I go? How would I live? The Witnesses closed off all exits, sincerely believing they were doing it out of love and a desire to protect you. During the five weekly meetings at the Kingdom Hall (being reminded that one should be willing to do anything, give up everything for Everlasting Life), I looked around me at the smiling and compliant faces as we sang songs of praise to God. What was wrong with me? Why did I struggle so much?

As the divorce proceeded, I left Jeffrey, and moved in with my parents. We argued as my mother saw me exerting my independence in ways that frightened her. I had a new job and began socializing with "worldly" people (as the Witnesses refer to anyone other than themselves). I came home late, sometimes missed going to meetings. My mother loved me and was very worried about me. My father was quiet, and I know now he was trying to give me some room.

After one particular volatile Sunday afternoon, I packed up my things and went to see my grandmother. I didn't tell her what happened, and only asked if I could stay with her for a while.

Olga asked no questions, made no demands. Her trust of me was a relief as palpable as if she had put her hands on my head or stroked my face.

I lived with my grandparents for three months. I no longer judged myself the errant child whose coming and going was suspect. When I was little, I would sometimes spend a few nights at my grandparents' home, along with my cousins. Olga would have the girls one week and then the boys. It was fun and free and I recall nothing but complete happiness, an overall awareness of being loved simply because I was her granddaughter. When I returned to her as an adult, she also seemed to know when I wanted to be a child again.

It was a luminous Indiana spring, Olga's lilac trees in full bloom. Each morning before I was off to work, I would quietly go into the kitchen and sit with Nonna Olga at that small table. She would pour me coffee, squeeze an orange, poach an egg and serve me my favorite—a piece of toast covered with ricotta cheese she sweetened with cinnamon and sugar. She'd come outside with me, waiting as I crossed the street and got into the car. She would wave from the porch, sending me off with a blessing.

Every evening, I walked up the steps onto the front porch and took a moment to watch my grandparents through the door. They always waited for me to have supper with them. They would be sitting in the front room (as Olga called it), she on the sofa crocheting, and Otto in his big, cushy leather chair, holding his pipe in his mouth or in his hand. *Jeopardy!* was blaring from the television. My grandmother would suddenly notice me and push herself up off the sofa to unlock the door. We kissed each other and I walked over to Otto, bent down and kissed him too.

The table would be set with a freshly laundered and embroidered tablecloth. There was the familiar and worn plastic coaster next to Otto's plate, holding the well used wine decanter. The rich aromas coming from the kitchen told me so much. Garlic and rosemary meant there was a roast of some kind in the oven. Tomato and basil promised a rich *sugo* for gnocchi or ravioli.

Otto would pour the wine, asking me in his quiet, understanding way, "Everything okay?" I would nod, and toss the salad with olive oil and red wine vinegar, and bring the steaming dishes to the table. And for the next couple of hours, we ate and drank and talked. Dessert would be a baked rice pudding sprinkled with nutmeg or a dish of spumoni ice cream or a slice of warm coffee cake.

After coffee, Otto got up and returned to his big chair. Olga and I usually continued to sit at the dining table and soon she would be pulling out old photographs or we would talk about Italy.

Sometimes she wanted music and she would pull an album from its cover and the dazzling voice of Luciano Pavarotti singing the arias of *La Boheme* or *Tosca* would resonate through the rooms of their small house. I never listened to opera unless I was with Olga and then it seemed like the most beautiful music in the world.

I was truly myself in her home. I didn't sense the eyes of Jehovah watching me as I did everywhere else I went.

I inhaled the scent of the sheets I slept on in that house, the light fragrance of soap and sweet tobacco lulling me into dreams . . . safe.

Shortly after I moved into my own apartment, Olga said she wanted to go to Italy one last time, and a light flashed in my heart that signaled *go with her!* I journeyed with my grandparents, my parents and my sister in the summer of 1978.

That trip to Italy worked a powerful change. On that maiden voyage, the dormant pagan in my soul came to life for the first time. I wasn't accustomed to being lusted after, and most certainly not by young Italian men pursuing me on the streets. This awakened a sensual longing I never knew I had. I felt beautiful, desirable.

I had been raised to believe the simple celebration of my own birthday was sinful. No wonder this kind of attention electrified. It was both terrifying and thrilling.

We went to Rome, Venice, Florence and finally, Carrara. The aromas emanating from the family table were familiar, but the complete immersion into the language, the dizzying display of theatre in the street, the beautiful drama of Italian life injected a passion into my soul that was an elixir of love. I was in love. My cousin Goffredo put me on the back of his motorcycle and the Colosseum soared above me as we leaned into fast curves around it. The austere had been swiftly replaced by the heady, and I knew somewhere deep inside me, in the dark soil of my nature, seeds of possibility had been planted.

And I saw that my mother became completely her "self" in Italy. As the Italian phrases flew back and forth and around a room, I was stunned when I saw that she understood nearly everything, yet I had never heard her speak a word of it. In Rome, I watched her laugh to the point of tears when Goffredo teased her. I took a photo of her as she stood, smiling, perhaps daydreaming, on the bow of a ship as we let warm winds take us to Capri. This carefree woman was my mother, and I knew she would disappear when we left, like people in fairy tales do when they depart a magic kingdom . . . but for those two brief weeks, we delighted in each other, walking arm in arm down narrow streets, marveling at what we saw, free from religious restraints, embraced by Italy and family. It was as if Italy was our magic kingdom, the only place on earth we could happily be mother and daughter.

We were at the train station in Carrara, all of us, waiting for the train back to Rome and our flight home. One of my cousins, Giorgio, white-haired, handsome, holding a cigarette, stood close to me. He blurted out a question that nearly knocked me off my suitcase.

"*Cara*," he said, "Why not stay here with us? You and my daughter are so close in age and it would be good for her to have a sister . . . besides, I could get you a job at the Embassy, you could learn Italian and we would be happy to keep you."

My answer froze in my throat. Did he see the longing in my eyes? I glanced at my grandmother. Her expression said, "And why are you looking at me? This is your decision to make." I looked over at my mother, whom I was sure had not heard him.

Every beat of my heart said "yes," as if a clear voice some distance away was calling for me. But my mind was still imprisoned by my beliefs . . . the train came and I let it take me.

I thought about my cousin's offer on the plane until it gave me a headache. My life, having been injected with a powerful dose of Italy, I now sensed as small, confining, even threatening. I knew I wasn't living an authentic life—I had one foot in the world and the other at the Kingdom Hall. But the Witnesses do not let people go easily. I wondered what I would do when I got home. I was changed, anxious and restless.

My parents came to my apartment the morning after we had arrived back home in Indianapolis and the look on their faces told me something was horribly wrong. My mother put her arms around me, crying. I pulled away in panic and yelled, "What happened?" Jeffrey was dead. He had hanged himself in a park a week before. He was twenty-seven years old.

The ending of Jeffrey's life was, quite literally, the beginning of my own. Something broke apart inside me. The demons that lived in his mind had suffocated him and now he was released. I wanted release from my own feelings of suffocation. I knew not how to create a genuine life, I only knew that I had to get out.

Within weeks, I wrote a letter to the elders, telling them I no longer wanted to be associated. Elation filled me as I let the letter fall into the mailbox. It was short-lived.

I realized that with the launching of the letter and my new life, I was saying goodbye to all the friends I had known and loved my entire life. At the time, I still had a relationship with my parents, because the Witnesses still allowed immediate family members to associate with those who left voluntarily. They tried very hard to help me "heal," never giving up hope I would return to my religious roots. But a few years later, the rules became stricter and there came the day when the ties were severed with my mother and father . . . and my sister as well. The news—that I was no longer welcome in their home unless I came back to the Kingdom Hall—shocked me, as if my parents had suddenly died. It was emotional blackmail, designed to move the "errant" one (in this case, me) to repent and come back. I could not.

When I looked back on all of that, I knew that much of the courage I needed to leave came from Olga, although she never uttered a word of opinion. She simply took me by the hand to Italy and showed me a bright world that woke all of my sleeping senses. *Don't be afraid!* Her messages still echoed inside me, even though I believed that when she died I had lost her forever.

My Aunt Joann showed me a packet of Olga's love letters, bound by a blue slipper satin ribbon. When I had them translated, I was astounded by what I read. The letters showed me a passionate side of my grandfather that I had never suspected. Part of me felt guilty, voyeuristic, but I also believed that if Nonna didn't want anyone to ever read them, she would have hidden them better.

If my grandfather's love letters were the foundation of the love our family is built upon, my grandmother's travel journals fueled my passion for my Italian heritage. I read them over and over. She seemed to be speaking to me, reminding me of how important it was to *remember*. Many of the passages were repeated; it was as if she was tapping me on the shoulder . . . it was the first sign of many more to come that she wanted me to do something about it.

Nonna died in June 1996. Four months later, my grandfather Otto passed away in his sleep. He was almost one hundred years old. He had the blood pressure of a teenager. He took up bowling with my uncles when he was eighty. He was a brilliant chef. He had all his teeth. He had loved my grandmother for seventy years and they had started a family that was seventy in number and growing.

After their deaths, there grew in me a conviction that I owed my grandparents so much. I deeply longed to honor them, certain that if it hadn't been for their love and support throughout my life, especially when I lost my immediate family, I would not have survived. Their love had been pivotal to my getting through the heartache. Especially my grandmother—she never lost faith in me, not even once.

I recalled the many times I had looked into faces in faded photographs, asking my grandmother, "Who is this?" The memories were fading like the photos. It haunted me to think that years from now, cousins not yet born would look at old family photographs and wonder who we were.

But what did I really have? There were so many gaps in my knowledge. A million times I said to myself, "You could have just asked her!" It would've been so simple. I was resolved in my desire to keep Olga and Otto's memory from fading.

But I didn't want to just draw up a tidy genealogical chart with names and dates and events. It was the living stories that mattered, and would need air and energy and passion to recall them to life.

I drove everybody crazy with my questions. I asked my great aunts, Annie, Laura and Maggie. My great uncle Joe. I couldn't ask Uncle Giorgio—he'd passed away in the 1980's and I realized I never had a single conversation with him about his life.

My great-great grandparents, Enrico and Cesira Giovannoni, lived and worked in Carrara, Italy in the last decades of the nineteenth century. He was a carver, she was a seamstress. Their only son, Aristide, studied Gothic architecture, and became *uno scalpellino*—a stonecutter. In 1902, when Aristide was eighteen years old, he made his first trip to America.

Years later, his family joined him, including his two children, Olga and Giorgio. Olga would become my grandmother, *mia nonna*.

I grew up hearing about my ancestors in Carrara from her, in stories embroidered in Italian when English wasn't up to the job; stories she told me as we sat across from each other at her kitchen table in the early morning quiet.

Whenever I found myself missing her—which was about every day—I brought back to mind those precious hours I spent alone with her.

Reading my grandmother's journals, I felt another tap on my shoulder: The only place to find that wellspring of my family's stories was in Italy. It's not as though I had not made recent trips to Italy, but only from a desire for the simple pleasure of being there. I was compelled to return and see it through my grandmother's eyes, walk in her footsteps. There was something in Italy I needed to capture and perhaps also to liberate. Her journals were like crooked fingers beckoning me to follow her.

In 1998, a couple of years after my grandparents' deaths, I moved to New York City. I had built a profitable service business in the Midwest along with partners and we had sold it to a group based in Manhattan. They asked me to work for them and grow the business internationally. I tingled all over in both fear and exhilaration. I had visited New York before, always in awe of it, never imagining I would live there one day. I plunged in. Between weekly business flights, I indulged my passion for opera at the Met, made the circuit of the best restaurants in the City, walked through all the neighborhoods, lingering in front of windows displaying chocolate, jewelry and impossibly high stilettos, many times going in and buying what I thought would satisfy me. I was no longer the little goldfish swimming around in a small world.

After two years of constant busyness, exhaustion, frustration and physical pain started paying me long visits. Buying expensive things gave me only short bursts of pleasure. Massage and Motrin helped me cope with the frequent headaches. The company went through a couple of agonizing mergers that seemed to mirror my own mental and emotional anguish over how the business was being run. At unexpected moments—especially at the opera— my eyes would close, music would stream through me, and I would remember my grandparents and their stories, the dream I still had to preserve them . . . never far away, but—where was the time to pursue it? Once more, it was like a clear voice calling to me, but again I ignored it. I was far too busy being successful in the most competitive city in the world.

One day, while walking around Soho with my Aunt Joann, who had come for a visit from Indianapolis, I was complaining about my frustration for the hundredth time. She stopped on a corner, in front of a bright yellow kiosk that was advertising writing classes. She pulled out one of the flyers, thrust it into my hands, looked me straight in the eye, and said firmly, "Do something about it." Being Olga's daughter, the same fire was in her eyes at that moment. I had my orders.

I took a memoir writing class on line, as I was still traveling all the time. I had a picture of my grandmother when she was about twelve and I imagined it had been taken shortly before the family came to America. Olga was standing next to her little brother, Giorgio, and looking fiercely at whoever took the picture. I began daydreaming about her as this young girl, whose life was about to dramatically change, wondering why she wasn't smiling, trying to read her thoughts. I wrote a story about the train ride from Carrara to Genoa, where the family would board the ship. I saw Olga sitting on the train, next to her own grandmother, Little Nonna, and what came to my mind was my Nonna's hands, remembering the way I used to hold and look at them.

The encouragement I got from my instructor to continue the story spurred me to action. Instead of poring over Excel spreadsheets on airplanes, I used the time to write more of the story. Instead of watching a late night movie to numb the stress of the workday, I climbed into bed with paper and pen.

When I finished this first story, another company merger was in the works and like a wildfire consumed all available patches of time. I put the story into a drawer, but once in awhile, I would pull it out, read it again to relive the pleasure of imagining the lives of the women who had gone before me. Often a pestering tap on the shoulder came along with it. The twelve-year-old girl on the train was waiting for me to take her somewhere.

I started rummaging through everything I had collected, especially my grandmother's worn cardboard box of mementos. I found the obituary of Salvatore Pezzullo, Olga's fiance who died of pneumonia. I looked at the tattered slip of newspaper and a young man looking back at me with tired eyes and a not quite handsome face . . . so very different from Otto as a bachelor, whose photos captured a quiet confidence, and a profile that would make any female heart flutter. What had Salvatore meant to my grandmother? She kept his death notice along with family pictures, postcards, special recipes clipped out of magazines, prayer cards . . . all clues to what she valued in her life. It was her secret, but it made me want to find him . . . go to Indianapolis and find him.

As I dug further, another yellowed piece of newspaper surfaced . . . an announcement dated 1944, of Leo Rizzuto's denial of parole from prison for manslaughter. I had heard many different versions of that story over the years, wild speculation over what really happened on that dark night. My grandmother had always insisted that she knew what others did not. Another secret taken to the grave, and these secrets were invitations to my curiosity.

I had already made plans to go to Indianapolis for Thanksgiving and was even more anxious to reunite with my family, especially Aunt Joann, to seek her guidance on filling in so many gaps in the family's history in Indiana. And to find Salvatore!

My Aunt Joann's home was always mine when I went to Indianapolis. There were remnants and keepsakes of my grandmother's life in every corner, on every table, in the kitchen, and in the bedroom, in her curio cabinet.

I had bought just such a cabinet also, a large one like Olga had. I filled it with mementos of my life, and of Olga's with a few of her treasures I inherited. It reminded me of when I was at her house, and asked her to show me those beautiful things. She would take them out one by one and tell me the story of how she came to have them.

There were small sculptures made of clay or marble, figurines of Murano glass and wood, crystal liquore glasses, each one a royal color and rimmed in gold, ceramic miniatures, creamy porcelain dishes. It was a menagerie of flowers, doves, angels, faces, hands, cats, children. They came from Paris, Rome, London, Amsterdam, Venice. They were bought in stunning arcade boutiques, given as anniversary or Christmas gifts, presented when friends returned from trips.

It was her life and when I gazed at the treasures in my "curio," I remembered her stories and how much her life was bound up in mine, how we both were "curious" souls.

I wanted to visit the old Italian neighborhood, which included the Holy Rosary Church, St. Joseph's cemetery and the home of my great Aunt Maggie, Olga's younger sister. She had invited Joann and me for a Sunday ravioli dinner, so we promised we'd be there after Mass and a trip to the cemetery.

As we walked up the steps to Holy Rosary and opened its heavy wooden doors, the giant bells in the *campanile* above our heads had begun welcoming worshippers. We found our places and my eyes swept up and down and across, taking in the white altar, the statue of St. Anthony, a bank of small flames from dark blue votives in front of him, and the prominent, jewel-colored stained glass windows along the sides of the church, inscribed with familiar Italian family names. It was the first time I had ever been in this church, where so many family events had either been celebrated or grieved.

My great Uncle Giorgio had been an altar boy there and I tried to imagine his young, strong tenor voice as he sang Ave Maria during a wedding ceremony. Aristide must have been so proud. Years later, Aunt Maggie was married there—the Italian event of the year according to the newspaper clippings I read. My mother was her maid of honor. Aristide walked down the aisle with Maggie . . . .

And of course, this was where Olga was to have married Salvatore, the poor young man who met an untimely death. Instead, his funeral Mass was given here, the church full of Italians dressed in black, my grandmother, only sixteen, sitting in one of those pews, also in black instead of wedding white.

Why did I feel the need to find Salvatore's grave? Why wasn't it enough to know his story and leave it at that?

Thoughts of Salvatore had begun to arouse old memories of my first husband, Jeffrey, and his own early death. I had never, in the twenty-five years since he died, visited Jeffrey's grave. My curiosity about Salvatore blended into a sudden yearning in my heart—to find them both.

It was bitterly cold and windy when we left the church and drove the short distance to St. Joseph's. The cemetery looked bleak and sad. Where to begin to find Salvatore?

First, we went to Aristide and Ione's graves. I found myself wishing there was a large white Carrara marble angel, head bowed toward earth, wings lifted behind, standing over them. We placed blossoms on their graves.

As we wandered Joann showed me the gravestones of all the Italian families she remembered as Olga and Otto's friends. DeMiceli, Rossetti, DeLuca, Santarossa, Guerini, Jardina. She pointed to the elaborately carved granite memorial of Dr. Lapenta, with Jesus, the Shepherd, holding lambs in his arms. The beloved doctor was only sixty-three when he died in 1946.

"He was our doctor, Carol," Joann said. "He took care of all the Italians. He delivered me when I was born . . . a wonderful doctor, but he died of a broken heart. Your grandmother told me he'd been wrongly accused of something during the war, and they put him in prison. He died just after the war ended."

But where was the Rizzuto monument? Joann pointed. "I remember waiting for my mother in the car while she walked up over that hill."

St. Joseph was a stark-white presence on the winter-dried grassy hill. I started walking in that direction, my heels sinking into the soft earth.

Ten minutes later, I called out to Joann. How could I have missed that? The Rizzuto monument, a massive block of stone, was crowned with the figure of a grieving woman, head down, in white robes, with her arm curling around a large white crucifix. It made me feel tender toward this family.

I scanned the names on the smaller stones—Leo, Amalia, son Salvatore, and daughter Simonetta. And then this odd white stone that looked like it didn't belong with the others, a round barrel that said, "Salvatore Pezzullo 1899–1924."

Joann came up and put her arms around me, and I couldn't stop the tears. I noticed we had a few stems of red carnations left, and I placed them on top of his strange monument. Joann said, "She must have been coming to see Salvatore while I waited in the car. All that time, she never said."

Why did this young man haunt me? The only reason I knew he existed was because my grandmother had kept his obituary, a slip of yellowed newspaper I came across in the box of mementos she left me.

Some days later, I went to the Washington East cemetery where Jeffrey was buried. I had to go to the caretaker's office to find out where he was. There was a light layer of fresh snow on the grass and as I walked to the place marked on the map, I was stunned to see there was nothing there.

I got down on my knees and began to wipe away the snow, then to tear away small clumps of weeds, thinking, is it possible nobody marked his grave? I pulled at the blades of frozen grass, wondering how I could bear it if there was simply nothing there. Then I saw a glint of metal. Jeffrey's name and the years of his life were engraved there on a bronze plate, flat against the earth, unadorned, small and unremarkable. I sat back on my knees and stared at his name. I closed my eyes and tried to remember him as the young and handsome man he was, when his demons weren't chasing him, when he wasn't angry. His alcoholic father had beaten him when he was a child . . . I remembered Jeffrey taking me to his childhood home and showing me the dents in the walls made by his own head when his father shoved him. Tears slid down my cheeks and I slowly allowed the grief I had kept inside to wash through me, grief I had not been able or willing to show for him before. I cried for Jeffrey and his unlived life. I put red roses on his grave and sent him love and thanked him because his death helped change my life.

I sat in my car there in the cemetery for a long time, wondering why I had finally come to see him, why looking for Salvatore caused me to want to find Jeffrey too. Ever since I began writing my grandmother's story, I also kept a journal of my thoughts. I was pouring out the words in ink that described the pain and frustration taking over my life, that was consumed almost completely by work, work that drained my spirit. With every admission on paper that I had to find a way to change my life, the string of my thoughts pulled me further and deeper into the past. It had been over twenty years since I left Jeffrey and my religion . . . twenty years since the anguish of my family closing me out had left its scars. I had built my life on top of that anguish and the confession of it stung.

Jeffrey's dying altered my life. Salvatore's dying altered Olga's life. Olga found joy in her life after Salvatore's death—yet she had carried a small torch in her heart for him because she made room for it. It was as if she had gently guided me to Jeffrey, so that I could properly say goodbye to him and begin to make room for the kind of life I longed for.

The next time Olga summoned me, I would listen—and follow. I could not have known how I would be pushed into answering that call.

I returned to New York and a few months later, in 2000, I started experiencing intermittent episodes of fever, migraine headache and searing pain throughout my body. Finally I was admitted to the hospital, where the doctors put me through many tests to try to discover what was wrong with me. As I lay in the hospital bed, in pain and dependent, I knew why I was ill. It was because my way of life was making me ill. I needed a long break from the relentless grind of sixty-hour weeks, working behind a desk or on an airplane, for a company whose goals I had long ago lost faith in, whose values I could not stomach.

I ached for the soulful, the spiritual, the creative. In the moments between sleeping and staring at the ceiling, I gave up. I asked for a way out. And so I surrendered—not to the exacting Jehovah, but to the compassionate, powerful presence I had begun to sense had always been there, waiting for me.

I couldn't quite imagine how I would walk away from everything, but I knew I could take some time off . . . a year . . . yes, a sabbatical. I could go to Italy. I would write the book about my family. With this thought, a sense of sureness and anticipation flooded through me, as if Olga nodded her approval. The mysterious virus vanished in a few days, and within a few short weeks, I had made a plan.

I would journey to Italy again, this time to seek out the places mentioned in my grandmother's journals. I wanted to discover where my ancestors dwelt, how they lived and worked a century ago. I would learn about marble quarrying and carving. Perhaps I would even cross paths with Aristide, Enrico and Ione, yes, and Little Nonna. More and more, I longed to sit at their feet and hear their stories. I put my affairs in order so that I could be away for months. I packed my Nonna's travel journals and love letters and bought a one-way ticket to Italy.

I traveled alone. I wanted to give Olga the room to push me into taking detours or encouraging me to stay longer some place. I was used to leading, now I would be led.

I set my sights on Carrara.

"So, signora, you are going to be with us for seven nights, si?"

La Passeggiata

A man's raspy voice came from the dark recesses behind the counter.

The blinding sun made the dim interior of the Hotel Michelangelo seem like a cave. I removed my sunglasses and peered across the counter. I soon found the face, the half-smile, weathered, dark skin and bright eyes of the owner, Luciano Lattanzi, with the requisite half-cigar stuck in the corner of his mouth.

The Hotel Michelangelo was "the only place to stay" according to several guidebooks I read. Fifty dollars a day including *la prima colazione*—breakfast. After the millions of lire I'd spent in Rome, this would give the AmEx card a breather.

My room was very small, but the bed was a double with a handsome antique headboard and there was a large window to the street. There was no air conditioning, but a fan provided a nice breeze. The bathroom was half the size of the lift, more like a thimble with a shower. The large mirrored armoire was better than a stuffy closet. I smiled at the Madonna over my bed.

I couldn't wait to get my clothes off, the heat from the train and the day clinging to me like hot glue. I stripped, got into the thimble and let cool water relax me. I was soon ready to take the evening *passeggiata*, the leisurely stroll around town.

I walked, found a *gelateria* in the town's main square, Piazza Alberica. The stones of the ancient piazza absorbed the warm rose light of the sun's descent. I took my pistachio gelato and walked around the fountain and statue of Maria Beatrice d'Este, the last Duchess of Tuscany.

One of the scenes sculpted on the pedestal showed Minerva, the Roman goddess of wisdom, practical arts and warfare. In this scene, she was presenting a young man who embodied the genius of sculpting. In legend, it is said the gods were fighting among themselves and Minerva threw a lightning bolt in a fit of rage, crashing it against the Apuan Alps, generating a vast river of pure white marble.

Earlier that day, on the way to the hotel, I had glimpsed these marbled mountaintops soaring above Carrara, thrilled to know I would soon be visiting the quarries, to see where Enrico and Aristide had left footprints.

But in the Tuscan summer night, sitting on one of the steps of the fountain, I happily thought that my grandmother, in fact my great-great-grandparents, had sat here many times also, washing off their sticky hands in this fountain as I was doing.

I walked a short distance from the Piazza and found *la Fontana della Sirena*, the Siren Fountain. How poor the homes looked along the *Ponte Lacrime*—Bridge of Tears. The laundry hanging outside windows was tattered, the windows had a dark, tragic air, the ancient walls were poorly patched, sad and neglected. The beautiful marble Siren watched over it all. I reached up, touched her where her arm had been broken off, ran my fingertips over the pockmarked surface. "I wonder how you looked when you were first made," I whispered. I let the soft waters that poured from the mouth of the dolphin she was riding on run through my fingers.

I walked to the *duomo*, the eleventh century cathedral made entirely from Carrara marble. Inside, I lit a candle and said a prayer. I spoke to my grandmother. "Nonna? I'm here!"

I sat in the sacred silence, as cool and still as the marble on the walls, drinking in the calm and thankful for the peace.

I thought that Ione and my grandmother, then only twelve, would have sat in these pews just as I did: grateful for the shelter of this place, yet anxious for the journey ahead.

"In the Piazza Alberica, il solleone
Mute, shoots darts at her dense flame"
~ Gabriele D'Annunzio

Il Solleone

~ The Lion's Summer Sun

It was going to be a hot day like the poem described, the silent sun throwing down darts of heat like a god who has lost his wicked temper.

I left the hotel early. It was market day and I brought Olga's journals along for company.

"It was Monday, and market day, la fiera. I remembered wandering the crooked streets with my mother and Little Nonna, admiring rolls of fabric and spools of colorful thread. I remembered her hands as she ran them over the textures, knowing exactly what she wanted.

I picked up a large yellow melon and was sure it would be perfect. As I pulled out the lire to pay for it, it suddenly

occurred to me. This was where I learned how to do that,
my mother putting fruit in my hands or under my nose."

I bought a spool of red thread in honor of Little Nonna before my attention was diverted by a display of fruits and vegetables— shiny, ripe to fullness, that made me believe I could taste their treasures with my eyes alone. I bought a plump pink peach—*una pesca*—and my teeth made a small delicious tear in its skin.

Palettes of soft pink, neon fuschia, sun coral, blues and purples of royalty, fiery crimson and purest white—the exuberant flowers of summer—splashed against crumbling corners of the Piazza Alberica.

The hot, bold breeze of late morning blew through a rack of soft cotton sundresses and above, under the booth's awning, a display of pinned-up bras, panties and all kinds of spandex undergarments—some in leopard prints, some in dangerous red or virginal lace. Sinful or sanctified indulgences.

I came upon tools and cookware for *la cucina*—cheese graters in all sizes and shapes, gleaming pots and colanders—all the time-honored and ritualistic vessels for pasta worship.

And the huge selection of cheeses! Thick wedges of *pecorino, taleggio, parmigiano reggiano*—the day's heat softening them to perfection. An array of sausages and cured meats was *una mozzafiata*—a mind blower. My favorite, *prosciutto di parma*, its slices almost transparent on the waxed paper—soft, a savory nothing on the tongue.

I went into a frame and old print store across the way to escape the sun's heat and fell in love with an old lithograph of the Siren Fountain, the one I stumbled upon in my wanderings. The owner's son, Mario, took it out of the frame for me so I could pack it more easily, something of *Carrara antica*.

I again sought refuge in *il duomo*. The cathedral was usually full of shadows, the marble absorbing the weak light from high windows. But later that evening at an organ concert, I would see the true glory of this *duomo*. On that dark summer night, the church was jubilantly lit from inside. Every saint, angel, crucifix and fresco came alive, as if they all decided to step out from behind their curtains and surprise everyone. A small crowd had filtered in and the size of the cathedral dwarfed us.

When the first notes were played, the reverberation was stunning, pulsing through my skin and scalp and colon. I let my eyes, when they weren't closed, roam and rest on all that had been hidden from me before. I discovered folds, textures, eyes, wings, crowns and faces I had only glimpsed in shadow before. And the colors! The pale and faded glowed golden and orange and crimson.

The ancient wooden crucifix suspended over the altar no longer looked like an obscure relic. It became a sacred shining symbol in this new light. The human-sized golden candlesticks at the back of the altar were highly polished and, like mirrors, reflected the faces of the admiring audience.

I stared at the whiteness of the two medieval marble sculptures of Mary and the Angel, their life-size shadows cast long and full against the frescoed wall behind them.

What a difference light makes. What has always been there hiding, satisfies all curiosity when illuminated by the light of the sun, the flash of knowledge, or the radiance of love. I've known that power in my own life, a sudden light like a gift falling on a dark corner, showing me something true. Olga was a light for me. The dark and fearful places I had known no longer haunted me as they used to. The bravery my ancestors displayed in facing the unknown gave me a sense of comfort—that I could be brave too. It also gave me an overwhelming desire to know more, and not only to know, but to illuminate it, write it down, to tell it, to put it in a reliquary of the heart.

The soaring notes put me into a trance. I let my body and spirit surrender to the echoes.

When the organist made his way to the front of the church to receive his applause, I could swear the notes he had played a minute before were still in the air, still in my body.

*"The angel. . . appeared before our eyes, a
shape alive, carved in an attitude of marble
grace, an effigy that could have spoken
words."*
~ Dante Alighieri
The Divine Comedy, Canto X: Purgatorio

Stardust on My Feet

I hired a fellow named Gianni to drive me to Carrara's
cemetery. He met me in the Hotel Michelangelo, and I liked him
instantly. He had a broad face with an equally broad smile. He
greeted Lattanzi with an exuberant *"buon giorno"* and put his
hand out to firmly grasp mine.

"This is Signora Carolina, Gianni. She wants to visit the dead
today." Lattanzi's deadpan delivery with his typical bemused
expression made everyone laugh.

"Andiamo," Gianni said. "I understand you also want to visit
the *cave di marmo*. I would recommend we do that in the
afternoon."

He escorted me to a big, shiny white Mercedes parked on
the street. As we took the short drive to the outskirts of town, we
passed along the *via Carrione*, "road of the carts."

Of course, I had Olga's journal in my handbag and I turned

to the pages where she wrote of her trip to Carrara forty years before.

"They were called ciabattoni, or shufflers. Tractors carrying blocks of marble that spewed black smoke as they shuffled slowly along the via Carrione. Young boys ran after them, climbing on the back for a ride before falling into the mud of the street."

Under Gianni's sure command, the car swung sharply up the curved road as we left the town. The cemetery appeared, its sturdy old iron gates were opened wide and welcoming.

Il cimitero was the most stunning I had ever seen. It looked like a beauty pageant of angels, so outstanding were the monuments in their sincerity and tenderness. The backdrop to this serene place were tall, noble cypress trees and the marbled Apuan Alps. I half expected to see a skier coming down one of the slopes, so much like snow did it look.

My relatives were buried there. Bruno, my great uncle who was just a little boy when he died, and my great-great grandfather Enrico. I had a rough idea of how and when they died. I wandered up and down rows searching for "Giovannoni," but didn't see even one with that name. If only Olga were here! I thought back to that first visit with her in 1978. We must have come to the cemetery. Did she show me the graves? Why didn't I pay some attention?

There were more than a dozen people working on the grounds, and I didn't know if they were workers or visitors, but all were devoted to their tasks: trimming, snipping, watering, in general tending the graves with love. I remembered the page from Olga's journal . . .

"In Italy, flowers are all over the graves, such a beautiful way Italians have to take care of their dead."

Most of the stones and carved figures were white, as one might expect, but because Carrara's quarries produce many types of marble, there were black and veined grey angels as well.

I stopped at the graves of one Fernanda Merli and her husband Renato. The angel that watched over them was holding a nosegay of carved roses before him. The angel was standing, his head tilted down, humble, sweet. His wings, though, were proud, high and arched behind him.

I was so drawn to angels with their heads turned down instead of up . . . perhaps I wanted to think that they looked toward the earth and saw us, watched over us, and that gave me more comfort than thinking of them with eyes toward heaven.

I found the caretaker, "Angelo," and asked him how I might find my ancestors' graves or at least a record of some kind. We went into the tiny office where I was greeted by a towering stack of massive, hard bound books, weighing down the wooden shelves. The books were arranged in order, starting sometime in the early 1800s. I had narrowed the time of death to a ten-year period for both Enrico and Bruno. Standing on his tiptoes and using both arms, Angelo muscled the ledger dated 1910–1920 in the middle of one stack and dropped it like a stone on the small table in front of me. His assistant pulled up a chair for me and they both stood back, smiling and anxious that I should find what I was looking for.

There were at least twenty records on each page. I focused my attention on finding either a large "E" or "B." I was halfway through the book and by this time, Angelo and his assistant were behind me, leaning over both my shoulders.

At last my eyes fell on the large looped E of an "Enrico" . . . I held my breath for a sharp moment, then was rewarded with the rest of his name.

"*L'ho trovato!* I found him!" I exclaimed, and Angelo cried out, "*Brava, signora!*" as I pointed to his beautiful name. It was a beautiful name. I had to be careful my sudden tears didn't fall on the black ink, still clear—and the care taken to record his death by someone who had lived then.

I scanned the columns, thirsty to fill the empty places of my knowledge of him. His occupation was listed as "*scultore del legno,*" wood carver, which surprised me, as I knew he also worked in the quarries. Enrico's address was listed on *via Carrione*, the old "road of the carts" that marble-laden oxen traversed in his day.

And then I saw his father's name, which had been unknown to me. Antonio Giovannoni. I pressed my fingertips along the name on this fading page, touching the fourth generation behind me in my family. That was all that remained of his and Enrico's existence, as their grave markers were long gone.

I was tempted to ask Angelo—who was still beside himself that I had found my family—for his help in finding Antonio, too. But I had come for Bruno, Olga's little brother, that small child who my grandmother spoke of so tenderly.

I didn't find him that day, and Angelo looked as forlorn as I did. But I wasn't truly unhappy. I smiled to myself, imagining Bruno as being shy; maybe he just wanted me to come back. I will. And next time, I will find Antonio, too.

I left, feeling blessed, feeling satisfied. Gianni drove me along

the *via Carrione*. There had been no house number listed in the
death record, but it wasn't so important to have it. As we drove
on that busy, winding street, any one of a hundred homes still
standing could have been where our family lived. I tried to imagine
what it was like in his day, the passing teams of peaceful oxen
loaded down with marble, instead of the huge trucks grinding
past now.

Desire fulfilled helps the imagination to embroider whatever
small details decide to stay hidden.

We made our way up into the mountains, to the famous
marble quarries of Carrara. My ears popped at the increasing
altitude and my heart beat faster as each curve in the road brought
me closer to the working quarries . . . where I would be able to
stand and walk, perhaps capture some mood, some image of
Enrico and Aristide as they worked there over a hundred years
before.

Our first stop was Torano. There are more than thirty
working quarries in the Basin of Torano. Every month, thirty
thousand tons of marble are removed from these quarries. The
marble found in Torano is of the very highest quality—*statuario*,
prized by sculptors. Other marble quarried there—*cremo, calacata,
arabescato, marmo azzuro* and *statuario venato*—these names
sounded and the marbles looked like flavors of gelato to me.

We drove on to the Basin of Fantiscritti, which also has thirty
working quarries and produces as much marble as Torano.

This basin is the source of ivory marble, *cremalato*, the
marmo nuvolato (ash grey, veined) and a very rare type—*zebrino*,
which is a smoky grey with green veins.

As we drove by the Fantiscritti quarries, the elegant and
arched Vara bridges stood like ghostly monuments to the past.

These bridges were part of the Marble Railway, used from 1876 until the 1930s, replacing the age-old method of using oxen as the means of transporting marble down the mountain to be loaded.

The marble dust I walked through in Michelangelo's quarries was like pale stardust on my feet. The soft and ancient powder was silky and clung to everything it settled on. I scooped some up with my hands, and picked up a statuary white piece, turning it over so that the sunlight made it a glowing thing in my hands. It was hard yet seemed crushable—enduring yet vulnerable.

At the current rate of production, there is at least another three hundred years worth left to quarry. Will Minerva throw down another lightning bolt to make more?

Gianni, who was comfortably plump with his job of driving people around Carrara, told me he used to work in the quarries. "Weight just drops off a man working the marble," he said as he patted his middle. "It keeps you fit, strong, but then I decided to do this; more money and I don't sweat away my life." He cranked up the air conditioning; I watched tiny particles of marble that covered my sandals swirl around my feet.

I liked the sensation of the marble dust between my toes, seeing it cling to my fingers. I had no desire to wash it away.

Gianni took me to an outdoor memorial in the quarries where we could view the two-thousand-year-old history of marble production.

I was surprised to be greeted by Aristide . . . there he was, looking right at me, chisel in hand, big smile on his face, his entire body melded against a large piece of marble, as if dangling from the side of a mountain . . . the slab was carved with inspiring words of tribute to the laborers, for the benefit of those visiting the memorial. But there was a special greeting just for me: "*Cara,* now you will see what it means to love this stone. This is where it all begins!"

I considered the astounding will of humans through the centuries as they relieved the mountains of their white gold.

They had first been worked thousands of years ago. Quarrying dated back as early as 177 B.C., when the Romans established the site for the sole reason of exploiting the marble and building temples for their glorious empire. When the "glory that was Rome" fell away five centuries after the birth of Christ, so did the marble industry. The peasants became farmers, cultivated their land, bred their animals and suffered during centuries of dominion by various and undesirable rulers: the Goths, the Visigoths, the Lombards. The political upheavals during Carrara's long existence caused great turmoil in the marble industry, the oldest in the history of the world.

Later, during the Renaissance, demand for marble became very strong again and Carrara grew as the premier source of the white gold. Michelangelo himself came to the quarries to find the perfect marble for his masterpieces.

Slaves were first used by the Romans to do this body-breaking work. There were those who quarried the marble, followed by those who shaped it, then those who used handsaws to cut the pieces into slabs and finally those who loaded it onto the ships.

The first group of workers, the *marmoraii*, used iron wedges that they forced into open places in the marble with hammers—a thousand times over and over until the piece was almost free. Sometimes the open places were not wide enough for detachment, so wooden wedges were pounded in and water poured onto them so that the wood would swell and widen the openings.

Iron balls were placed under the piece as it was about to be cut free, so its massive weight could be rolled.

The *quadratarii*, the group in charge of shaping the newly detached piece of marble, took over at this point. The hammer and chisel were their tools of trade. As I ran my fingers over these ancient tools, I imagined a slave's browned face and arms—muscles strained and flexed, a lifetime of labor under a white sun.

Then the only way down from the quarry was to let the detached piece go headfirst—*abbrivatura!* Broken and fractured, many blocks were ruined.

The next step in the process belonged to the *sectores serraii*, pairs of men who cut the broken blocks into slabs by using simple saws. Again, for centuries the technique remained unchanged.

Next came getting the pieces to the ships with the help of oxen. The great white beasts pulled the *carro romano*—a Roman-style cart. The carts of that day took the same route to the sea as the trucks of today by way of the *via Carrione*, "road of the carts."

Loading the marble onto ships was yet another ordeal of moving immensely heavy stone. Cables, pulleys and slides were used, backed by super-human muscle to accomplish the loading. Imagine, then, before the piers were built, getting the freighted ship back into the waters to begin its journey to Rome or other destinations.

In ancient times, when all marble was going to Rome, the cargo of white gold would have to be transferred again to smaller ships once it reached the mouth of the River Tiber.

> *"Today we went to see the cave di marmo, the quarries.*
> *The beauty of the marble, the white gold is a wonder.*
> *Marble, serene . . . ."*

I studied the displays of old and rotting equipment, the collections of ponderous hand-held chisels. Did Enrico and perhaps his father use these tools? Did they go up into these mountains every morning and work until their hands bled?

We got back into the car to head back to town. I was still holding the piece of marble I picked up in the quarry and I looked at it glinting in the sunlight.

We gaze upon miracles of marble in art museums, only seeing the sculptor's genius shine forth. In Rome's stunning Galleria Borghese, I've stood for hours in front of Bernini's sculpture of Apollo and Daphne, enraptured by the almost transparent leaves sprouting from the nymph's lithe figure as she flees. They appear to be rustling, so delicate and perfect are they. Stardust held together by genius and enchantment.

But what of the invisible hands of slaves, quarry workers, sawyers, squarers, carvers, polishers? With each step of revelation, loving hands guided the raw beauty until it reached the sculptor. Like skin stroked tenderly by a lover over and over, marble surrenders when it is desired.

Surrender. Something I used to consider a weakness.

As Gianni drove me back to the hotel, I shut my eyes and brought to my mind's eye all I had seen and sensed that day. The journey of art, of turning a block of marble into a masterpiece of sculpture seemed quite like the journey of one's life. Both are spiritual quests. Both are about finding truth. Both require surrender.

The pouring of healing water into resistant places so gentle openings can be made . . . then freeing it, only to see it sometimes come crashing down to be fractured . . broken . . . in ruins . . . but then lifted again and shaped, lifted again and transported, delivered into caring hands that chisel away the unnecessary and excessive, so that a true life can begin to emerge . . . carving into delicate and vulnerable places to reveal spirit and beauty . . . and then the surrender that comes from the long practice of polishing and refining all that has been done.

I wanted to surrender like that. I wanted to be released from the hard places that still kept me imprisoned.

I then surrendered to a glass of wine Lattanzi handed to me when I walked into the hotel. I went up to the roof. It was going to be a glorious evening. The coral sun was fading into pink as it set, the air was cooling and the first stars over Italy appeared. I looked up at the white quarries high in the mountain I had just journeyed through. Stretching out on a chair, I was happy to be alone there. I closed my eyes and could still see the blinding whiteness of marble in my mind. I fell into dreaming.

Michelangelo, bruised, scraped and bloodied, makes his way along the deserted via Carrione into Carrara. He has been at the quarry to find the marble for his work, and has narrowly escaped being crushed by crashing blocks. He finally finds himself in the Piazza Duomo. He looks for the welcoming light of a candle in the window of the apothecary, Pelliccia, with whom he is staying, but it is as dark as abandonment.

He is exhausted and discouraged because yet another day has gone by and his perfect statuario eluded him. Everyone is angry with him. From the quarrymen to the Pope, they are all exasperated with him over his search for perfection. And time is his greatest enemy, as always.

It is late and he wants to wash his wounds, put his head down and forget his own existence. He finds the Siren and leaning against her smooth marble face, allows the water from her fount of tears to heal him. She hears his tired heart because it is so open to pain, as hers is. She weeps more for him than she has for others.

"Your solitude imprisons you as the marble imprisons me," she tells him. "The wrath of a goddess turned me into a statue and took away my freedom forever, but you free the soul within the marble forever by revealing it."

He is grateful in his anguish. The Siren retreats into her marbled web and for the first time in hundreds of years, glimpses her own beauty in his eyes.

Aristide speaks to me . . . "If you want to find me, look for me at the opera."

An Exquisite Evening

On my final evening in Carrara, I found myself at a concert of Italian opera in Piazza Gramsci, set in a beautiful park filled with lush green trees that gave shade to life size sculptures.

There was one empty seat next to me and I imagined it was for Aristide. Since I had arrived in Carrara, I had detected my great-grandfather's presence subtly, like soft footsteps behind me. But on that evening, he was right there, as if he had followed me down from the mountain.

It was an exquisite night; the first stars of the evening twinkled. The sky was nearly dark, the violet and pink summer sunset swiftly slipping away.

I closed my eyes and listened to the music of Italian conversation, neighborly voices, and thought how natural a thing it is for Italians to love opera.

My reverie was broken as someone handed me *il programma*: Maestro Sergio Bologna to conduct the *Filarmonica Giuseppe Verdi di Carrara*. The three-hour performance would have selections from every famous Italian opera I'd heard of and some

I hadn't. "Un bel di" from *Madama Butterfly*; "Vissi d'arte" from *Tosca*—of course many by Verdi, but also Donizetti, Mascagni and Leoncavallo. My eyes took in *Pagliacci, Nabucco, Lucrezia Borgia, La forza del destino, Turandot, La Traviata*—I was surprised and embarrassed to feel tears springing in my eyes as I anticipated being swept away.

In that hyper-romantic mood, I was overcome as I listened to Violetta sing "È strano" from Verdi's *La Traviata*, as her passion for Alfredo fills her with bewilderment.

È strano! È strano! In core sculpiti ho quegli accenti!	Strange! Strange! Those words are engraved on my heart!
Saria per mia sventra un serio amore?	Might it be a serious love, to my misfortune?
Che risolvi, o turbata anima mia?	How will you decide, my confused soul?
Null'uomo ancora t'accendeva. O gioia . . .	No man has ever set you aflame! O joy . . .
Follie! Follie! Delirio vano è questo! . . .	Madness! Madness! This is a vain dream! . . .
Sempre libera degg'io folleggiare di gioia in gioia.	Forever free, I must dash madly from joy to joy.

I floated back toward the hotel from the concert, Aristide still at my side. I stopped for a gelato, sat at a table outside and watched couples hold hands. I was glad to be in the darkened street so my tears were not noticed. How I desired a man "to set me aflame." The potent cocktail of romantic Italian opera mixed with loneliness and desire resulted in unwelcome memories.

I was transported once again to Olga's kitchen, the setting of many of my life's lessons. She said to me, "You may not be lucky in love, but you're strong. You are a survivor."

When I parted ways with my former life, I lost my immediate family. It was as though some great glass mirror had suddenly lost its anchoring from a sturdy wall, and fallen with a deafening crash . . . the pieces of who I was, where I belonged, scattered everywhere. I couldn't pick them up by myself, and often ended up in the arms of men who I wanted to believe could help put me back together. It was always too much, for me and for them. I lived like Violetta in *La Traviata*. She said she wished to perish in a vortex of pleasure. There were times when I thought I could.

But there were angels and teachers and guides, and the raw block of marble that I was began to take shape.

I put another spoonful of gelato in my mouth as I remembered one of those teachers. Alex, many years younger than I, appeared in my life when I was in my early forties, and feeling powerful in only one way: my career. My head was full from building that career. My heart was full of desire for genuine love, some of those healing waters that could pour into my soul and free me. Despite the social taboo of the age difference, I yielded and let myself be taken care of by Alex.

We were not meant to be lifelong lovers. But for more than three years, Alex taught me how to love myself, to not be ashamed of anything, to let the girl who lived inside me out to play, because I was good and beautiful exactly the way I was.

I cried often during that time. A beautiful sunset or a particular look Alex would give me could set me off. I grieved for the years I spent living in fear of a God who I had only recently discovered wanted reconciliation with me too. I grieved for the loss of my mother and immediate family. And I cried for joy, the pure joy of being loved by a good man.

I began trusting my own wisdom by excavating my intuition, listening and responding to it. After all, if my mind had made the decision and not my heart, I would never have allowed Alex into my life. An important lesson.

Olga would have loved Alex. Maybe she had a hand in it.

Here Aristide gave me a nudge to tell me it was time to go, enough drama for one evening. I finished the last bite of gelato and walked the small streets to the hotel.

I considered that no one in the world knew where I was at that moment, which is why I think I was aware of Olga and Aristide so close to me. I had left a career behind in which I was always connected, available, responsible. There were other voices calling me now.

My dreams that night were filled with visions of beautiful Italian sopranos in glittering gowns, with the voices I still heard singing in my head, of the smile I saw on Aristide's face.

My grandfather, Otto, had never told me even one story about his life.

The Maremma

I was on the train from Carrara to Rome, as this thought popped into my head. *Not one story about his life . . . .*

Or what it was like to come to America at age sixteen. He answered questions put to him, but unlike Olga, he said little, as if there was something very troubling about remembering it.

I knew he had a very poor childhood and that he grew up with ten siblings on a remote farm in Tuscany called Sant'anna. Otto was child number eight, following Settimo, child number seven. Not all of the children were named by number, but I wondered if his mother was just too exhausted at the time to do anything else.

I also knew that Otto's father, Alessandro, went missing during his service in World War I. This was the extent of my facts.

My curiosity about Otto's life, plus the fact that the Italian relatives I knew in Rome were on his side of the family, added up to the opportunity to find and visit the farm.

These Roman cousins, Goffredo and Alma (Otto's niece) and their two daughters, Rossella and Monica had, over the years during a few of my earlier visits, become very close to me.

I met them the first time, of course, in 1978, when Olga brought me. Goffredo, a Charles Boyer look-a-like, had won my heart back then, showing me Rome on the back of his motorcycle. He was devoted to Olga and Otto, whom he addressed as *zia* and *zio*, aunt and uncle.

He had taken them in his car everywhere on their first trip back to the old country in 1962. I had read all about this in Olga's journal.

Almost forty years later, and to the very same day, I found myself with Goffredo in a small car, Alma in the backseat, speeding along a tightly curved road, in excess of a reasonable speed and nearly scraping the metal road posts that went flying by my window.

I winced and turned my attention to Olga's journals, which as usual, were sitting on my lap.

I laughed at the entry I happened upon:

> *"Imagine six people in that midget car of Goffredo's! What a ride! He went so fast all the way, we marveled at how fast these little cars can go. His hands were in the air, not on the wheel as he talked and looked back over his shoulder at me, laughing. Goffredo did everything in a big hurry!"*

Goffredo craned his neck, wanting to know what was so funny.

"Well, a lot of it is about you."

"*Davvero?*" he grinned.

"Let's just say your driving methods haven't changed in forty years."

He shrugged as if to say, And why should they?

I glanced over at him and smiled. His dark good looks were

still intact, the eyeglasses and graying temples the only signs of age. He was seventy going on thirty.

Alma sat in the backseat, quiet and after all these years still wondering what Goffredo would do next.

I had no idea exactly where we would go, where we would stay. I wasn't concerned. Goffredo always took care of everything.

We drove along the rocky ancient coast of Tarquinia and then inland to traverse country roads. I was mesmerized by an endless field of sunflowers, my eyes almost closed when suddenly there was a sharp turn through gates and onto a gravel drive. Goffredo said this was where we would be staying for two nights—with another "cousin" whom I'd never met, Rosina, her son Massimo and his child, Francesca.

They seemed to be expecting us and welcomed me warmly. Eleven-year-old Francesca was the only one who spoke even a smidgeon of English, and I knew that my Italian was going to have to improve immensely. I'd started to understand Goffredo and even Alma when she spoke slowly, but at the dinner table that night, my head spun from the words flying across the table. This was good for me—complete baptism!

Rosina had prepared a wonderful pasta *pappardelle* with a sauce made with *cinghiale*—wild boar. It was like a Bolognese, but richer and more savory. The fresh figs came out later, plucked from their trees that afternoon. I almost swooned while I ate them.

Goffredo stood up from the table, smiling, and announced *il programma* for the next day, which was to get up bright and early, have our *espresso* and hit the road. "*Buona notte!*"

So, after this very sensual meal and the most intense Italian lesson I'd ever had, I was ready for bed.

My room was on the second floor of the large farmhouse

and when I opened the window to look out over their property, the white magnolia tree that grew in front of the house seemed to reach up to embrace me. I could almost touch the giant blossoms. The moon was full, the night was silent and the pale blooms had a sheen that was missing during the daylight. Sighs came easily, as did sleep.

I woke the next morning early to the crowing of a rooster. I eagerly got out of bed and opened the shutters to look upon a sparkling day, eager for what new discoveries awaited. Every single day Italy gave me gifts that delighted, stimulated or challenged me. That day, I would be looking for Otto.

I descended the staircase, following the heavenly scent of brewed espresso. I could hear Goffredo talking and making Rosina and Alma laugh.

As Rosina placed some flaky sweet pastries on the table, Goffredo turned to me and said, "We're going to visit Pitigliano today. This is where Alma was born and also where Otto's father came from."

I said, "I know very little about his father. And I thought Otto was born and raised on a farm."

Alma nodded my way in agreement.

"So where is the farm?" I asked. "Is that Sant'anna?"

Alma nodded again.

"So can we go there too?"

Goffredo frowned and said, "I honestly don't remember where it is, *cara*. The last time I was there was in 1962 with *zia* and *zio*."

I knew he felt bad about it, so I kept my disappointment to myself.

"*Va bene!*" I said. "*Andiamo!*"

I read Olga's pages about that 1962 visit to Sant'anna. Otto's older brother Memmo and his family all lived there then. I thought with dull resignation that Memmo had to be dead by now, and probably everyone else moved away.

I changed my mood and thought about Pitigliano. I had read up on the city and had been astounded by its history. Pitigliano was built by the Etruscans four thousand years ago. It was one of several Etruscan cities in the Maremma (the Latin for "water"), which is what that region of Tuscany is called because it is a fertile land, abundant with sulfurous thermal springs. Fabled people called the Pelasgi, a cult of water worshippers, lived in this area long before the Etruscans appeared.

I looked out the window and indeed, the evidence of the *Etruschi* was there on the side of the road, signs pointing to tombs and springs and passageways, inviting exploration.

When I was researching this civilization in anticipation of making the trip, I read an interesting passage in *The Cities and Cemeteries of Etruria* by Sir George Dennis, written in the mid-1800's. He spoke of the role of women in that culture:

In physical comfort and luxury the Etruscans cannot have been surpassed by any contemporary nation . . . Much of it is doubtless owing to their extensive commerce, which was their pride for ages. In their social condition, they were in advance of the Greeks, particularly in one point, which is an important test of civilization. In Athens, woman was always degraded; she trod not by the side of man as his companion and helpmate, but followed as his slave . . . But in Etruria, woman was honoured and respected; she took her place at the board by her husband's side . . . she was educated and accomplished and sometimes even instructed in the mysteries of divination; her children assumed her name as well as their father's; and her grave was honoured with even more splendor than that of her lord. It is not easy to say to what Etruria owed this superiority. But whatever its cause, it was a fact which tended greatly to humanize her, and through her, to civilise Italy—a fact of which Rome especially reaped the benefit by imitating her example.

It really was not such a surprise to learn the Etruscans admired and venerated their women. In the Maremma, this land of fertility, the Divine in ancient times was feminine.

I found myself sitting up, as if it was important to pay attention. Goffredo's uncharacteristic silence left me to my own thoughts as we sped past fields of green and gold.

The road we were on had to be the same one Olga traveled with Goffredo and Otto forty years ago. It made me wonder what she would have been thinking about as she entered this land of the feminine. Did she recall her own life or that of her mother and grandmother? Did she think about their bravery, their strength, how they had kept both their spirits and families intact?

These remarkable women, strong and many times just plain fearless, made the necessary sacrifices for family during times of hardship and separation. The loving relationship Olga and Otto had lasted seventy years. What sustained the love between Aristide and Ione when they lived apart for more than ten years? When the time for reunion came, it was the women who left the home, got on the ship, crossed an ocean into a country where they could not imagine what life would be like, but were willing to go into the unknown because *family came first*.

They also had religious faith, but it never severed family.

"When your mother left the Church, it broke my heart, but I never stopped talking to her." These words of my grandmother were spoken to me long ago, as we both tried to make sense of a religion that would demand such a thing.

I know that my grandmother agonized over the rift, with my mother on one side of a chasm and me on the other. She must have decided it had gone far enough. There would be no further widening if she would stand between and hold closely onto us both. And she did, for the rest of her life, never openly revealing what it cost her.

Yet, during intimate moments between us, often a sad silence would linger, as we both longed to have my mother there too, at the table, sipping coffee with us. Our eyes would meet, and we read the same thoughts in each other. Then I would say something to distract her . . . there was a threshold neither one of us would cross.

My grandmother was patient beyond belief. So many times she could have complained or withdrawn her affection, but she did not put conditions on her love of either my mother or myself. Then, I took it for granted. Now, I could understand what an unselfish heart she had.

As we drove along the Etruscan roads that curved up ever higher, I thought about my parents. How loving they had been to me as I was growing up . . . yet their religion, joyless and oppressive, was a cement wall that had come between us, preventing the expression of their love towards me. If only my mother could be with me again in Italy—I found myself romanticizing—maybe the wall could come down for awhile. Wouldn't Olga smile then!

Pitigliano appeared suddenly like a page in a book of fables. It was built high on a precipice, and blended into its foundations as if it sprang from a volcano. The city was three hundred feet above a gorge that brought two rivers together, the Lente and the

Meleta. Pitigliano looked as if had been and would be there forever.

"*Molto impressionante, si?*" Goffredo said quietly.

When we pulled into the main piazza of Pitigliano, I immediately recognized—of all things—the sign on the *albergo* where my grandparents stayed during their visit. I had looked at the photograph many times.

> *"It was almost 2:00 a.m. when we went back to the Albergo Guastini. As tired as I was, I couldn't sleep, everything went around and around in my mind, thinking about what had happened that day—going to the farm at Sant'anna and meeting Otto's brother Memmo and family! Eating those wonderful cherries in their orchard. It was so hard to say goodbye. Fifty years since Otto left them. Memmo is very sick, he had a stroke and cannot speak. He was sobbing for Otto to see him like that. I could not sleep when we finally got into bed. And that donkey! Crying in the middle of the night! I gave up and stood by the window as the sun was coming up and Otto came over by me. He pointed out things in the city to me— the school, the church where he was baptized. Such a beautiful town, Pitigliano, so old and so beautiful."*

We took our lunch at a trattoria next to the albergo. Goffredo ordered a bottle of the locally produced wine, Bianco di Pitigliano. This golden white wine, made from the Trebbiano and Chardonnay grapes, was chilled but not cold and as I took a first sip, I tasted the subtle flavors of lime and honey. The delicate ravioli swirled in a simple sage and butter sauce, melted in my mouth, enhanced by the light crisp wine. The heat of the noonday intensified. The wine "went to my legs," one of Olga's favorite sayings. I gave in to it and relaxed into that one simple hour of life. That's one of the things I loved about Italy: time there seemed to last as long as you willed it to last.

We saw no one as we walked the narrow streets. The ancient fortress town was quiet—it was as if it had suddenly been abandoned. Everyone had finished up lunch and found their napping place at that hour. The morning's fresh laundry hung high above our heads between windows, like cotton rainbows against an indigo blue sky.

My love of history bubbled up in that place as I encountered traces of Orsini counts, the Knights Templar, the Medici. I was determined to learn more and come back. But more than its history, it was my family history that mattered most to me. I imagined Otto leaving the farm and coming to Pitigliano to meet his friends, flirt with girls, make plans to go to America.

Where was that farm? Why couldn't I find Sant'anna on a map?

It seemed I had one last living relative in Pitigliano, an elderly lady whose name was Renata. Goffredo led the way to her house. She lived alone, her husband was dead and her children had moved away to Rome where a living could be made.

Goffredo rang her doorbell and she was ecstatic to see us. She lived at the top of a very narrow flight of stone steps in a few rooms that were tiny, as she was. She was still a beautiful woman. Her profile was like a carving despite the hair growing wild from her head and face. Her home reflected her love of her family, photos gracing every surface. I wondered who still came to see her.

As we were leaving, Renata gave me a charming set of hand-painted ceramic miniatures made in Pitigliano—bottle, cup and saucer and a pitcher, all in blue and white.

As we drove away from Pitigliano, I made a promise to myself and to Otto that one day soon, I would come back here and find Sant'anna.

Rosina had prepared another lovely meal. I smelled the garlic when we entered the house and we sat down to *involtini*—veal scallopine layered with prosciutto, fresh sage and thin slices of hardboiled eggs, then rolled up and simmered in wine and the juices of the meat. Olga had made this dish and for a sweet couple of hours I was at her table again.

"*Buon appetito!*" Goffredo said with robust voice and we all repeated it. He laughed at me as I took the first bite and rolled my eyes.

After helping clean up the kitchen and finally being persuaded by Goffredo to "have just a little grappa, *bella*," I was more than ready to fall into that inviting bed.

The windows of my room were open wide to the summer night and the magnolia's heavy perfume. It was silent except for crickets chirping. I thought about the day. While I was not unhappy, I had to admit very few of my questions were answered that day. I had so many questions about my grandfather. I had so few real answers, only clues left in a journal.

I got out the ceramic pieces Renata had given me. I let them spill on the sheet so I could study them. The teacup had a small chip in the handle, the vase a hairline crack. The bottle was painted a different shade of blue. They were not perfect and that was why I liked them.

If I had all the answers, I would not be there.

The end of my Italian odyssey lay ahead.

Michelangelo's Walls

It was with some alarm that I realized only five more weeks in Italy remained and that I didn't have a single page of the book I intended to write. I had filled a journal with notes and musings along the way. I had earmarked books on Michelangelo, marble production, historical accounts of Carrara and Pitigliano, but hadn't seriously put pen to paper.

I had suspected that it would take weeks of cultivation before any real writing could take place, which was why I had made arrangements before leaving New York to rent a villa for those last weeks.

I chose Florence for its perfection, but I needed quiet. I discovered nearby Settignano, and learned that it was where Michelangelo was raised and where he first learned to work with stone . . . I believed it would be the best possible setting for what I wanted to accomplish. *Va bene.*

I hauled my luggage off the train in Florence and hopped into a taxi, which within minutes had maneuvered through city center traffic and was ascending into the hills. It always was magical to me that one can depart a bustling and noisy city like Florence, or New York for that matter, and all of a sudden be in the midst of quiet winding roads and green trees.

Via della Capponcina became narrow, so narrow in one place that the driver closed off the side mirrors. My eyes opened wide as we passed an impressive home with the name Villa Michelangelo prominently carved into the stone columns supporting a huge bronze gate, ornate and befitting the greatness behind the name. We turned through another tight bend and arrived in front of the home that would be mine for five weeks.

The iron gate protecting the property was large and elegant also, but less ornate, more welcoming. It said "come in" instead of "keep out."

I was greeted by Signora Marchetti, an attractive middle-aged woman with thick blond hair and a lively step.

We exchanged our greetings of "*piacere*," and I followed the signora to the back portion of the villa where I received a first glimpse of my terrace. There were my noble cypress trees, which rose high up above the villa into the sky. I saw a long, oval, stone table that looked impossible to move, and instantly imagined an evening dinner party, the candelabra glowing and lighting the faces of happy and tipsy guests.

The signora unlocked the door of the darkened home, shuttered against the intense heat of the day.

La cucina was grand, with a large, long marble table where I imagined pasta laid out in rows and dusted with flour, just picked fruit resting in bright ceramic bowls. In fact, every room in the entire house matched the vision I had for my home.

Signora Marchetti left me to my unpacking and then, finally, I just let myself stand still and breathe and listen. Houses have their distinct smells and so much of what I smelled in my grandparents' home was there. Hints of garlic and sage, clean smells of freshly sun-warmed laundry, even the fragrance of the morning espresso lingered in the air. It was quiet except for the occasional barking of Gina, the dog, and other sounds behind walls . . . the faint voice of a woman, the clink of cooking pans told me others lived close by.

This was home.

Later, Signora Marchetti's daughter Alessandra drove me through Settignano, which is situated on top of the hill above the villa. On the two-way road, wide enough for only one vehicle, Alessandra honked her horn at every turn. Along the way, she pointed out all the property once owned by Michelangelo, really the whole hillside along via della Capponcina. I sat transfixed as she told me Lionardo, Michelangelo's nephew, had lived in "our" very house, some of the original walls still intact.

The Tuscan sun was about to kiss the horizon, radiating a tropical pink light that bathed the countryside and warmed the ancient walls. A celestial brush swirled the olive and ochre of noonday into a surreal watercolor washed with twilight shadows.

What writer in history has ever visited Italy and not mentioned the extraordinary light? It's a delicious surrender that overcomes you the very first morning you fling open your bedroom window and gaze upon green hills and country towns.

The signora invited me for dinner on this first night. I walked around the corner to their part of the villa, a cold bottle of *vino vernaccia* in my hands. The sky was dark, the stars making faint appearances. The humid heat of that day had retreated and the cool air caressed my arms.

The signora and her daughter were in the kitchen, which

was like a closet, but seemed to contain as many cooking accessories as mine did—hanging from hooks and stacked, but everything within immediate reach.

The signora had made pasta with a garlicky *pomodoro* sauce.

"*Ah, sugo!*" I said as I inhaled the sauce in the pan.

"*Si! Brava, cara!*" Signora Marchetti said and it made me stand up a bit on my toes, happy to have pleased this wonderful woman in such a small way.

We drank the *vernaccia* with the rest of the meal—*fried zucca de fiore* (those buttercup-yellow flowers of the zucchini, plump and crunchy with delicate tempura, coated lightly with grated *parmigiano reggiano*), an egg frittata made with caramelized onions, followed by fresh tomatoes dressed with the olive oil the Marchettis produce on their land. The onions in the frittata dissolved in my mouth, tasting of sugar; the signora explained it was most important to cook them slowly, very slowly until they became so soft they almost disappeared.

Dessert was a little bit of fruit—*poca frutta*—biscotti and *vin santo*. The coppery-colored sweet wine was deceptively strong, like honey going down the throat and into the veins. I kept licking my lips, expecting some to still be clinging to them.

I told them that my great grandfather had been *uno scalpellino* in Carrara, and Alessandra's face lit up.

"I intend to begin writing a book while I'm here about his life and the stories my grandmother told me while I was growing up."

"That's really wonderful, Carolina," Alessandra said with a genuine smile. "So you have been to Carrara, then?"

"Oh yes, I first went with my Nonna years ago and I was there just last month. I want to know everything there is to know about marble, stone and sculpture. I can't believe I landed at your house!"

"The walls will speak to you here," she said. "Come, I want to show you something."

It was almost *mezzanotte*. Alessandra took me to a small glass shed in the garden lit by moonlight. Alessandra pointed to a broken white marble column leaning against the corner. I placed my palm on its cool surface.

"There is an old man here who is a sculptor and a restorer. We have spent a lot of time digging up places on the property looking for clues of Michelangelo." Alessandra said.

"Is this his?"

"Who knows? The sculptor says it is from the sixteenth century. Isn't it splendid?"

It was splendid. In that light, it took on an enchanted quality as the stone both absorbed and reflected light at the same time.

Alessandra and I exchanged the Italian cheek kisses and said *buona notte*.

"*Grazie per tutto*," I said.

"It's nothing. We are happy you are here, Carolina."

So was I.

For the next five weeks, I gave over the days and nights to my moods, my desires and daydreaming. For so many years, much of my life had been driven by agendas, routines and others' expectations of my time. Here, I let myself be taken by the natural current.

Sometimes I would take day trips. A drive through the Chianti region, stopping in small towns on an impulse, was a frequent pastime. I visited Siena and San Gimignano, its towers like medieval skyscrapers. I navigated my car up to Settignano and from there took the small orange city bus into Florence where I would wander the entire day.

The thought that I should be writing plagued me at times, but I continued to let myself be drawn away during the days. After all, it was all research.

On one of those leisurely days, I climbed to the top of the marbled *duomo*, the cathedral of Santa Maria del Fiore, to the crown of Brunelleschi's famous dome, to take in the expansive view from that tallest point in Florence. Sienna-colored roofs fell below me, encircling the Duomo and protecting Florentine homes, both humble and grand. This jewel of a city, the birthplace of the Renaissance, was cradled by the hills surrounding it, the hills where Leonardo da Vinci conducted his flight experiments . . . it was as if nothing had ever touched it since.

From the *duomo*, I headed across the way to the Baptistry where Ghiberti's bronze doors invite crowds of people to marvel at a masterpiece that consumed one man's lifetime. Michelangelo named them the Gates of Paradise.

Encountering the word "paradise" made me pause, as I thought about what that word used to mean to me and what it meant to me now.

As I stood among the crowd, I saw that one door was made of panels depicting Old Testament stories. There were Adam and Eve, Abraham, Jacob and Esau. Scenes from my childhood swept into my heart as I let my eyes fall on Eve, walking away from Paradise, looking back with all regret and loss in her face, punished because she ate of the tree of knowledge and her eyes were opened.

It seemed a symbol of my own lost paradise, the paradise of being safe in the world. A very early memory surfaced.

I was five years old and at my Aunt Joann's kitchen table. Her back was turned to me as she prepared my lunch and I was turning the pages in a book, a rather large book with a flamingo pink cover. The gold letters of the title were "From Paradise Lost to Paradise Regained." The book, published by the Jehovah's Witnesses, was filled with illustrations of Bible stories. It was written simply for reading to children.

I remembered kneeling on the chair, leaning on the small table and flipping the pages. There were pictures of kings, angels and prophets. There was Daniel and the lions in the den that do not open their mouths to harm him. There was Delilah holding the head of Samson in her lap, ready to cut his hair. There was Noah leading animals into the Ark.

I kept turning the pages and once in a while, my Aunt turned around to smile at me. As I got closer to the back of the book I began to get nervous. There were scary pictures in there I didn't want to see. I turned the pages anyway, as if it was important to be brave. The black ink of the words came through illustrations drawn in purple ink. It was shocking to suddenly see these, as if a hand had come out of the book and grabbed me by the throat.

I was too young to read the words. The purplish scenes told me how horrible Jehovah's wrath would be.

There were skyscrapers falling down on people in the city. The streets were flooded and people were screaming. There was hail falling on more people who in their panic crushed one another. Homes were burning and children were running from them in terror. Another illustration showed the earth opening up and into the big crack you saw people falling in, along with bicycles, handbags and shoes.

Armageddon was a big word for a five-year-old. But I knew how to pronounce it and I knew what it was. Jehovah's war, the end of the world . . . I also believed that unless you went to the Kingdom Hall, God would destroy you as a wicked person.

I felt sick. My knees started to slide on the seat and I began to cry. My aunt was alarmed and rushed over to me. All I could do was point to the pictures and say, "I don't want you to die."

"Honey!" She took me in her arms. "I'm not going to die!"

The crowd in front of the Gates of Paradise had changed. I'd been standing there longer than anyone else. But this memory, so seldom recalled, and so visceral, made me stand motionless and wonder how much of that fear still ruled me.

I no longer lived with the fear that God was out to get me. It was no longer the terrifying thought I woke up with every morning, and it had stopped feeding the apparitions in my dreams.

How had this happened? Had I just wakened one day and not been afraid? For years after I left the Witnesses, I continued to believe in their dark prophecies. They had a hold on me, cold clammy fingers gripping the back of my neck.

I became exhausted with the battle and resigned myself to whatever fate God had in mind for me. For whatever time I had left, I would try to be happy. I practiced living the kind of life I would have if I weren't afraid. The edges of my fear softened a little at a time over many years and eventually, the life was real and the clammy fingers released.

The softening in myself was compassion, and made it possible to ask myself: How could God be less compassionate than I? This sudden knowledge opened my eyes.

What surprised me so much during that time of my sabbatical were the sudden personal insights into my own journey. As I stood enthralled before ancient sculptures and paintings, their beauty unleashed emotions that wakened something ancient within myself . . . a longing to live a creative life, the desire to end the famine of my soul, a hunger for a passionate existence, a repossession of something I lost a long time ago. I had stunning, yet very simple revelations that helped me retrieve painful moments from my past and see them under the healing light of the present . . . and even more poignantly, I began to see how the connections to my family and their life stories intertwined with my own. My grandmother was the guide, had always been my guide . . . and Italy was my Paradise.

One day, Olga guided me onto the road back toward Pitigliano. I hadn't planned to go back in that direction again, but something was unfinished, like one of Olga's crocheted washcloths left unraveling and tossed aside. I had continued to buy and fruitlessly pore over maps for Sant'anna, the farm where Otto had been born. Had it been swallowed up and made part of a local wine producer's vineyards? The questions taunted me from the pages of Olga's journal where she had so beautifully described the farm. The questions reminded me of stubborn children, arms crossed, refusing to admit what they knew.

It wasn't so far to travel there from my Florentine villa and it didn't much matter. Olga seemed to be the one in charge. I giggled out loud as I imagined her the last time she rode in a car with me . . . . her small frame filling the seat, as I helped buckle her in snugly, pocketbook on her lap, fiddling with her hearing aid, complaining about its high-pitched whistle in her ear.

So it really did feel like Olga was leading me, as we rounded the final curve and Pitigliano came into view. The late morning sun was just emerging from the shadow of a big white cloud, and it illuminated the stone city so that it seemed to burst upon my eyes. It was as thrilling as the first time I had seen it.

Since I had no idea how much time Olga would want to

spend there, I decided to check in at the Albergo Guastini. I walked part way out of town to sit on a bench along the road to the cemetery, which generously offered up the full panorama of the old city.

Pitigliano looked as if the reddish-yellow volcanic rock had sprung out of the ground and showered itself with green shutters. Birds flew to and from the crevices of the city, dark birds flocking to tall ominous towers and out again. For centuries, the same dance.

I continued the five-minute walk to the cemetery down a lane of ancient shade trees.

I couldn't wait to get there. I wanted to find my grandfather Otto's mother, Maria.

Words from Olga's journal came to my mind, as if she were telling me the story:

"We went to the cemetery to find his mother's grave. The tombstone was cracked. We put some pink carnations on her grave and I wished I had known her. Otto paid the caretaker to repair the stone and as we walked out of the cemetery, the entire city of Pitigliano stretched before us, teetering on a cliff, a site that I'm sure was the same a thousand years ago. I looked at Otto and I know he was glad we came."

We passed through the small iron gate to find humble gravesites generously adorned with flowers, candles and photographs. I searched for the caretaker and discovered the small, stooped *vecchio* digging in a patch of grass, his work clothes stained with soil. I spoke with him in Italian as best I could, so I was met with a flurry of a response. He wouldn't slow his speech, but was willing to repeat himself.

He led me into the "office," a small, windowless room with a desk, chair and the now familiar sight of sturdy shelves loaded down with old record books the size of big accounting ledgers, dating from the early 1900s forward.

"No, I don't know the year of death. Sometime after 1920 and before 1960."

His eyebrows arched and his head shook a little in the face of my task. He pointed to the books as if to say, Knock yourself out.

He left me alone, and unlike Angelo in Carrara, was not remotely interested in my search. I took a sweeping look at the stacks of books facing me.

"*Mamma mia,*" Olga and I muttered in unison.

Since logic would not be offering any assistance, I simply pulled and opened the book within easiest reach.

A puff of fine dust escaped, a musty smell that had been trapped in the pages for decades. As I became acquainted with the layout of columns, I began equating the quality of handwriting with how much the recorder had cared about his job at the time.

I scanned the left margin for "Maria Faenzi," who would have been my great grandmother. But something was nagging me. Olga was tapping on my shoulder hard.

I sat back, closed my eyes and remembered a conversation. I was sitting with Olga in her front room, and she was telling me the names of Otto's family. She started giggling.

"My mother-in-law's name was Maria and she had a funny maiden name, didn't she Otto? Your mother."

Nonno sat placidly in his leather easy chair, nodded his head as he chewed on his pipe stem.

She said, "Mangiavacchi! Do you know what that means, Carol?"

"Hmm, eat something, right?"

"*Si*! Eat cows! What a name to have, my goodness."

Now, this is not a name easily discarded from memory.

I returned to my search, now armed with another name, pleased that I knew Italian women used their maiden names. I took a deep breath and closed the book firmly, returning it to the shelf.

The handwriting in the next book I opened was elegant, almost floral, and when I saw halfway through it the large sweeping M's of "Maria Mangiavacchi," I started laughing. Olga was laughing with me. There she was—Maria Eat Cows! Maria died November 15, 1941. She was sixty-nine years old. Her parents' names were listed as Teodoro and Lavinia Maglione.

My grandfather left in 1913 and never saw his mother alive again, like countless other young Italian men seeking a way out of their poverty.

But where was the grave? The archive listed the quadrant and row number and I imagined that's how Otto and Olga had found her when they visited forty years ago. I put this question to the caretaker and he explained, in a respectful tone, that after thirty years, room has to be made for others.

I imagined Olga right next to me, and slowed my long-legged walk to keep pace with her quick short steps—as I used to—and we made the *passeggiatina* back to Pitigliano. It had been a deeply satisfying moment, finding Otto's mother . . . I looked back over my shoulder, expecting to see Otto trailing a few steps behind us as he always did, slow and deliberate, nodding at me benignly, his fedora set just so, and his cigar smoke gently floating into the air. *Tutto bene.*

I was hungry and followed my nose to the piazza where the baroque cathedral sat like a decadent old king, casting its shadow on a charming *trattoria*. Colorful umbrellas cooled the few tables that spilled out of the little restaurant. It was wonderful to sit in the shade and slip off the sandals for a while. Even at lunchtime, Pitigliano was quiet as a whisper; the tinkling of glasses and plates sounded almost like wind chimes. It was a fairy tale town and blissfully unknown to mass tourism. I opened the small menu and every one of the ten simple selections made me lick my lips. I chose the *gnudi*, a type of gnocchi made with ricotta cheese instead of potatoes, drizzled with sage butter sauce. They were like down pillows filled with cream, those darling naked dumplings.

We drove out of Pitigliano after that divine lunch, in search of my grandfather's farm. A sense of urgency came over me, although I had no idea which direction to go. The rocky terrain of the area, so ancient, so unchanged, beckoned me to slow down. The curves of my thoughts followed the curves of the road.

The ship manifest I had found through the Ellis Island archives clearly stated my grandfather Otto's city of residence as Sorano, which had completely puzzled me, since I expected it to say Pitigliano or Sant'anna. I recalled again that in 1962, my grandparents visited his brother Memmo, in what Olga referred to as Sant'anna.

I then remembered the rest of the conversation with Olga and Otto that day, after the Mangiavacchi revelation.

"*Nonno*, you were born in Pitigliano, right?" I asked my grandfather.

Otto nodded and said, "Yep."

Olga fidgeted, "Otto! You were not born in Pitigliano. Your father was, but you were born in Sorano."

He took his pipe out of his mouth. "No, Sant'anna! It was Sant'anna."

This went on, back and forth, while I began to wonder if any conclusion would be reached. Dinnertime arrived and the mystery of Otto's birthplace lingered. After a glass or two of Chianti, these things gather less importance.

I was remembering this with a smile as I passed into Sorano, another Etruscan city near Pitigliano, and the town listed on Otto's Ellis Island record. I was immediately charmed. Something of how the stone entry was carved and the way bright flowers tumbled called me to walk through it.

A humble doorway invited me into a shop selling olive wood products—spoons, cutting boards, cooking utensils of all sizes filled cases and were suspended overhead. Two men, both smoking, talked with each other near the entrance. Ostensibly trying to decide on some of the spoons, I thought . . . was I going to speak up? Was I going to ask?

"Ask!" Olga chimed in, impatient with my timidity.

As the owner wrapped up my purchases in stiff white paper, not allowing this task to interrupt the flow of his conversation or cigarette, I spoke.

"*Scusa signore.*" He stopped his conversation and just looked at me.

"I—I have family here in Sorano." I struggled with the Italian.

"*Si?* What is the name?

"Faenzi. My grandfather was born near here in Sant'anna." Recognition lit his face.

Cigarette still hanging from his lip, he said, "Catia Faenzi works in the bar, near the bank."

"*Molte grazie! Buona giornata.*"

"*Buona fortuna, signora.*"

I thought Catia Faenzi, whoever she was, must be related. All I had to do was walk into the bar where she worked.

A woman, perhaps in her late thirties, with long blond curly hair, was behind the bar making a *caffè freddo* for a customer seeking refreshment during the sleepy part of the afternoon.

She looked at me, ready to take my order.

"*Si chiama Catia Faenzi?*" I asked.

She nodded.

"I am your American cousin!"

She put her head forward as if she had not heard correctly.

In Italian I said, "Catia—I am Ottavio's granddaughter!"

Her eyes had that saucer look.

I opened Olga's worn journal to the page with a list of Memmo's children, and put it on the bar so she could read it.

"*Guarda*—look," I said.

Her hands came to either side of her cheeks, she pointed at the names and said, "This is my father and this is my grandfather! *Mamma mia!*"

The next thing I knew she had grabbed the phone on the wall behind her. A customer came in and while she punched in the number, she pointed to me, then waved her hands, so he would understand there were amazing things happening here. He would have to wait for his drink.

Catia got her mother on the line and instantly she was relating the news in a rapid-fire exchanges. For the second time that day, a minor miracle had occurred.

Catia hung up, hurried around the bar, and embraced me with the instant affection that comes upon you when you realize the same blood flows in your veins, even if minutes before, all that might have passed between you was the transaction of a drink and a couple of euros.

Knowledge itself may be devoid of emotion, but it's a door that can take you in a flash from being a stranger into being in someone's arms.

In my world, it did feel like a miracle.

The lingering Italian townsfolk stayed in their seats, remained glued to the bar or stood in the street. They didn't intrude, but wanted to watch this small spectacle.

A pint-sized dusty car roared up and screech-stopped in front of the bar. Two old men emerged and again, embraces and hugs went around as introductions were made. Ghino and Gino, brothers—both sons of Memmo.

Lines from Olga's diary flashed in my head.

"Otto pointed out different places he remembered on the farm at Sant'anna and his brothers agreed he was right. We went into the house to take a few movie pictures with the camera. We had to leave before it got dark, to drive back to Pitigliano. We said good-bye to all and it was so sad for Otto's sick brother to leave him again. His two boys Ghino and Gino followed us on their motorcycles to the square in Sorano. They invited us for an ice cream and then they were gone."

Ghino, a small brown man with a smile I was sure seldom left his face, was Catia's father.

"Andiamo!" either Ghino or Gino said. Let's go!

I climbed into my car and followed the small brown men in theirs, trying to memorize the turns and saying aloud to Olga, "I hope we're going to Sant'anna."

And just as the words came out of my mouth, I saw the tiniest of signs, a slender piece of weather-beaten wood with the name and an equally small arrow.

The farm came into view. It was as if Olga's journal had sprung to life. Olive trees and vineyards were what I noticed first, as they framed each side of the farm, with a few sleek horses grazing behind a fence. I saw the cherry trees Olga had described, and in and around all the lush vegetation were separate homes. Small terraces were filled with pots of pink and orange summer flowers. The entire family lived there and over the course of the next couple of hours, highly excited relatives showed up one or two or ten at a time.

I met Telma, Ghino's wife and Catia's mother. Telma was bouncing a baby on her hip and I learned it was Catia's child, Alessandro. The Faenzi tradition of naming the firstborn son of each generation Alessandro was alive and well over here, too.

Gino's wife, Luigina, was the undisputed matriarch and respect had to be paid. She was a squat, strong woman with a red complexion, not from the sun, but from what I suspected was pure enthusiasm or extreme annoyance, depending upon the circumstances.

She was barely five feet tall, wore a blue printed dress, and walked with a bit of a waddle. Her iron hand stayed latched onto my forearm as she guided me where she wanted me to go. I remembered her name from Olga's journal too.

"I sat with Memmo's daughter-in-law, Luigina. She was such a nice woman and wrote down everyone's names for me. We promised we would write to each other."

Drinks were poured, snacks were produced and then the questions came like lasers, everyone trying to understand exactly who I was, where I lived, how I came to be there in the first place, if I was married, and why not? A brief thought flashed in my head, that in America the first question would have been, "What do you do?" In Italy, it's always about who one is and how one lives.

After a while, things calmed down. We walked around the farm, under the cherry trees. I looked out over the land. The lush rolling hills of Toscana went on forever into the horizon, olive trees and grape vines basking in the slant of the sun's rays, cypress trees like exclamation points on slopes.

Then Gino said he had something to show me. He guided me into what looked like a work shed. It was open, tree branches serving as a shady canopy. A few narrow steps led down to the door of the wine cave.

The dark of the cave was a shock, as was the plunge in temperature. The damp, odorous stone room was not offensive to the senses, but rather was fertile and smelled sweetly overripe.

Gino said they grew *sangiovese* grapes as he handed me a bottle.

"*Un regalo*," he said. Wine is such a noble gift.

"Your grandfather, Ottavio, liked our cave," he said.

And I was immediately transported to my grandparents' home, following Otto down the steep, narrow and shallow basement stairs, placing my feet side by side so I wouldn't fall face forward. My nose led me to the cool damp. His oak wine barrel was down there, the red wine fermenting until Christmas came around. The wine came from his backyard Indiana vineyard and the taste would bring tears to my eyes, it was so bold in its youngness. I imagined the trip here in 1962 was an inspiration for him to begin his own grape-growing enterprise. After all, he had done well with his fig tree—if he could get figs out of Indiana soil, hard as rock in winter, grapes would have been easy.

I always believed that somehow the portion of their home that was their garden was magically sustained by the Toscana sunshine and climate they had both grown up with. Their back yard burst, not only with grapevines, basil and the miraculous fig tree, but also with different kinds of lettuces—like the red bitter one, radicchio—arugula, even dandelion, the leaves of which were bitter but delicate when we ate them. The Italian *pomodori* for *sugo bolognese*, and the zucchini, whose flowers were a delicacy in the late spring, sizzled in Olga's pan. A peach tree grew in the center of the yard and its shade gave us rest on Sunday afternoons.

Herbs grew abundantly as well: thyme, mint, sage and rosemary. My hands were fragrant with them as she plucked off pieces and handed them to me, telling me what their therapeutic or—more important—culinary, uses were.

Olga loved roses and she had many varieties. We would walk through and take the time to water and smell them. Lilac trees in blue, pink and white popped in the spring and every vase in her house would be filled with them for those few precious weeks when they bloomed.

I supposed it was fitting that her last desire, before she fell and was taken to the hospital, was to water her roses.

We were in the cave long enough for our eyes to have trouble readjusting to the afternoon sun. The few sips of wine I had taken crept along my veins and made me want to stay there on the farm forever.

The indomitable Luigina pulled out old photographs, spoke of my grandparents' visit and how much she loved Olga. I looked at her lined, sun-browned face as she pressed my grandmother's letters, spanning forty years, into my hands. Olga and Luigina had kept their promise to write to each other.

Holding those letters reminded me of how much time my grandmother spent writing to people. I would say, "Nonna, why not just pick up the phone and call them?" She resisted and would say it's too late or too early "over there" to call. I didn't understand her reluctance until later.

As I sat there with these warm and wonderful people, I

realized what a treasure I had inherited in Olga's journals because she took the time to write. What a treasure were her letters to her friend Luigina! Even in death, Olga lived on because I could read her words a thousand times and hear her speaking to me.

I wouldn't have found this part of my family if Olga had not left clues for me in her journals . . . and if I had not been willing to let her lead me there.

I knew it was my turn, my time to write, to keep Olga's voice and her stories alive. I could almost feel her placing a mantle on my shoulders.

Like taking slow deep breaths and deliberately feeling the air come in and go out of the body, writing slows the racing pace of thoughts, allowing everything to be experienced, understood and conveyed deeply, sensuously, genuinely.

I was persuaded to stay with the family that night. They would have let me stay there for as long as I wanted, but I was eager to get back to my villa and begin writing.

My heart was in my throat as I walked out to the car in a gaggle of newfound Italian relatives. Luigina still had a death grip on my arm. Even the dog looked at me with large sad eyes. I wished that Olga really were still alive so I could have left her there for a few days to visit with her friend, Luigina. All I could do was promise that I would come back. I would return and sit in the garden with Luigina, sharing bits of Olga's life from those letters, letters that contained more of her soul.

I had no clue how to get back on the road toward Florence. Amidst the vigorous gestures and disagreements arising over the best way to go, Catia got into her car and told me to follow her.

"I'm going to take you not only the fastest way, but the most beautiful," she smiled.

Each curve in the road revealed ever more breathtaking vistas, like a beautiful woman who slowly lets her veils fall from her. The sun was now finishing its journey across the sky and the yellow light turned to sensual gold and copper rays descending into emerald-green hills.

Catia put me on the right road, waving and sending profuse kisses from the car. I stopped only to take a last photograph before going on.

Olga was quiet the rest of the way back. I was *contentezza*.

It was time to get serious and actually write something. There was a beautiful, feminine writing desk in my bedroom next to a window overlooking the exquisite terrace. I propped up the lithograph of the siren fountain, lit some candles, filled a small vase with a few strands of summer flowers. I pulled out photographs of Aristide and Ione, Olga and Otto. It was an inviting shrine to call up my muses. I poured myself a glass of wine. Toasting them, I announced, "It's time to go to work!"

They all just looked at me.

Scraps of paper began to accumulate in the wastebasket. My neat and expanded list of names, dates and known facts sat there impatiently waiting for me to bring it to life. My task fled from me, even though I could not have been in a more inspirational spot on earth. No muse appeared. The walls didn't speak. The wine supply was becoming depleted.

I became anxious. It was familiar, the kind of tension I used to feel when I had an impossible list of business tasks to attack. I shuddered to remember how hard I tried in those days . . . was it only a few short months before? . . . trying to make things happen . . . forcing, manipulating, coercing . . . exhausting.

Remembering how helpful meditation was during those times, I abandoned the writing desk for a cushion in the garden. I closed my eyes and saw myself sitting at the edge of a clear, still lake, peering in and asking, "What do I need to know?" Yet after many seemingly fruitless sessions, I could still feel rigid edges in my body and mind. Finally, I let go of trying.

It was after midnight, when the moon was high, and I leaned my head back against the cool stone garden wall. To my delight, I found that Aristide had quietly come to sit beside me.

I didn't see his face, only his hands. I looked at them as he began to speak and wanted to take them into mine. They were large for such a small man. They looked as if they had been carved . . . distorted but fine hands.

I told him my desires, and that I longed to know him. That I always looked for him at the opera, but didn't know what else to do.

He said that he would tell me his stories, that I needed to keep still and everything I wanted would come to me.

He reached over to take my hand in his and said, "One more thing, *cara*. You need to be closer to the family. Like me, you have moved around too much, and been alone for too long."

The startling truth of these last words moved me to tears. He did know me.

I repeated "keep still" to myself like a mantra over the next days. I laughed, remembering that was exactly what Olga had told me to do at least a million times during my life. *Keep still.*

I found many wondrous places in my neighborhood where I could practice keeping still. I visited the gardens of Villa Gamberaia on the edge of Settignano and sat by its green pools and lemon trees. I sat in small churches I stumbled across in the streets of Florence. I drove aimlessly through the hills of the Chianti.

It came to me clearly one day that the stories I found so compelling, yet that evaded my grasp, were not to be written from my point of view, in my voice. No. Aristide's voice was strong inside me. It was his voice that wanted to be heard.

This shifted my entire outlook. No longer did I try to fashion a sensible, perfect narrative from fragments of stories and genealogical records. Suddenly, it was a matter of deep listening and looking. I listened to opera and let the soul-searing notes of impassioned tenors course through my body, imagining it was Aristide's voice singing the arias. I studied his eyes in photographs and saw his fatigue. I looked at his hands and perceived strength and tenderness. I read his expressions and glimpsed his humor and optimism. I re-read Olga's journals and listened to her feelings, not simply her descriptions. I spent time in *la cucina* and attempted some of her recipes, so I could smell and taste and remember what it was like to sit with her as she spoke of things past. I transported myself back to Carrara, still a fresh memory, and again imagined Aristide walking those same streets as a young man, full of dreams of going to America.

Keeping very still indeed, I began to write in the dense quiet of the Tuscan summer night.

Once I began writing in Aristide's voice, other voices spoke up. First was Ione, then Salvatore. The only quiet ones were Otto and Little Nonna. Olga's voice, clear and strong, moved me to think of her as a young girl, leaving her home and falling in love. The sense of separation was acute as I wrote about Olga's ten-year separation from her father, and remembered how painful it was for me to not only leave home, but take leave of my immediate family.

When I sat down to write, it became a festive occasion. I played recordings of entire operas . . . *Tosca, Rigoletto, L'Italiana in Algeri.* I poured chianti. I placed family photographs in a circle. This wasn't a shrine. It was a family gathering.

It was as if I could open a door into Olga and Otto's living room any time I wanted. Every seat would be filled with all my ancestors having a great time talking about the old days. Little Nonna Cesira embroidering in one corner, Ione sitting with her pocketbook on her lap and Aristide smoking one of his little Tuscan cigars, waving me in to come join them.

I loved taking this journey with them, going to unexpected places, back to the times of Puccini, Michelangelo, even Mussolini. I did an exhaustive amount of historical research to give the stories a time and a place, and became absorbed in the thrilling episodes I read about . . . the turbulence of Italy's unification, the violence and discrimination toward immigrants as they labored to create lives for themselves and their families, the horrendous ocean journey itself and the terror of passing through Ellis Island.

When I came to places in a story and did not have all the "facts," I listened to the voices of my family to guide me to the truth. Often, I would hear Aristide say, *"Non preoccupati, cara! Don't worry so much!"*

I heard Olga's voice within her journals, which I reread many times. I would notice something I hadn't seen before every single time. I realized there would never be an end to this. Letting the mysteries remain was part of what made the stories so enthralling. I hoped I would never be satisfied.

The five weeks flew and so did the stories. As I came to the end of my Italian summer, the prospect of going back and resuming my life was becoming almost dreadful. What would I do? How would I live? I decided that those last precious days would have to be spent in Carrara.

I wanted to go again to the place where the stars melted.

Carrara

All seemed as I had left it at the Hotel Michelangelo. Lattanzi was still standing behind the desk, the ever-present dark cigar stub molded into the corner of his mouth. His wife Eileen was sitting at the small desk hunched over paperwork. Their floppy little dog was lounging in the same spot in the lobby.

"Hey! Look who's here," Lattanzi said, his eyebrows reaching almost to his hairline.

Smiles, hugs went all around as I drank in the welcome that made me feel at home.

I went for dinner at the Leone d'Or, a restaurant in the Piazza Alberica where I had dined several times before. The owner, Umberto, and his wife welcomed me back as warmly as if I had been invited into their home for supper. Sitting at what was now my usual spot, I ordered the *tagliatelle con pesto* and a glass of *vino bianco*. Umberto kept bringing out more savory dishes despite my protests and his insistence that I try everything.

Needing to walk off dinner, I strolled away from the Piazza toward the Duomo. It was closed at that hour. I glanced over at the building nearby which was the site of the apothecary, Pellicia, Michelangelo's host when he visited Carrara. I looked for a light in the window, but it was dark.

I found my way through the familiar narrow streets, to the Bridge of Tears and the Siren Fountain. I placed my hands through the healing waters, closed my eyes and thought about what that lady might have meant to my grandmother when she was a girl. Did she come to her for healing? Was that why I stood there? I looked at the face of the beautiful mermaid and asked for her help, that the waters might release me from what I was resisting.

Sadness stole over me, the kind of sadness you feel when you come close to the end of a movie or a book that you really want to go on forever because it's so beautiful. Just a few moments more, just a few pages more! I was already missing the odyssey I'd had, gloriously free of burdens and obligations . . . the long weeks in Italy, all my senses soaked with its pleasures . . . with every tender bite of pasta savored at a corner table draped in pink, every wicked glance of a dark stranger on the via Condotti, every moment spent in wonder at Caravaggio's Magdalene, the stroke of my fingertips over Bernini's cold marble masterpieces, shivering at the touch of a cream silken garment spun lighter than air, the pealing of bells on a clear Sunday morning while I dreamt Italian dreams . . . with every drive along country roads, silvery green terraces of shimmering olive trees and golden faces of flowers made from the sun, seducing me for as many miles as I desired to go . . . Italy was where I had always found paradise. I wasn't ready for it to be over. I wasn't ready to go back.

I imagined facing some of my friends, friends who knew me because of my work. I could hear them say, "You had a wonderful vacation. And you're writing a book now, you say? That's a nice hobby, Carol, but . . . what are you going to do for a living?" I knew it was career death to wait too long to get back in the "game," to do anything other than what you know. *So what do you know?*

I said good-bye to the Siren and her Dolphin and took this question with me. I was in kind of a daze as I walked. I passed the antiques store where I'd found the Siren lithograph a few weeks before. The shop owner, Mario, was locking up and he greeted me with "*buona sera, come sta?*" and a big warm smile. It made me feel proud that I was at home in Aristide's and Olga's birthplace. I returned his smile. "*Sto molto bene, grazie, Mario!*"

So what do you know? Olga's persistent taps prodded me harder this time. I could almost see her little face looking up at me. *Che cosa sai?*

I knew that I loved writing, had always loved it, whether I was composing a business memo, creating a poem, scribbling in a journal or pouring out my heart in a love letter. Spending hours weaving words together caused me to lose myself, so that each moment was something alive, something that spoke of longing and desire.

I had spent many years creating and honing my business competence. Pride coursed through me when I remembered my humble start in the working world, not knowing my next steps, then years later finding myself admired and respected for having "made it." I had invested so much into my career, to the detriment of my health . . . *yet part of who you are was bundled up in all that too.* If not, I couldn't have known so much satisfaction as my work helped other women succeed. But I also had to admit that I had compromised many times, selling off pieces of myself to survive in that world. I had stepped out for awhile, because I had to . . . but in stepping out, I could see that the world I left wasn't completely uninhabitable . . . was it possible to find my place, where my work belonged, where I belonged? I was nervous. I wasn't sure I knew how to go back in and stay intact. What if I got caught up in it again and lost all that I had learned during this precious time of recovering the forgotten pieces of myself? *Don't be afraid!*

Sidewalks made of marble appeared under my feet and directed me back toward the Piazza Alberica, where a pistachio gelato was waiting for me. The young woman who always served me asked, "*Desidera gelato al pistachio?*" Another friendly smile that told me I was remembered.

I licked at the cone quickly, as the lowering sun was giving off its final blast of heat. I sat tiredly at the feet of the Duchess, on the steps of the fountain and its wise lion.

My thoughts flowed back and forth across time, like the water over the stone of that centuries-old fountain. I had come again to Italy to find the remaining traces of my ancestors and the stream of my own life had joined with theirs.

As I looked back through my own history, I thought about the first time I had sat on the fountain's steps. It was in 1978 on that trip with Olga, when I had barely begun to awaken to my life.

And it gave you the courage to turn your life upside down when you went home, didn't it?

During the fifteen years that followed that trip, I grew into the life I was creating, by trial and error, still believing in imminent doom in the private chambers of my mind, yet showing the world a brave face and a normal, even successful existence. My grandmother, my aunt Joann and others, never let go of me and I slowly began to see myself through their eyes. *You are strong. You are a survivor.*

So here I was again in Italy and feeling another seismic shift inside. Within the last few weeks, I had been led to a group of people who instantly embraced me as family, who begged me to return, whose very presence said *you have a home here.* I remembered the words spoken to me in 1978 by my cousin at the train station . . . "*We would be happy to keep you, cara.*"

I thought of how wonderful it would be to have that choice, to make the sabbatical permanent. Another dark place was illumined . . . *but you're really not on a sabbatical, are you?*

A new place inside me was opening up as I let the meaning of this sink in. I had a choice. I could stay on this path and choose how I would live, how I would work. It did not have to be a prison unless I made it one. And what about all that stuff that lived on a resume, *carved in stone?* That stuff might show what I've done. *That's not who you are.*

Another tap . . . *and you're not just writing a book about the family either.*

"But I wrote the book for you . . . out of love for you," I said out loud. Yet I was there, sitting by that fountain, because I was part of this one family. Who and what I was came from who and what they were . . . brave and caring souls, willing to go on journeys into the unknown. Their lives showed what it meant to have courage and steadfastly take care of family. Their blood flowed in my veins, from a beginning deep within marble quarries and green Tuscan hills. Once more, it was in returning there, to know Italy's ardent embrace and gentle acceptance, so much like my grandmother's very presence, that I had found courage.

I had sought my ancestors in their stories . . . found them by walking in the stardust of ancient quarries, by turning the faded pages of cemetery records one by one, by sitting in a park and listening to arias . . . and in doing so, I found myself, too. *Brava, cara!*

There is an aria from Puccini's opera, *La Boheme*, that has never failed to pierce me. Rodolfo tells Mimi about his life:

È una notte di luna	It's a moonlit night
e qui la luna	and up here we have
l'abbiamo vicina.	the moon near us.
Aspsetti, signorina,	Wait, miss,
le dirò con due parole	and I'll tell you in a couple of words
chi son, e che faccio,	who I am, and what I do,
come vivo. Vuole?	how I live. Would you like that?
Chi son? Sono un poeta	Who am I? I'm a poet.
Che cosa faccio? Scrivo.	What do I do? I write.
E come vivo? Vivo.	And how do I live? I live.

As I strolled slowly back to the Hotel Michelangelo in the moonlight, humming the melody of that sweet aria, I was calm and peaceful, as if indeed the Siren's healing waters had washed away my anxiety and dread. I was surprised at the stirrings of anticipation within me at the thought of returning to New York and immersing myself in this expanded vision for my life . . . even though I could not know how it would develop. I only knew that it would be joyful and it would be genuine.

I listened to my footsteps on the pavement and imagined both Aristide and Olga beside me, arm in arm. I found myself wishing my beautiful mother were there too, as I recalled those sunny days long ago, when Italy gave us paradise. That is the image of her that I would keep in my heart, chiseling the rest away—grateful that Olga had taught me, by her example, the power of forgiveness, that I might remember with love.

In the early morning, I drove up the steep winding road to the marble quarries. On a Sunday, it was quiet and cool before the heat beat down on the countryside. The rising sun reflected every diamond facet of the pure white gold. I walked through ancient white dust and . . . yes, it was as if stars had melted.

The clearness of the day opened vistas before me, to the far reaches of the *Mediterraneo* where sky and sea come together, then across the mountains and up the sparkling coast.

I thought of the passing centuries here, where poets, princes and popes walked, where masterpieces were born, and ocean journeys were begun to America, journeys filled with hope, love and longing for a different life. I thought of Aristide, Enrico and now Antonio, all of them in the mountains, in the quarries, three men who belonged to me. And now I had become part of those stories by walking in their very footsteps, through stardust.

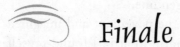

Finale

The sun is low behind the mountain, so it is still dark. Soon, the first rays of sunlight will bleed into the sky and I am anxious for it to light my footsteps, to see it make the white marble of the mountain's face shine.

But for now, I hardly see the path. It somehow feels familiar to me. I am not afraid that I will slip or get lost. No.

I have to hurry. They're already there, ahead of me, in the quarry, have probably had coffee and bread.

I have my chisel and it's hanging from a leather belt around my waist. I hold it steady, so it doesn't hit me in the leg as I climb. I like how it feels. I like the weight of it.

The path is becoming lighter every minute. I look up and see a patch of dark blue sky, streaked with light pink. I stop for just a moment to breathe in the pure alpine air, the still air . . . the chill of it clears my head.

I climb for another hour or so. The day is now in full procession and the dark blue is brightening. The gleam of the crystalline mountain is blinding, even in the crevices and ravines where pieces of broken marble have fallen and collected. They sparkle like facets of diamonds.

I bend over to pick up a flat piece, turn it over in my hand, hold it up to the light, which glows through it and is held there. Everything here is unchanged by time.

I hear men's voices, so I know that I am close now. My heart beats a little faster. I keep going.

The voices I hear are like a chorus that sings low in the background of an opera. I cock my head to see if I hear Aristide's voice. Surely, his would rise above. And he would be singing.

I hear him call from above, "Up here!"

I look up. The sun's in my eyes, but I see the outline of his small wiry body. He's smiling and the dimple has disappeared into his chin.

I climb faster to reach him. There are tears in my eyes and now he is holding me and it feels like he'll never let go of me.

Who are the others standing behind him? The man I can see is tall. He has dark hair and a curling moustache. His eyes twinkle. He's coming over and puts his arms around us both.

"*Finalmente!*" he says in a big booming voice and I know who he is. It's Enrico.

"Are you ready?" he asks me.

"Yes, I am." And we all go into the mountain together, to the place where the stars melted.

Bibliographical Sources
for *The Stonecutter's Aria*

PRINT

Barzini, Luigi. *The Italians*. Penguin Books, 1964.

Black Dog Opera Library. *Rigoletto*. Black Dog & Leventhal, 1998.

Black Dog Opera Library. *Tosca*. Black Dog & Leventhal, 1998.

Bleiler, Ellen H., ed. *Famous Italian Opera Arias*. Dover Publications, 1996.

Canali, Daniele. *Carrara: The Quarries, The Marble, The Sea*. Casa di Edizioni, 1992. (Carrara, Italy)

Canali, Daniele. *Archivi del Marmo—Marble Archives: L'archivio fotografico Bessi*. Aldus, 1997. (Carrara, Italy)

Carrara Marble: Touchstone of Eternity. National Geographic, July 1982.

Conti, Alessandro. *Il Marmo: Ieri e Oggi*. Societa Editrice Apuana, 1996. (Carrara, Italy)

Dennis, Sir George. *The Cities and Cemeteries of Etruria*. John Murray, 1848. (London)

Divita, Professor James J. *The Italians of Indianapolis: The Story of Holy Rosary Catholic Parish, 1909-1984*. 1984.

Ferrucci, Katherine. *Limestone Lives—Voices from the Indiana Stone Belt*. Quarry Books, Indiana University Press. 2004.

Jones, Maldwyn A. *Destination America*. Holt, Rinehart and Winston, 1976.

LaGumina, Salvatore J.; Cavaioli, Frank J.; Primeggia, Salvatore; Varacalli, Joseph A. *The Italian American Experience*. Garland Publishing, Inc., 2000.

Mangione, Jerre, and Morreale, Ben. *La Storia. Five Centuries of the Italian American Experience.* Harper Collins, 1992.

Musa, Mark. *The Portable Dante.* Penguin Books, 1995.

Palla, Marco. *Mussolini and Fascism.* Interlink Books, 2000.

Perkins, Charles C. *Historical Handbook of Italian Sculpture.* Charles Scribner's Sons, 1883.

Vasari, Giorgio. *The Life of Michelangelo Buonarroti.* Translated by George Bull. The Folio Society, 1965. (London)

Weaver, William, and Puccini, Simonetta. *The Puccini Companion.* W. W. Norton & Company, 1994

INTERNET SOURCES

Carrara, City of the Marble: Its Monuments Between History and Legends.   http://www.massacarrara.net/lsgmarconi

Hart, E. St. John. *A Marble World.* Pearson's Magazine, 1903. http://www.cagenweb.com/quarries/articles_and_books/a_marble_world.html

English/Italian Marble Glossary. http://ww.marblefromitaly.com/marblefaq/glossary.htm

Marble.   http://encarta.msn.com

What is Marble?. http://www.vivincitta.it/artedelmarmo/marble1.htm

Phillips, Kyle. *La Lizzatura.*   http://www.italianfood.about.com/library/weekly

Noether, Emiliana P. *Risorgimento.*   http://www.ohiou.edu/~Chastain/rz/risorgim.htm

The Island of Ischia.   http://www.ischiaonline.it

Life and Times of Giuseppe Garibaldi. http://www.reformation.org/garibaldi.html

Vizetelly, Ernest Alfred. *The Anarchists—Their Faith and Their Record*. Turnbull and Spears, 1911. (Edinburgh).
http://dwardmac.pitzer.edu/Anarchist_Archives/vizetelly/vizetelly10.html

The Anarchist Encyclopedia: Alberto Meschi, Italian Anarchist.
http://recollectionbooks.com/bleed/Encyclopedia/MeschiAlberto.htm

Italian Anarchists: Luigi Galleani.
http://www.radio4all.org/anarchy/galleani.html

Wilson, Peter Lamborn. *Brand: An Italian Anarchist and His Dream.* 2003.   http://www.anarchist-studies.org/article/articleprint/46

Gori, Pietro. *Addio A Lugano*. 1895 (Anarchists song).
http://www.nelvento.net/addio-lugano.html

Canti Anarchici Italiani.
http://www.utenti.lycos.it/Guctad.gori1.html

King, William E. *The Stonesetters—The Men Who Built the University.*
http://lib.duke.edu/archives/holdings/campus/stoneset.html

Divita, James. *The Italians of Indianapolis.*
http://www.italianheritage.org/church.htm

A Hundred Years of Terror. A special report prepared by the Southern Poverty Law Center, Montgomery, Alabama.
http://www.unf.edu/dept/equalop/oeop11.htm

Invisible Empire, Knights of the Ku Klux Klan.
http://www.encarta.msn.com/index/conciseindex/2A

Biographical Sketch of Andrew W. Mellon.
http://www.ustreas.gov/opc/opc0056.html

Jewish Culture of Pitigliano. The Jewish Community.
http://www.pitigliano-ferien.de/pr.jerusalem-e.html

Levenson, Gabe. *Tuscany's "Little Jerusalem." The Jewish Week*.
http://www.thejewishweek.com/news/newscontent

Winter, Rebecca. *The Virtual Jewish History Tour, Pitigliano*.
http://www.us-israel.org/jsource/vjw/Pitigliano.html

The Theatrical Magic of Giacomo Puccini, Biography.
http://www.hearts-ease.org/cgi-bin/conservatory_bio.cgi?ID=57

Mitchell, Brian. *Giacomo Puccini: His Life. Investor's Business Daily*.
http://www.r-ds.com/opera/pucciniana/life.htm

Biography of Giacomo Puccini.
http://www.geocities.com/airepuccini_english/Biography.html

Shargool, Ernestine. *Maria Lavava (*Song: *Mary Busy with the Washing)*.   http://www.mamalisa.com/world/italy.html

On a personal note . . .

During the four years I spent writing *The Stonecutter's Aria*, there were many who cared about my dream and supported me. I would like to thank you.

In Carrara: Carolina Nicoli of the Carlo Nicoli Sculpture Studios and Renato Carozzi, Director of the *Accademia di Belle Arti di Carrara* for enlightening me on how Aristide would there have become the artisan he was; sculptor and family friend, Monfroni; Luciano Larranzi for painting vivid images of Carrara's history.

I am indebted to the late great author, Barbara Grizzuti Harrison, who generously read a portion of the manuscript and who, as an Italian-American and former Jehovah's Witness, encouraged me, in the months preceding her death, to bravely tell my story.

Mille grazie to: Professor James "Giacomo" Divita for Holy Rosary parish history; the wonderful staff at the Columbia Club in Indianapolis; Duke University Archivist Thomas Harkins for his reverence for the stonecutters; Luciana and Alessandra Marchetti for Michelangelo's walls.

My aunt and muse, Joann Wilson; Rebecca Giovanoni for Giorgio's stories; great aunts Anna, Maggie and Laura, and great uncle Joe, for memories; Goffredo and Monica Ricci in Rome and many other family members, including Ron, Scott and "Danilo" Wilson. And my father, William Whalin, for teaching me the importance of remembering stories.

For additional and invaluable help: Janice and Joan Phelps for shaping the first stories, Germana Marchese for correcting my Italian, Arturo Brunetti for translating Otto's love letters, and to my brilliant editor, Kedron Bryson, for her virtuosity and humor.

And dear friends: Rita Michaelson who opened her home to me; Pat and Dr. David King for a month of peaceful writing days in France; Laurie Wilton, Patricia Pardon, Eileen Lambert, Jerrilee Lucas, Frederica Thea, Lisa Catton, Silvio Pastore-Stocchi, Hazel Stroth, Christine Rosen, the Deiningers and my creative mentor, Joseph Weishar.

I wanted to write a true story of love, compassion and courage. For those readers who find themselves in these pages, whom I hold in deepest respect, I ask your understanding if my truth differs from yours.

About the Author

Carol Faenzi conducted extensive research into the history, art and culture that framed her ancestors' lives. In Carrara, she collaborated with the director of Accademia di Belle Arti and local sculptors and visited the vast quarries to study technical aspects of marble production. She met with the owner of the oldest marble-sculpting studio in Carrara to gain a working knowledge of the art form and its rich history. In the U.S., she interviewed sculptors, academic authorities, Italian-American historical societies and prominent authors, most notably the late Barbara Grizzuti Harrison, author of *Italian Days* and *Visions of Glory*.

Visit the world of the Stonecutter's Aria at
www.TheStonecuttersAria.com
To order copies, please call: 800–345-6665